Creating Maintainable APIs

A Practical, Case-Study Approach

Ervin Varga

Apress®

Creating Maintainable APIs: A Practical, Case-Study Approach

Ervin Varga
Expro I.T. Consulting, Kikinda
Serbia

ISBN-13 (pbk): 978-1-4842-2195-2   ISBN-13 (electronic): 978-1-4842-2196-9
DOI 10.1007/978-1-4842-2196-9

Library of Congress Control Number: 2016959187

Cover image designed by Freepik

Managing Director: Welmoed Spahr
Lead Editor: Steve Anglin
Technical Reviewer: Jaroslav Tulach and Sverrir Sigmundarson
Editorial Board: Steve Anglin, Pramila Balan, Laura Berendson, Aaron Black, Louise Corrigan, Jonathan Gennick, Robert Hutchinson, Celestin Suresh John, Nikhil Karkal, James Markham, Susan McDermott, Matthew Moodie, Natalie Pao, Gwenan Spearing
Coordinating Editor: Mark Powers
Copy Editor: Teresa F. Horton
Compositor: SPi Global
Indexer: SPi Global
Artist: SPi Global

Distributed to the book trade worldwide by Springer Science+Business Media New York, 233 Spring Street, 6th Floor, New York, NY 10013. Phone 1-800-SPRINGER, fax (201) 348-4505, e-mail orders-ny@springer-sbm.com, or visit www.springeronline.com. Apress Media, LLC is a California LLC and the sole member (owner) is Springer Science + Business Media Finance Inc (SSBM Finance Inc). SSBM Finance Inc is a **Delaware** corporation.

For information on translations, please e-mail rights@apress.com, or visit www.apress.com.

Apress and friends of ED books may be purchased in bulk for academic, corporate, or promotional use. eBook versions and licenses are also available for most titles. For more information, reference our Special Bulk Sales–eBook Licensing web page at www.apress.com/bulk-sales.

Any source code or other supplementary materials referenced by the author in this text are available to readers at www.apress.com/9781484221952. For detailed information about how to locate your book's source code, go to www.apress.com/source-code/. Readers can also access source code at SpringerLink in the Supplementary Material section for each chapter.

Printed on acid-free paper

To my family (my wife Zorica with my sons Andrej and Stefan),
who put in the lion's share of the effort to make this book a reality. I'm grateful to them!

Contents at a Glance

Contents

About the Author

Ervin Varga has been in the software industry as a professional software engineer since 1994. As an owner of the software consulting company Expro I.T. Consulting (www.exproit.rs), he is always in touch with production software. He is an IEEE Software Engineering Certified Instructor, and an assistant professor at the University of Novi Sad, Faculty of Technical Sciences, Novi Sad, Serbia. He was the primary technical reviewer for the book *Thinking in Java* (4th ed.) written by Bruce Eckel. He was also the co-author with Bruce Eckel of the book *Thinking in Java* (4th ed.) *Annotated Solutions Guide* published by MindView LLC in 2007.

Ervin actively participates in open-source projects. He is the author of the Docker image (evarga/jenkins-slave) to serve as a Jenkins slave node in distributed builds.

He has an MSc in computer science and a PhD in electrical engineering. His thesis was an application of software engineering and computer science in the domain of electrical power systems.

LinkedIn profile: linkedin.com/in/ervinvarga

E-mail: e.varga@ieee.org

About the Technical Reviewers

Jaroslav Tulach is the founder and initial architect of NetBeans, later acquired by Sun Technologies. As creator of the technology behind NetBeans, he is still with the project to find ways to improve design skills among the programmers who contribute to the success of the NetBeans open source project.

Sverrir Sigmundarson has more than 15 years of industry experience building high-performance, mission-critical software for the finance and software industries. He holds an MSc degree in Computer Science from Reykjavik University in Iceland. He is currently on a special assignment as a stay-at-home-dad living in Strasbourg, France, with his wife and son. He can be contacted through his web site, `coruscantconsulting. co.uk` or via `linkedin.com/in/sverrirs`.

Acknowledgments

Publishing a book is a team effort. I am really thankful to the team at Apress, especially Steve Anglin, Mark Powers, Laura Berendson, Alexander James, and Amrita Stanley for their tremendous support and professionalism. Their experience in the book publication domain was indispensable.

I am also happy and indebted that Jaroslav Tulach accepted the role of the technical reviewer. His comments and mathematically precise methodological reviewing approach made huge quality improvements in the text. I would also like to thank Dr. Heinz Kabutz for recommending and introducing me to Jaroslav.

Many thanks to Sverrir Sigmundarson for reviewing Chapters 10 through 13 and his useful remarks.

Introduction

The goal of this book is to teach you how to design maintainable application programming interfaces (APIs) with reuse in mind. Of course, by reuse I don't mean simply visiting http://www.programmableweb.com and starting to search the API directory, although if you find something interesting there, then it might be a good source of inspiration. It is hard to encompass everything regarding APIs in a single book. It is even impossible to fully cover just one particular type of API (like REST) in one book. Therefore, the focus here is solely on the gist of producing evolvable APIs. Nevertheless, learning the foundations is the most important thing before crafting more complex solutions (including a business model around APIs using some of the available API platforms, like the one provided by Apigee).

The book is made up of four logical parts: basic principles of API design in the realm of object-oriented design (OOD) and object-oriented programming (OOP), HTTP REST APIs, messaging APIs, and JSON API as a concrete, powerful hypermedia-driven media type. These parts can be read in any order, but I suggest you start with Part I. This presents some essential topics, which are required to understand the rest of the text. Part III is independent of Parts II and IV. I would recommend reading Part II before Part IV. Of course, the best result is achieved by following the text in a linear fashion.

The book tries to balance stability and pragmatism. The main ideas are presented in a form that will hopefully remain valid for the next couple of years. On the other hand, to make the elaborations practical, I was forced to stick to concrete versions of frameworks, which will surely change much quicker than the accompanying principles and methods. On the other hand, without practical case studies, the reader will have a hard time mapping high-level concepts to everyday situations. To compensate on the side of volatility for the referenced frameworks, the book also has a Github repository belonging to Apress. This will be updated as new versions of the frameworks are published. Some novel, interesting projects, like GraphQL (http://graphql.org), were not examined as they are mostly in draft form, so considerable changes are expected in their specifications in the near future.

The book also tries to introduce the reader to the Semantic Web technology in a very lightweight manner. This is done in an attempt to demonstrate the semantic gap problem in current REST APIs, and how it could be mitigated by using linked data concepts. Many advanced topics, like semantic inference and reasoning, aren't scrutinized, although they are the most beautiful and powerful aspects of the Semantic Web movement.

CHAPTER 1

■ ■ ■

Information Hiding and APIs

Encapsulation, information hiding, interface segregation principle, *dependency inversion* principle, and the list goes on. Is it really the case that they talk about fundamentally different things? Can we find some common denominator? How does this relate to application programming interfaces (APIs)? Certainly, there are object-oriented design (OOD) and object-oriented programming (OOP) principles that aren't directly applicable to APIs. There are some that are hard to apply in the correct way. Without entering an endless fight about rationalism versus empiricism (for more details visit `http://wiki.apidesign.org/wiki/RationalismVsEmpriricism`), we will discover universal principles to create maintainable and evolvable APIs. As we will see, all of them aim to tame complexity and control changes.

I still remember as a student an enlightening lecture about the basics of electrical power systems. The professor told us that we should forget those complex and convoluted formulas to reason about physical processes. If we wanted to understand why we need shielding, to get a feel about the level of the needed shielding, to judge about the size of the wires, then we needed something much simpler. In other words, we have to touch the crux of the things. In this case, it was the relationship $P = UI$ (these are electrical engineering symbols). If we want to operate an appliance (having some fixed power) with a lower voltage, then we will need a higher current and thicker wires. On the contrary, if we use thinner wires, then we will need a higher voltage, but also more protective shielding. In this chapter, we try to find the $P = UI$ equivalent to maintainable APIs. Our quest here is to unearth the essential forces behind changes, and to illuminate some techniques to control those changes. To make the whole discussion comprehensible, we also present a simulation about what typically happens in the software industry during development and maintenance in relation to APIs.

Electronic supplementary material The online version of this chapter (doi:10.1007/978-1-4842-2196-9_1) contains supplementary material, which is available to authorized users.

---

[1]Does it help if I say that reactive power exists in an AC circuit when the current and voltage are out of phase? Or maybe to say that the presence of capacitors or inductors in a circuit would create such power? Or even better, that reactive power helps active power flow through the network? None of these are satisfactory, nor illuminate the essence of reactive power. However, everybody agrees that reactive power is crucial to maintain the operation of a power grid. The same is true with an API. Even if you don't fully understand it, it will still dictate the destiny of your software system, so it is advantageous to grasp it!

© Ervin Varga 2016
E. Varga, *Creating Maintainable APIs*, DOI 10.1007/978-1-4842-2196-9_1

■ **Tip**   We also need to outline what we mean by an API. In some ways, it is hard to define, like asking someone to explain what the *reactive power* is in power transmission and distribution networks.[1] Whatever definition you use it must embrace an important goal: It is the responsibility of the author of the API to make it right! There can be no excuses that users misused it and no excuses that the previous version was bad, and we needed to break compatibility. I would recommend you read Jaroslav Tulach's excellent book *Practical API Design* (Apress, 2008) to get a better insight into the types of APIs we're going to talk about in this part of the book. His book will also equip you with concrete technical knowledge (with a focus on Java) about evolving APIs. At any rate, we will leave the question "What is an API?" open for now, and let you synthesize the definition of it by yourself (after reading this book).

Why is there a need to give so much attention to an API? It's predominantly because APIs cannot be treated as an afterthought of development; that is, it isn't straightforward to bolt them on top of existing applications and expect that everything will just work out well.[2] An API has to grow from inside by letting an application expand around it. To create maintainable APIs, we first need to analyze what forces influence our decisions, and what happens to a software system during its exploitation.

The maintainability of an API entails the search for likely changes in the future. The idea is to make the system more flexible and thus easy to modify, in the areas where we expect those changes to happen. The requirements should reflect those concerns (give some hints), as it is nearly impossible to design a system with pieces that are all straightforwardly malleable. Therefore, we start with an initial set of assumptions and group them into two broad categories: those that remain relatively fixed, and those that are expected to be in flux. Of course, at any given time ostensibly all assumptions are rock solid. The next quote sets the stage between assumptions and induced changes in a system.

> *Death is very likely the single best invention of Life. It is Life's change agent. It clears out the old to make way for the new.*
>
> —Steve Jobs, *2005 Stanford Commencement Address*

This is exactly the driving force behind changes, the death of assumptions about the state of things inside the software and its surroundings (see the sidebar "Types of Software Systems" to better understand how an environment affects the software). Figure 1-1 shows a continuous sequence of changes during the software's life cycle. We see here that a die out of an assumption triggers a change, which results in the establishment of a new (possibly better) assumption about the real world, hence our software. If this assumption turns out to be unstable, then it will eventually expire. That would initiate a new cycle (this is similar to the notion of systems with a feedback control loop). Another way to look at this is like an evolutionary race, where the goal is for stakeholders to reach the Nash equilibrium[3] in regard to assumptions.

---

[2] One of the biggest mistakes is to take an existing implementation and simply treat it as an API. That doesn't work. On the other hand, it is possible to develop an API for existing applications. For example, Amarok (see `https://amarok.kde.org`) has a JavaScript extension API: you can add new menu items, modify a list of songs, and so on. Originally it had no API at all. Another superb example is the hue demonstration video of adding a hypermedia-driven REST API on top of an existing non-hypermedia-based API (see reference 1 in Chapter 7).

[3] For more information see `https://www.khanacademy.org/economics-finance-domain/microeconomics/nash-equilibrium-tutorial`.

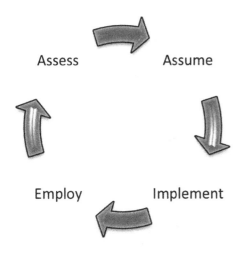

Figure 1-1. *The perpetual cycle of changes initiated by invalidated assumptions. We can name this cycle Assume-Implement-Employ-Assess, where during an assessment phase we discover the death of assumptions.*

TYPES OF SOFTWARE SYSTEMS

We can classify software systems in various ways. One such approach is especially useful from the viewpoint of maintenance, and is based on the nature of a system's interaction with its environment. This model suggests that the necessity of changing software is directly proportional to the intensity of such interactions. By *intensity* we mean the strength of the environmental influence on the software. We can even extend this model by saying that a software system might also affect its environment, and trigger changes in it. Systems highly dependent on their environment could even have an API for self-adapting mechanisms, if such autoregulation is feasible for the matching system.[4] At any rate, this classification might help us to better understand the potential sources of changes.

The following are the three categories of software systems.

1. *S type systems:* The environment is only taken into account during the initial requirements specification. Systems of this type are static, and solve some well-defined problem. There is no interaction with an environment during execution (we don't assume providing input data by a user as a classical interaction). If initial conditions change, then a brand new system is realized. For example, the popular Tic-Tac-Toe game is an S type system. The problem space is totally searchable (all possible moves can be easily enumerated and evaluated in real time), and there is a straightforward optimal strategy for both players. In other words, if both players play optimally, then all games will end in a draw.

2. *P type systems:* These systems have a very complex and vast problem space. There is no way to iterate over all positions in real time (in case of a board game, like chess or go). For this reason, a system of this type employs a simplified abstract

---

[4]Self-adapting systems are commonplace in distributed control systems, with an API to tune configuration parameters, or other aspects of self-adaptation. The JMX technology (for a good overview, visit https://docs.oracle.com/javase/tutorial/jmx/) might be handy for exposing management characteristics of a system to tune control parameters.

model as a replacement of the original domain. Of course, solving this simplified model will not necessarily result in producing an optimal answer. Therefore, model improvement efforts are an extra source of changes compared to the previous S type systems. Nevertheless, the original problem domain doesn't change over time.[5]

3. *E Type Systems:* These are the most complex systems. They have a complex problem domain, so simplified models are needed as in the case of P type systems. However, the execution environment (i.e., real world) is an integral part of it. Many times, especially in regulated markets, the environment is the principal reason for a change. For example, accounting software definitely must follow all financial rules established by a government. The problem is that those changes cannot be always predicted with 100% accuracy. They do sometimes pose a huge challenge, when the solution cannot nicely fit into an existing architecture.

If we treat these categories (established in Lehman's law of software evolution; see [3]) as indicators of how much we can assume about the future, then as we move from S to E type the amount of "stability" declines. The main problem with most university curricula[6] and software books is that they dodge E type systems. On the contrary, reality loves them.

The former Sun Certified Java 2 Developer certification process (I got certified before Oracle took over Sun) exhibits a lot of the cycle from Figure 1-1. The requirements specification for the assignment was intentionally written in a vague manner. The goal was to leave plenty of opportunities for assumptions, and to somehow simulate E type systems. The beauty of the certification process was that all assumptions were supposed to be properly documented. Any unmentioned assumption was treated like an omission, as if the developer didn't even think about it during the implementation. For example, if pagination (as a technique to control the amount of returned data) was not mentioned, but the implementation returned all data at once, then this was an *unconscious assumption* (one of the wickedest sort).[7] The assessment phase was basically the evaluation of your submission, together with the set of associated assumptions. Of course, documented but wrong assumptions were also penalized. All in all, the soundness of the solution heavily depended on the initial set of assumptions. The points loss rate was directly proportional to the assumptions die-out pace (unconscious assumptions died instantly).

Entropy and Its Impact on Assumptions

Entropy is a fundamental phenomenon that permeates our physical world. We have all experienced its effects in our everyday lives. Murphy's law (you can find lots of references of this kind at http://www.rationality.net/murphy.htm) even states that "things will go wrong in any given situation, if you give them a chance." The truth is that you don't even need to do anything; entropy will spontaneously raise the chance above zero. Entropy is the degree of randomness of a system; that is, the level of its disorganization. Nature will always strive to dismantle any organized system into a total fuzziness. A software system is also on an entropy's target list.

Suppose we start with an uninitialized computer system. Its memory is filled with garbage. When you turn on your computer (assuming the memory gets initialized arbitrarily), then the probability is actually zero that the bytes will arrange themselves into a useful program. If we would like to use this computer, then we need

---

[5]Well, this is not quite true, as the rules of chess did change over its history. However, such changes are extremely rare, and nobody anticipates further alterations to chess rules in the future.

[6]Just imagine the reaction of a student, after she or he is informed (at the last minute) that some of the settings in her or his semester project was changed! I, as a professor, would surely have consequences.

[7]For another example of a wicked assumption (undocumented software features) you can read my LinkedIn blog post at https://www.linkedin.com/pulse/instead-rules-tell-story-ervin-varga. The example in the article is tightly associated with an eager empirical programming, where perceived behavior prevails over the specification itself.

to fill its memory with instructions and data, which entails bringing order into a system. By increasing order, we basically defy entropy. As a positive side effect, we also acquire efficiency. At least we can use the computer now for our own purposes. On the other hand, this is the moment when the fight begins. We constantly need to push back entropy's attempts to rob us of the pleasure of further exploiting our computer system. At any moment, what stands between us and the computer is an API, which enables us to reach out to the features of our computer system (we hand wave a bit here, as we equalize API and the user interface).

The corollary is that if you don't invest energy in keeping something useful, it will simply rot over time. *Broken windows theory* is a good allegory for what happens to unmaintained buildings as well as to messy software. Entropy is an inherent state of nature.

Figure 1-2 shows the three major intents we like to achieve in relation to an API, taking entropy into account. As long as we maintain order we defy entropy and preserve efficiency. As we invest more energy into an API, we actually combat the natural tendency of disorder. There might be entropy and disorder on the left or right side of the universe (see Figure 1-3), but the goal of the API is to prevent it from flowing from one side to the other. The API is a gatekeeper. It also gives us a simplified view of how things look on the "other side." We might not fight the entropy in the whole universe, but if we invest correctly into APIs at right places, then we'll be able to keep entropy in isolated locations, where it cannot do as much harm. In general, an API has two goals:

- *To protect client programmers from changes inside a target system:* A well-defined API hides the internal details of a system and localizes the effects of a change behind an API. Client programmers don't need to worry about being endangered by the ripple effects of a change in the system.

- *To protect the target system from whims of client programmers:* A well-organized API prevents client programmers from bringing disorder into the system, because a weak API allows loose behavior. If we expose too many internal details, then we need to bring in futile rules and expect people to follow them. Entropy will kick in and ruin everything. Therefore, by exposing less we actually reduce the surface area over which entropy can penetrate (through an API) into a system.

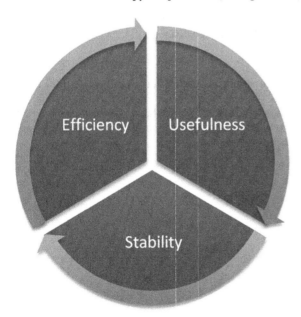

Figure 1-2. *We would like our API to be stable, efficient, and useful. These have to be balanced in the context of entropy. We can always create a supergeneric, but utterly useless API (I used to call microservices of this sort neutrino-services). Conversely, it is not hard to make a superefficient but totally unstable API.*

Figure 1-3 illustrates the previous two points, which have mentioned *exposure* for the first time so far. Hiding details not relevant for external parties (other components, or a client programmer) is what information hiding is all about. Without it we wouldn't be able to control the development and operation of a software system, as entanglement (both static and dynamic) would be unbearable. The main message is that the author of an API must be responsible for both directions. If you expose a field directly, without shielding it with methods, then that is your decision. If, for some reason, the user sets the field in a wrong way, or at a wrong moment, then this is your fault. All this boils down to the entropy of assumptions. If more is exposed than necessary, then the number of safe assumptions drops; that is, we have reduced the set of assumptions for which we can surely state that they will remain valid over some period of time.

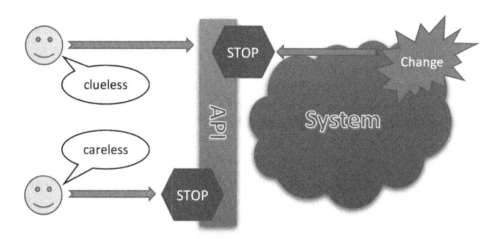

Figure 1-3. *The API protects clients from internal changes, and allows them to be clueless. Also, the API protects the system against careless usage. Be aware that the same client could be both clueless and careless. However, all of them will relentlessly criticize you and your API if things go amiss.*

Entropy, assumptions, and information hiding also explain the *amoeba effect* (see [1] for more details), which is a dichotomy between the actual state of a software system and our expectations (how we think it behaves[8]). The expectations are nothing but assumptions. If the system is sloppy in regard to information hiding, then our ability to safely set valid assumptions is rather limited. This will have dire consequences later on, when we start to discover that our previous assumptions were wrong. In other words, a high die-out rate of assumptions will trigger lots of code changes on both sides.

---

[8]The behavior of software is what determines whether it is *functionally compatible* with its past or possibly future versions.

It is tempting to combat entropy by making an overly generic API. If we mechanically parameterize every aspect of a function, then we will miss an opportunity to make clients' lives easier. The API, as well as the client's code relying on it, will become cumbersome. Here is a concrete example, using MIT Scheme (a variant of Lisp, and my favorite language) to illustrate the point (it is always beneficial to cultivate the polyglot programming principle). Suppose we came up with the following `accumulate` function:

```
(define (accumulate combiner null-value term a next b)
  (if (> a b)
      null-value
      (combiner (term a) (accumulate combiner null-value term (next a) next b))))
```

The Scheme is a functional programming language treating functions as first-class citizens in the program. The `accumulate` accepts the `combiner`, `term`, and `next` functions as parameters. The idea is to return an accumulated value of the `combiner` function (starting with an initial value of `null-value`) over an interval [`a, b`], where points inside the interval are converted by the `term` function. The `next` function is used for stepping through the interval. The `accumulate` is a recursive function, where the first point of the current interval is combined with the result of the accumulation over the rest of the interval. In Scheme (`<operator function>` `<argument-list>`) applies the operator function over the given arguments (these could also be expressions).

Using this version of `accumulate` we can easily calculate the maximum value of the `sin` function (this is quite a *brute-force* tactic):

```
(accumulate max -1.0 sin 0.0 (lambda (x) (+ x 0.1)) 4.0)
```

We will get the result of 0.9995736030415051, which is indeed close to 1. Despite the power of `accumulate`, it is hard to decipher what the given call is supposed to achieve. It begs for a comment, which is a clear sign that the code isn't comprehensible; that is, it isn't self-documenting. The corollary is that an API should serve a clear purpose, the utility of which has to be judged in the context of the target "audience." It might be the case that this version of `accumulate` is perfect in some low-level framework intended for experts. Obviously, it is a blunder to use it directly inside a high-level application code. In the next chapter we more systematically couple APIs with *abstraction*s, and illuminate how proper abstractions restrict entropy's negative effects.

■ **Note**   There are two opposite forces that you as a software engineer need to keep in balance. One is entropy with an aim to ruin the stability of assumptions, and the other one is the desire to keep the API stable. The API cannot just simply "follow" the entropy. Once an API is published it must be available forever.[9] Therefore, any change of an API needs to be done, at least, in a backward-compatible manner, annulling the effects of entropy.

---

[9]My favorite example for this is Java's `Thread` class. Since its first version it contains the next four deprecated methods for synchronizing threads: `resume`, `suspend`, `stop`, and `destroy`. They are deadlock-prone, and unsafe (see a detailed explanation at `docs.oracle.com/javase/8/docs/technotes/guides/ concurrency/thread-PrimitiveDeprecation.html`). As far as I know, nobody is using them, but they are still with us even in the latest edition of Java!

Case Study: API for Calculating an Integral of a Function

This case study demonstrates how the leakage of implementation details jeopardizes an API's stability. I also clearly circumscribe what I mean by a stable API (people often fallaciously think that stable necessarily means fixed). The task here is to specify an API for calculating the definite integral of a function f (with one real argument) between the limits a and b. We do not delve into implementation details, but keep our focus on only the API.

The API presented in this section is intended to be used both by client programmers and framework providers. These parties are at the opposite end of a spectrum; that is, they "subsist" at different sides of an API. Therefore, they have a diverse perception of what a compatible change means. We, as designers of the API, must be aware of this situation, and take it into account. The upcoming examples illustrate what conflicts might arise by not following the counsel that the API for clients and providers shouldn't be mixed (we separate them in Chapter 2).

The case study sheds light on a couple of aspects of maintainable API design. The goal is to put those aspects into a proper context for you to be able to find matching techniques (optimized for your programming language) to achieve them. Most of the time errors stem from improper usage of otherwise sound techniques, due to misunderstanding the preconditions for their application.

Version I: Direct Summation (Riemann Sum)

The integral can be approximated numerically, for relatively small values of dx, using this formula:[10]

$$\int_a^b f = \left[f\left(a + \frac{dx}{2}\right) + f\left(a + dx + \frac{dx}{2}\right) + f\left(a + 2dx + \frac{dx}{2}\right) + \cdots \right] dx$$

It is enticing to be fast, and come up with the next variant of an API (we will use purely Java interfaces here inside the default package[11]):

```java
import java.util.function.Function;

/**
 * API for calculating an integral of a function.
 */
public interface Integral {
    /**
     * Calculates the definite integral of a function between the limits a and b.
     *
     * @param f the integrand.
     * @param a the lower bound of the limit.
     * @param b the upper bound of the limit.
     * @param dx a small step size for iterating over the specified interval.
     * @return the numerical approximation of the definite integral.
     * @throws IllegalArgumentException if b <= a or f is null or dx <= 0.
     */
    double calculate(Function<Double,Double> f, double a, double b, double dx);
}
```

---

[10]The summation continues until the argument to f is lower than b. We are using middle values here, therefore this is the middle Riemann sum.

[11]For production you will need to introduce unique package names.

At first glance, nothing is wrong here. The interface `Integral` is properly documented (forget now the `@author` field), the method `calculate` has a meaningful signature, and again it is decently described. You are ready for the next steps:

1. Write unit tests.

2. Provide implementation according to this API.

3. Package up your stuff in the form of a jar file.

4. Publish the jar together with the `javadoc` documentation in some repository.

If creating APIs were be so easy, then you wouldn't need books about them. The major hindrance in designing a maintainable API is that you usually don't realize your mistake until it is too late (after the API is already published). Can you spot a problem? Is there a problem at all? That depends on what is going to happen in the future. If this will be your sole version of the API, and you don't plan to evolve it ever, then you're really done. However, a software framework's life truly begins after the publication of its first version. The first version is always easy, as that is when people feel like artists. However, once you switch into a so-called *sustaining mode*, all the freedom is gone. Only a tough engineering job remains for the future.

Version II: Simpson's Rule

Soon after the release of the first version, clients reported issues with performance and accuracy. The natural choice was to harness *Simpson's Rule*, which uses the following formula:

$$\int_a^b f = \frac{h}{3}\left[y_0 + 4y_1 + 2y_2 + 4y_3 + 2y_4 + \ldots + 2y_{n-2} + 4y_{n-1} + y_n\right], h = \frac{b-a}{n}, y_k = f(a+kh)$$

The first idea that usually comes to mind is to simply keep the current API, and replace the implementation behind it. Unfortunately, we cannot do this. Simpson's Rule expects an even number n instead of dx. We have a problem, and none of the following choices are adequate:

- *Let the client provide an equivalent of* n *in the form of* dx: The client would need to calculate the step size, which would give back the number of steps for the given interval. For example, if n should be 10 for the interval [0,1], then dx would be 0.1. This hack is just seemingly appropriate, and backward compatible. The ugliness of the API is not even the biggest problem. The main issue is that old clients would get different results, as the new version of the framework isn't functionally compatible with the past version.

- *Add a new overloaded* calculate *method taking* n *instead of* dx: Adding a new method to an interface is not a backward-compatible change. Framework providers will complain that their code doesn't compile anymore. Here is the visible consequence of not separating the client and provider APIs.

- *Announce that* dx *from now on represents* n: This is perhaps the worst incompatible tactic here.

Faced with this riddle, a typical reaction of most developers is to start looking at programming language mechanisms as a remedy. They will start to read blog posts, articles, and books, and stumble across the following pieces of advice:

- Interfaces are bad, bare classes are better.

- Bare classes are bad, abstract classes are better.

- Abstract classes are bad, final classes are better.

- Final classes are bad, Java 8 interfaces with default methods are better.

Some even get so emotionally attached to interfaces over abstract classes or vice versa, that they will vehemently defend their "baby" under all circumstances. What they fail to notice is that all of these statements are meaningless when taken out of context. They do have a value, but only when considered in the context of higher level principles.

■ **Caution** No technical magic can compensate for the leakage of an implementation detail into an API (in our case the dx parameter). Most technical advice written down in books and articles contains a section explaining the prepositions of their usage (just like design patterns). You cannot neglect the context!

An API is all about clarity (see http://wiki.apidesign.org/wiki/ClarityOfTypes). It is about the communication between the writer and users of the API. If the communication isn't clear, it will generate noise. How to eliminate such noise? An effective tactic is to make sure that the API can be used in only one correct way. Clearly, Version I is far from being evident. For example, there is no guidance about how to get an implementation for the interface. In Chapter 2 we will see how to solve this conundrum in a standard fashion. Moreover, the method calculate has an overloaded meaning.

At this moment, an alluring strategy is to bite the bullet, and come up with the proper solution (despite the fact that it will not be backward compatible).[12] After all, it seems better to improve the situation now than to defer the inevitable rework for later. Postponing this task will just make it harder. What should we do?

Well, we must be responsible, and preserve backward compatibility. Compatibility is a matter of an attitude and will, rather than a pure technical skill of the API designer. Hence, we will mark the first version of our API as deprecated (using the @Deprecated annotation), and clearly document the reason. Moreover, we will point users to the new version. Nevertheless, we will have to support this old version forever.

In the new version (note the introduction of the IntegralV2 interface), we need to separate the definite integral's definition from its implementation-related part. The implementation aspect must be a wrapper with a new abstraction, so that clients may explicitly choose the algorithm and specify custom parameters. This approach is embodied in the principle called *separation of concerns*. A similar principle is the *separation of a mechanism from its policy*. All in all, instead of dx or n we need to pass an instance of the matching portfolio for grouping algorithm-specific parameters (see more about the *Portfolio* pattern in [4], which is also close to the Request/Response pattern as described at http://wiki.apidesign.org/wiki/RequestResponse). The type of the portfolio will implicitly designate the desired algorithm. Here is the new API with the full definitions of portfolios (only the entity names shown in bold):

```
import java.util.function.Function;

/**
 * API for calculating an integral of a function.
 */
public interface IntegralV2 {
    /**
     * Calculates the definite integral of a function between the limits a and b.
     *
     * @param f the integrand.
```

---

[12]As you've seen, even this innocuous example contained a hideous trap. Imagine how hard the API design endeavor for complex frameworks is (e.g., Netbeans integrated development environment [IDE], Java collections framework, etc.).

```
 * @param a the lower bound of the limit.
 * @param b the upper bound of the limit.
 * @param spec the algorithm and its associated parameters.
 * @return the numerical approximation of the definite integral.
 * @throws IllegalArgumentException if b <= a or f is null or spec is null.
 */
double calculate(Function<Double,Double> f, double a, double b,
            IntegralPortfolio spec);
}


/**
 * The base portfolio marker class from which concrete algorithm specific
 * versions are derived.
 */
public abstract class IntegralPortfolio {};


/**
 * The portfolio for the Direct Summation method.
 */
public final class DirectSummation extends IntegralPortfolio {
    private final double dx;

    /**
     * Creates a new immutable instance of this class.
     *
     * @param dx a small step size for iterating over the specified interval.
     * @throws IllegalArgumentException if dx <= 0.
     */
    public DirectSummation(double dx) {
        if (dx <= 0) {
            throw new IllegalArgumentException(
                    "The step size must be greater than zero.");
        }

        this.dx = dx;
    }

    public double getDx() {
        return dx;
    }
}


/**
 * The portfolio for the Simpson's Rule method.
 */
public final class SimpsonsRule extends IntegralPortfolio {
    private final int n;
```

```
/**
 * Creates a new immutable instance of this class.
 *
 * @param n an even positive integer representing the number of summands.
 * @throws IllegalArgumentException if n <= 0 or not even.
 */
public SimpsonsRule(int n) {
    if (n <= 0 || (n % 2 != 0)) {
        throw new IllegalArgumentException(
                "The number of summands must be a positive even integer.");
    }

    this.n = n;
}

public int getN() {
    return n;
}
}
```

The `IntegralV2` interface can be implemented by using a switch over the instance type of `IntegralPortfolio`, or via the *double-dispatch* approach. Nonetheless, this decision isn't completely hidden from implementers (see the next version). Figure 1-4 shows the class diagram of our new API (for a good overview of the UML you can visit `http://holub.com/goodies/uml/index.html`).

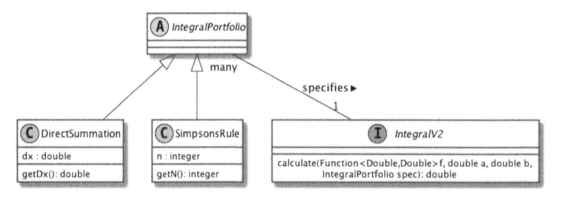

Figure 1-4. *The class diagram of the improved API (Version II) for calculating an integral of a function. Recall that the old interface (not shown here) is still available for clients.*

The various portfolios contain selectors (getters) for the private instance field(s). In general, getters and setters should be avoided, but here getters are returning the parameters that the matching portfolio is supposed to hold. They are okay here, as a portfolio is reminiscent of a *data transfer object* (see `http://martinfowler.com/eaaCatalog/dataTransferObject.html`).

Version III: Romberg's Method

Some sophisticated clients demand more control over accuracy and performance. They've specifically requested the implementation of Romberg's method. It is not unusual that clients drive the evolution by also proposing solutions (besides just reporting problems, or asking for extensions). The formula is recurrent, and you can read about it in some good books about mathematical analysis. It is interesting to note that Simpson's Rule is a special case of Romberg's method. All in all, the method is fully specified with two positive integers: n and m.

Luckily, this is now easy for us to support. We just need to introduce a new portfolio type, RombergsMethod, and we are done. This change is absolutely backward compatible. Figure 1-5 shows the new class diagram of our API.

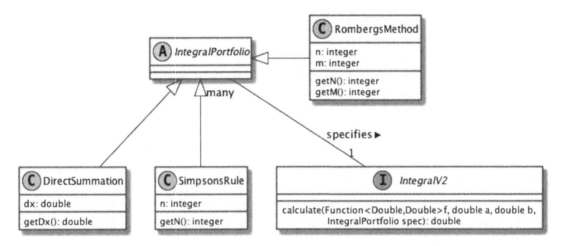

Figure 1-5. *The class diagram of the latest API (Version III) for calculating an integral of a function. Again, the old interface is still alive.*

■ **Note** If your API isn't ready for evolution, then you could easily lose your users. It is especially important to respond quickly to requests and incorporate all changes in a backward-compatible manner. Responding to requests quickly brings you new users, but making the changes in a backward-compatible manner keeps the existing users. Finding the proper balance is the delicate art of doing good API frameworks. Preserving compatibility builds up trust, which is the key enabler for the growth of your community and your software. Trusted clients will be motivated to formulate constructive feedback, and that is the best way to know what to include in the next version.

The code for the new portfolio is shown here:

```
/**
 * The portfolio for Romberg's method.
 */
public final class RombergsMethod extends IntegralPortfolio {
    private final int n;
    private final int m;
```

```java
/**
 * Creates a new immutable instance of this class.
 *
 * @param n a positive integer representing the first dimension in the formula.
 * @param m a positive integer representing the second dimension in the formula.
 * @throws IllegalArgumentException if n <= 0 or m <= 0.
 */
public RombergsMethod(int n, int m) {
    if (n <= 0 || m <= 0) {
        throw new IllegalArgumentException(
                "The dimensions must be positive integers.");
    }

    this.n = n;
    this.m = m;
}

public int getN() {
    return n;
}

public int getM() {
    return m;
}
}
```

We have just witnessed what is a *stable* API. Stability entails that an API can be straightforwardly evolved in a backward-compatible manner. Stable doesn't mean fixed; quite contrary, it designates a flexible, dynamic and maintainable API. The principal mechanism to achieve stability is to properly judge the potential *vector of changes*. These vectors indicate the directions from which changes will most probably emanate. Never assume that your API is finalized. It isn't. Always think about what you'll do, when it is found to be insufficient.

At any rate, many open questions are still unanswered (we will see in Chapter 2 how OSGi might help us in getting suitable answers):

- How can a client find out that a particular implementation of the IntegralV2 interface supports the Simpson's Rule algorithm (or any other for that matter)?

- What will a client receive after making a probationary call (to check the previous guess)? Is there a way for a client to avoid making such a call?

- Will a client get an exception? Is this documented?

Summary

What is then the P = UI equivalent for maintainable APIs? This expression tries to formulate the answer:

<Assumptions> = <Information Hiding><Software Type (S, P, or E)>

In other words, the set of valid assumptions is directly proportional to the achieved information hiding in the context of the type of a software system. This is tightly related to entropy. For an E type software, the surface area over which entropy may penetrate into a system is much larger than for an S type software. This means that this surface area has to be reduced by careful abstractions and information hiding. We always have to strive to control an E type software as it would be an S type one.

This chapter has highlighted the importance of information hiding and some other associated principles in creating maintainable APIs. The next chapter builds on this one, and explains the role of abstractions and modules to control complexity. Again, the focus will be on APIs rather than on implementation.

MONTE CARLO INTEGRATION

The Importance of Proper Naming

Monte Carlo integration relies on the Monte Carlo simulation to estimate the integral. This is a totally different approach than we have seen so far. It belongs to the class of probability methods, where the output value cannot be exactly predicted. Instead of an integrand, the method generally expects a predicate function. A canonical example of Monte Carlo integration is the estimation of π.

Consider adding support for this kind of integration into our API. Does it fit nicely? If you would choose to add an additional API to this nondeterministic group of methods, how would you name it? Does it hurt that we already have such a generic name as `Integral`? Wouldn't be better if we would have named it differently, like `RiemannIntegral`?

This exercise tries to drive your attention to the fact that improper naming can cause havoc in an API. Always try to avoid exceedingly generic names. The ancient Egyptian people were possessed with names, and they invented the *cartouche* to write them down. We should be equally preoccupied about naming software artifacts.

THE LIFE OF A CLIENT

Practicing Empathy

As an API designer you need to care about both developers and users. If you solely optimize the solution to be developer friendly (easy to implement), then it might be a nightmare for clients to use. Version III isn't quite a user-friendly proposition. Imagine that you did introduce an exception, in case the requested algorithm isn't supported (a usual practice in Java is to throw an `UnsupportedOperationException` exception). The client code would look similar to the following code snippet (this just illustrates the problem rather than hinting that you should code in this manner):

```
try {
// RombergsMethod
} catch (UnsupportedOperationException e) {
    try {
    // Simpson's Rule
    } catch (UnsupportedOperationException e) {
    // Fallback to Direct Summation
    }
}
```

Your task here is to come up with a revised approach by separating the client and provider APIs. The client API can go along the following line:

```
public final class IntegralClient {
    public double directSummation(...) {...}
    public double simpsonsRule(...) {...}
    public double rombergsMethod(...) {...}
    public Capability supportedAlgorithms() {...}
}
```

The `Capability` would contain a description about the available algorithms. You would also need to have a pluggable service provider interface part as follows:

```
public inteface IntegralProvider {
    double calculate(...);
}
```

This interface would be implemented by different providers, such as `RombergsMethodImpl`, `SimpsonsRuleImpl`, and so on. Each provider's implementation should be linked with an instance of a client API class.

The client API class could even try to simulate various integral methods, if they aren't supported by a particular implementation. For example, if the `simpsonsRule` is called without the matching provider, it might convert its argument for the direct summation routine (this is assumed to be the default method). Think about how the client would signal the acceptance of this behavior through an API.

The preceding API would be a mediator between the caller and implementer. The selection of the right integral method wouldn't be a contract between the user and the implementer of the API, but rather an internal "protocol." This is far simpler from the outside compared to Version III.

References

1. Tulach, Jaroslav. *Practical API Design: Confessions of a Java Framework Architect.* New York: Apress, 2008.

2. Niku, Saeed Benjamin. *Engineering Principles in Everyday Life for Non-Engineers.* Synthesis Lectures on Engineering #26. San Rafael, CA: Morgan & Claypool, 2016.

3. Pfleeger, Shari Lawrence, and Joanne M. Atlee. *Software Engineering: Theory and Practice, Fourth Edition.* Upper Saddle River, NJ: Pearson, 2010.

4. Fowler, Martin. *Analysis Patterns: Reusable Object Models.* Reading, MA: Addison-Wesley, 1997.

5. Abelson, Harold, Gerald Jay Sussman, and Julie Sussman. *Structure and Interpretation of Computer Programs, Second Edition.* Cambridge, MA: MIT Press, 1996.

CHAPTER 2

■ ■ ■

Modular Design

In the previous chapter, we analyzed information hiding as a mechanism to hide implementation details from external parties (clients and providers). However, we haven't spent a lot of time looking at our subjects as physical entities. We were complacent with the notion that we do possess some logical entities that need their own API. We have merely struggled to reduce the amount of exposed implementation details to conceive an evolvable API. In this chapter, our focus is on the kinds of entities we usually manage in large software projects, and how such entities are materialized as a unit of use and reuse. Nowadays, these entities are well known by the name of *software modules*. Nonetheless, this doesn't mean that we only deal with one predetermined type, as software modules are quite diverse. They have different granularity, scope, life cycles, and so on.

In essence, a software module is a by-product of a program design technique called *modularity* (see [1] for more details). The idea is to apply encapsulation to group-related pieces into an independently deployable unit, and leverage information hiding to shield them from each other. Each unit is then allowed to communicate with dependent units solely via well-defined interfaces (APIs). Apparently, a module is made up of a publicly exposed part (API) and an internal implementation. At first glance, we have just repeated what the *class* is in an OOP language. Despite the similarity, these are two different things. A class is purely the blueprint for creating objects; it is meaningful only in the context of object-oriented languages, and has a fixed scope, granularity, and life cycle (dictated by the rules of the matching programming language). A module doesn't have these limitations. At the highest *modularity maturity model* level (see [2] for more explanation) it may could even exist in a form of an independent service. To make the discussion more pragmatic, this chapter introduces examples of software modules using Racket (a functional programming language) and OSGi[1] (a mature modularity solution for Java).

At any rate, we are here interested in to see how modularity helps us in creating better APIs as well as to investigate how APIs may become separate modules having completely independent life cycles from their realizations (usually an official implementation of an API is called the *reference implementation*). In other words, we will amalgamate modularity as a design technique with OSGi as a modular technology to shape our APIs. Modular design complements object-oriented design, where physical design decisions influence purely logical ones. All this has a profound effect on APIs, as well. For example, only through modularity we can start thinking about the environment (the required environment of a module is usually expressed by its dependencies as elucidated at `http://wiki.apidesign.org/wiki/Environment`), and its configuration aspects comprise a separate API. Such a thing doesn't exist in logical design artifacts (classes and packages).

---

[1]Another good alternative is the NetBeans module system, which is fully OSGi-compliant since version 6.9 (`http://wiki.apidesign.org/wiki/NetBeans_Runtime_Container`). The Eclipse Equinox is an implementation of the OSGi core framework specification (`http://www.eclipse.org/equinox/`). Java 9 will come up with a modularity support called Jigsaw, but at the time of this writing, it is too early to say how it is going to be accepted. I have a feeling that it will come too late, and will share the destiny of the JDK logging framework. The latter appeared well after Log4J was already established as a de facto standard Java logging solution.

© Ervin Varga 2016

E. Varga, *Creating Maintainable APIs*, DOI 10.1007/978-1-4842-2196-9_2

Without proper APIs, and their backward compatibility, modularity has a very limited scope. It is still applicable inside a single project, without sharing in mind, but the true benefit comes with reusable modules. The only benefit of modularity without proper APIs is variability; you build a product once, and then distribute it to various users in different configurations (set of enabled modules). This scenario might tolerate the absence of appropriate APIs because the product is always built and distributed as a whole, but once you start leveraging a truly distributed development with diverse schedules (`http://wiki.apidesign.org/wiki/Distributed_development`), then having adequate APIs is a must.

API-Driven Development

To understand APIs and their associated entities (classes, modules, or applications and services), we first need to analyze the metaprocess that substantiates all APIs. Furthermore, we have to describe the following terms (these are crucial from the viewpoint of modularity and APIs): *abstraction, encapsulation,* and *data.* The biggest challenge, what most books silently skip, is how to acquire the material to work with and apply to it all those principles, patterns, and techniques that books are so happy to talk about (see [5] for an insightful introduction into this topic). Figure 2-1 shows the UML activity diagram depicting the metaprocess of creating an API. A real (concrete) process would be an instance of this metaprocess configured with a set of principles, patterns, and techniques applied at each activity. A real process would also have additional activities, but those are omitted to keep the diagram lean and focused.

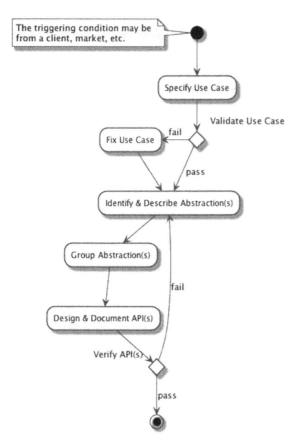

Figure 2-1. *The use-case-driven API metaprocess is similar to the rational unified process, where use cases play a central role in shaping the architecture.*

The creation of a clean API cleans the associated implementation, too. Therefore, focusing on an API (API-driven development) has a profound effect on code clarity. In other words, it exerts a powerful force on later design decisions. In some way, an API serves the role of a system specification, a kind of a mediator between requirements and implementation. On the other hand (in sustaining mode), the need to preserve backward compatibility might lead to ugly solutions inside the API implementation.

Use Case

Here are the most salient benefits of starting with an underpinning use case (for a more detailed treatment of use cases see [3]):

- It encompasses behavioral requirements.

- It has a clear goal from the primary actor's perspective.

- It has a designated level helping to identify the target software layer, where this use case belongs.

- It lists all the stakeholders interested in the use case.

- It describes the main scenario, possibly with alternate flows.

■ **Note**   The life of an API must start with a compelling use case; that is, no use case => no API!

The use case must be validated to properly reflect the intention of the primary actor. The use case later on serves as a reference to verify the API (whether it truthfully reflects what is stated there). A use case is the generator of abstractions, which will become part of an API. Note that a single use case could entail multiple APIs if someone decides, for example, to apply the *interface segregation principle* (see [4] for more details), to enhance maintainability, usability and reusability (this is reflected in the *grouping abstractions* meta-activity).

A use case may be issued for a new feature, a bug fix (where it describes how to reproduce a bug), performance improvement, and so on. All in all, it justifies the reason for change.

The use case description must follow an agreed-on template, and should comply with the same quality standards as all the other software artifacts. The description should be taken from the main success scenario with some alternate flows (error situations, variations in the main scenario, etc.). Each step in the description must clearly state who is performing that step (you will see an example of a concrete use case later exhibiting one simple template). It is bad practice to put conditional steps in a particular use case scenario. All these must be placed into alternate flows with pointers about what steps are modified in the parent scenario (you should also avoid deep nesting of flows). An ambiguous use case description is a sign of a lack of commitment from the initiator. You cannot produce a proper API if you don't know exactly what the user wants. Guesswork rarely pays off, as anything you publish as part of an API will need to remain forever.

As use cases are just pure textual descriptions, following some predetermined format, they can be stored in basically any issue tracking system. They could also be part of the documentation, as it should start with use cases (see also http://wiki.apidesign.org/wiki/Maven#What_Do_API_Users_Say.3F). If there are lots of interrelated use cases, then you might accompany them with corresponding UML use case diagrams. You might even model the users (e.g., some use cases are solely offered to users with higher privileges). However, use case diagrams should never replace the textual description.

Abstraction

The acts of the mind, wherein it exerts its power over simple ideas, are chiefly these three: 1. Combining several simple ideas into one compound one, and thus all complex ideas are made. 2. The second is bringing two ideas, whether simple or complex, together, and setting them by one another so as to take a view of them at once, without uniting them into one, by which it gets all its ideas of relations. 3. The third is separating them from all other ideas that accompany them in their real existence: this is called abstraction, and thus all its general ideas are made.

— John Locke, *An Essay Concerning Human Understanding* (1690)[2]

This quote nicely defines an *abstraction*: It is a principal mechanism to cope with complexity, like a living cell capable of combatting entropy. It purifies noise from the real world, and illuminates only the pertinent details. All this happens in the context of the use case; that is, we can judge the power of an abstraction only by relating it to the use case. One persuasive way to test the soundness of an abstraction is to identify it with a name. A troublesome name implies a problem; for example, `GenericGenerator`, `LoopComponentManager` (I have found this in the superb collection of enterprise naming madness at `https://github.com/EnterpriseQualityCoding/FizzBuzzEnterpriseEdition`), and so on. If these samples are all you can come up with, you should immediately stop. Would you like to use an API filled with such "cool stuff"?

Abstraction is a precious and scarce asset. It might sound strange that I'm advising you to be sparing with abstractions, as they don't consume computer resources; they instead consume someone's ability to keep them in her or his head while browsing your API. More is not always better. Miller's rule states that we can simultaneously keep 7 ± 2 facts in our memory. If you use more than this, scrolling up and down in your IDE starts to be your main activity.

One way to reason about the quality (power) of abstractions that you aim to put into APIs is to estimate how many design and implementation decisions can be deferred to a later time without affecting the APIs. If there is an impact, then you should estimate how big it is. Recall Version I of our integral example from Chapter 1. The dx parameter leaked into an API, and it was a pure implementation detail. However, it should have been a decision postponed for a later time. This is why use cases are so important: They emphasize the primary actor's goal, not the technicalities around it. All abstractions of an API must be goal-oriented.

Invest in the abstraction, not the implementation. Abstractions can survive the barrage of changes from different implementations and new technologies.

— Andrew Hunt and David Thomas, *The Pragmatic Programmer*[3]

Data

In general, we can think of data as defined by some collection of selectors and constructors, together with specified conditions that these procedures must fulfill in order to be a valid representation.

— Harold Abelson, Gerald Jay Sussman, and Julie Sussman, *Structure and Interpretation of Computer Programs, Second Edition*[4]

---

[2]You may read the whole book at `https://ebooks.adelaide.edu.au/l/locke/john/l81u/index.html`.
[3]For more information about this book visit `https://pragprog.com/book/tpp/the-pragmatic-programmer`.
[4]See [10].

One approach to rigorously formulate the concept of data was introduced by C. A. R. Hoare (1972), known as the method of *abstract models*. In this model, abstractions are built on top of each other, very much like Lego pieces are arranged into bigger forms. Reasoning about complex data objects is then performed by analyzing the underlying building blocks (checking assertions about the constituent data objects).

This is a very powerful idea, bringing closer the notion of data to the other elements in the system. Even more, data is nothing else than an abstraction with a well-defined API, and an accompanying implementation. In Java, int is a *primitive* data type. Why primitive?[5] This is stated in the javadoc for the Integer class: "The Integer class wraps a value of the primitive type int in an object." So, what is Integer then? A nonprimitive data type? The Integer class undeniably appears as a kind of data abstraction, with a public API and implementation behind it. However, this is also true for int. The only difference is that int's API, and the same is true for the other built-in Java data types, is part of the Java language specification, and implemented by the Java virtual machine (JVM) itself. Hoare's abstract models method is depicted in Figure 2-2.

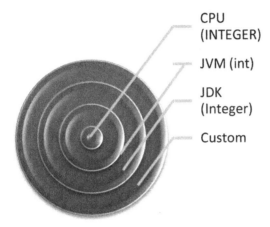

CPU
(INTEGER)

JVM (int)

JDK
(Integer)

Custom

Figure 2-2. *Hoare's abstract models in action. Each layer contains its own set of abstractions exposing a data API to the layers above. Outer layers are implemented on top of inner layers. Java's Integer class is realized using facts about the primitive data type int.*

■ **Note** Modules need to communicate with each other, and most communication entails passing data around. How you treat data has a fundamental impact on the API. If you pass a primitive data type, then you are relying on a low-level abstraction provided by the JVM. At any rate, each data type is accompanied with by API, and this is passed around together with the value.

Sometimes the runtime environment helps in converting between various data representations. For example, Java offers *autoboxing* and *unboxing*. The former is the automatic conversion between the primitive types and their corresponding object wrapper classes. *Unboxing* is the opposite process. At any rate, what happens is that a client programmer is provided with a suitable API to work with the same underlying value. Of course, some clever optimizations might happen in the background, like caching of instances, but users are usually clueless about these minutiae.

---

[5]It is an indication that the type isn't a subclass of java.lang.Object, has special treatment in the Java virtual machine (JVM), and so on. The notion of primitive types was an attempt to make Java acceptably fast in the 1990s. Nowadays, optimizing compilers (like Graal; see http://openjdk.java.net/projects/graal/) don't need such a hint, and can generate fast code even with "normal" subclasses of Object. The notion of primitive types just complicates the JVM. Nobody should design a new language with primitive types anymore.

Alonzo Church, the father of lambda calculus, invented a method called *Church encoding.*[6] Here, natural numbers are represented using lambda notation, and are named *Church numerals* (see the exercises at the end of this chapter for an example). Data, as we normally think about them, totally "disappear" in this method, though. You should keep in mind that in memory, executable code is stored as data. A self-modifying code (a popular technique in malware) even treats code as ordinary data.

Encapsulation

Encapsulation is probably one of the most misunderstood terms.[7] The computer community usually uses it interchangeably with information hiding, and this is wrong. Encapsulation is a technique to group related entities (in our case abstractions) together, sharing a common cause for change. Proper encapsulation is the enabler for achieving high cohesion. It is important to remember that encapsulation is applicable at all granularity levels (class, package, module, and application or service).

A properly encapsulated set of abstractions in an API establishes its unique abstraction level. This might self-protect the API, as nobody should make modifications that are inconsistent with this level. For example, a high-level API should not be polluted with raw device access details. This also applies to exceptions: It is wrong to put a "raw" IOException exception into a method signature in a high-level API. By raw I mean a very implementation-specific IOException, like java.net.SocketException, which would reveal too much. A high-level consumer would be puzzled by such an implementation detail.

Type Coercion Case Study

To make these concepts clearer, we will analyze a small segment from a symbolic algebraic manipulation system (for the full source code, visit https://github.com/evarga/algebraic-manipulation) pertaining to type coercion. I am going to use Racket (https://racket-lang.org) with the Scheme dialect (the modules here are intentionally simplistic without using Racket's more advanced features). Using a functional programming language gives me the freedom to focus only on the gist of the material without distractions due to syntactic sugar to satisfy the language compiler. This will allow you to see only the abstractions, and nothing else. Additionally, you will experience how the borders between data and procedures simply vanish. Learning to program in a real functional programming language is very important, as it totally transforms your way of thinking and enhances your problem-solving capabilities (you can read more about the *blub paradox* at http://www.paulgraham.com/avg.html).

The functional paradigm is gaining momentum in most mainstream languages, and Java is no exception. To use the power of lambda expressions in Java you need to make a paradigm shift (this is not easy). Finally, this case study emphasizes the fact that modularity is not Java related, but having a support from a modular framework[8] is very important. For example, Racket ensures that module relationships are acyclic, and emits an error otherwise.

As a starting point, we assume that our system already has the following modules:

- *type-tagging:* Handles the tagging of data types. A data type is represented as a pair (<type tag>, <contents>). There is a special *bridge* data type called 'scheme-number. Its purpose is to provide a transparent autoboxing and unboxing between built-in scheme numbers and our custom data types.

---

[6]See [10].

[7]Another one is the stability of an API, where people think that stable means fixed or unmodifiable. In the case of an API, stable means its readiness for backward-compatible evolution. For a module, greater stability implies bigger resistance to change. Modules with a high number of incoming dependencies (afferent coupling) are said to be stable. The number of outgoing dependencies (efferent coupling) defines the module's weight. A higher weight ruins usability and testability, as you would need to handle many dependent parts to use and test the module.

[8]For information about Racket's modular framework, visit https://docs.racket-lang.org/guide/modules.html.

- *function-composition:* Creates new functions from existing ones by composing them together.

Here are the listings of these modules. Each module is packaged in a separate file (e.g., `type-tagging.rkt`), and clearly announces its public API. We see that the unit of release is the unit of reuse. This mapping is only effective when the grouping of abstractions (encapsulation) is properly done. Mixing unrelated things together immediately spoils this relationship. Of course, it is possible to circumvent the agreement, and peek into internal details using intrusive techniques (e.g., someone could use reflection in Java to access private stuff of an object). However, in this case the developer must do such things intentionally and neglect what the design is trying to say. After all, somebody can even patch the compiler-generated code to make forbidden contraptions possible.

```scheme
#lang scheme

(provide attach-tag)
(provide type-tag)
(provide contents)

(define (attach-tag type-tag contents)
  (if (eq? type-tag 'scheme-number)
      contents
      (cons type-tag contents)))

  (define (type-tag datum)
    (cond ((pair? datum) (car datum))
          ((number? datum) 'scheme-number)
          (error "Bad tagged datum -- TYPE-TAG" datum)))

  (define (contents datum)
    (cond ((pair? datum) (cdr datum))
          ((number? datum) datum)
          (error "Bad tagged datum -- CONTENTS" datum)))
```

The function car returns the first element of a pair, and cdr the second one. The predicate pair? tests whether the argument is a pair. The eq? predicate compares symbols for equality. Symbols in Scheme are prefixed with '. Finally, define is used to define a function, and cond is the switch statement. However, the most important is the provide directive. It lists what is exposed in this module. In our case, type-tag and contents are selectors (getters in Java), and attach-tag is the constructor. Next is the listing of another module, function-composition.rkt:

```scheme
#lang scheme

(provide identity)
(provide compose)
(provide repeated)

(define (identity x) x)

(define (compose f g)
  (lambda (x) (f (g x))))

(define (repeated f n)
```

```
(cond ((= n 0) identity)
      ((= n 1) f)
      (else (compose f (repeated f (- n 1)))))))

; Couple of test cases.
; We define here our auxiliary increment and decrement functions.
(define (inc x) (+ x 1))
(define (dec x) (- x 1))

(inc 1)
; The output is 1.

((identity inc) 1)
; The output is also 1.

((compose inc dec) 1)
; The output is 1, since we are applying the composition (inc(dec(x)) to x=1.

((repeated inc 5) 1)
; The output is 6, since we are applying the composition (inc(inc(inc(inc(inc(x)))))) to
x=1.
```

This is perhaps the first time that you are totally puzzled, especially if you've never been exposed to the charms of functional programming. There is no difference between functions (procedures) and data. This is the same now in Java 8 with lambda functions. The compose is returning a lambda function applying f to g. The expression ((compose inc dec) 1) means that we are applying the result of composition (compose inc dec) to the first argument. The repeated function is recursive. It says, repeating the function f n times is basically composing f with its n-1 times repetition. Notice how the auxiliary inc and dec functions are not visible from outside of a module.

Another thing to observe is how the abstractions (identity, compose, and repeated) nicely complement each other. Obviously, they naturally fit together, and provide a cohesive unit.

■ **Caution**   Note that there is no safety check (validation) of input arguments in the code. For example, calling repeated with a negative number would induce an infinite loop. Never allow an API to be exposed to such attacks. You always need to apply the *defensive programming* technique (see [6] for more details). Also, you need to clearly document your APIs, including the exceptional conditions. Here, all this is omitted to save space.

Use Case: Coercing Arguments

We start with the use case definition using a very simple template (see [3] for more details about writing suitable use cases). Our use case has no alternate flows. Steps 2 and 3 may be rewritten into one, which would be even more correct to keep all the steps at the same abstraction level. Nevertheless, the current form's advantage will be revealed later. This use case is issued by the user of the symbolic algebraic system, and she or he has a request for a new feature.

Use Case: Coercing Arguments
Goal: Arguments are of mixed type, we want the module to coerce them into a single one. This allows us to sum up a complex number, rational number, and integer directly, and get back a complex number (as this is the most powerful type in this sample).

Scope: Symbolic Algebraic Manipulation System
Level: Primary task
Preconditions: All input argument types are known.
Success End Condition: All arguments are converted into a single type.
Failed End Condition: Internal system error.
Primary Actor (Caller): Algebraic engine subsystem.
Trigger: When an expression is evaluated containing arguments with mixed types.

MAIN SUCCESS SCENARIO:
1. The caller passes the arguments with mixed types to the module.
2. The module decides what the target type is by leveraging the tower of types.
3. The module converts all lower types into the target type.
4. The module returns the coerced arguments to the caller.

The *tower of types* is illustrated in Figure 2-3. To move up in this hierarchy, the algebraic system provides a polymorphic function raise. For example, a real number can be converted into a complex number by letting its real part take the value of the real number, and setting its imaginary part to zero. This function will be provided as input to the type coercion module.

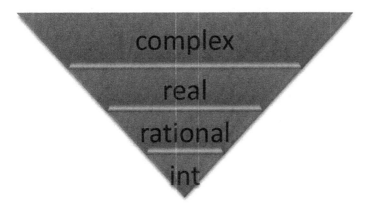

Figure 2-3. *As we move up in the hierarchy the types are more powerful; that is, they are the superset of the types below.*

Type Coercion Module

The new feature request use case unambiguously describes a compelling business case for us to create a new module. We know exactly what the user wants to achieve. Use cases are a perfect mechanism for you to get acquainted with your users, as they are most probably distributed all over the planet. Here is the listing of the new module called type-coercion.rkt.

```
#lang scheme

(require "type-tagging.rkt")
(require "function-composition.rkt")

(provide coerce-args)

; The levels are: integer (0), rational (1), real (2) and complex (3).
```

```
(define (type-level x)
  (let ((type-of-x (type-tag x)))
    (cond ((eq? type-of-x 'complex) 3)
          ((eq? type-of-x 'rational) 1)
          (else
           (if (exact-integer? (contents x)) 0 2)))))

; The 'raise' is an input function raising its argument into a higher level type.
; Each line in the implementation below is mapped to the corresponding use case step.
; Step 1.
(define (coerce-args raise args)
  ; Step 2.
  (let ((target-level (foldr max 0 (map type-level args))))
    ; Steps 3-4.
    (map (lambda (x) ((repeated raise (- target-level (type-level x))) x))
         args)))
```

The require directive indicates what the outgoing dependencies of this module are. The type-level internal function returns the data type's level in the hierarchy (the full system also supports polynomials of type 4). However, the effectiveness of functional programming languages is best exemplified in the implementation of the coerce-args function. The steps of the use case are essentially part of a pseudo-code documenting the inner details of this function. The code is nothing but a sequence of abstractions (built-in and custom) arranged into an engineering novel. You just need to speak the functional language, and all the rest unfolds automatically.

Let us see what happens in Step 2. This line says that the target-level variable should receive the result of evaluating the right side expression. That expression says that the input arguments list is first transformed into a new list using the type-level function (each element in the new list will have a value of (type-level x), where x is an element of args). Finally, by folding the transformed list using the max function, we will get the maximum element. In other words, we will find what the maximum type level of arguments is.

The line for Steps 3 and 4 is more interesting. It says to transform the input arguments using the specified lambda function. That lambda function receives an element from args (represented as x), and repeatedly applies the raise function to it. The number of such applications is equal to the difference between the maximum type level (kept in the target-level variable), and the type level of x.

■ **Caution**   Don't be seduced by beauty! It is okay to seek it until the first version of your API. Once you publish your API, you need to switch over into a maintenance (sustaining) mode. This means that you are obliged to only make backward-compatible changes in the future, even though that sometimes goes against beauty.

You're now hopefully aware of the importance of abstractions and encapsulation in creating evolvable software artifacts. An API is exposing the most salient abstractions, and these must be carefully postulated. Any rush work will have negative, long-running consequences. You have also seen that data is another type of abstraction with an associated API. At any rate, when an API exposes appropriate cohesive abstractions, the clients' code will use them in the most natural way. This is evident from the implementation of the coerce-args procedure. The imported abstractions nicely interplay with built-in abstractions (foldr, map, etc.), and together boost the expressive power of the language. When designing an API, make sure that you follow the patterns and conventions of the surrounding system. Following the same conventions and interplaying well makes it easy for programmers to get used to your API. An awkward API will spoil even the most decent client code. Therefore, as an API designer you have to put yourself into a client's position when leveraging your API. If you force the client to use strange, unnatural constructs in a code, chances are that she or he will switch to a competitor. An inept API cannot lower the cost of ownership for a client, as all the savings realized by reusing your library will be spent maintaining shoddy code on the client side.

Here is what can we conclude from this case study using Racket's module framework (which is really tiny compared to the potentials of OSGi):

- A module is the unit of reuse. In Racket, it is the file containing your artifacts. If the API isn't cohesive, then reuse isn't going to be economical, and use will be troublesome. In this case, you need to rethink your logical design and better group abstractions.

- Each module clearly signals what it exposes, and what it requires (imports) from other modules. The exposed part is the published interface (API).

- A module framework helps in managing a module's life cycle. For example, Racket automatically loads a module into memory when you reference it. It protects you from introducing dreaded cyclic relationships between modules.

Standard Java's Limitations

We switch now into the world of Java, which is currently the most popular programming language. All published versions of Java so far (at the time of this writing Java 8 is current) have a serious limitation regarding modularity. In Java, a module is physically represented as a jar file. Even if you come up with a perfect logical design (with properly encapsulated powerful abstractions), there is no way to enforce information hiding when packaging your artifacts into jar files. Obviously, producing a jar file is inevitable if you would like to share your module across applications. Figure 2-4 depicts a canonical example of the issue.

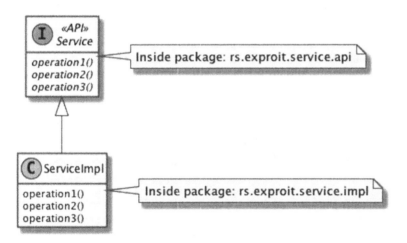

Figure 2-4. *There is no way to hide the* Service Impl *class, if it is declared as public. In other words, you cannot exclude it from your API. You can put it into the same package as* Service, *and make it package private (this would solve the visibility issue). However, for more complex scenarios you would want to keep the API separate from implementation.*

If you package the artifacts from Figure 2-4 into a service.jar module, then there is no way to hide from users the presence of the implementation class. Moreover, if you publish multiple different versions of this module, and someone has transitive dependencies that on them, only one will "win" on the classpath. This causes the infamous *jar hell* problem. Of course, we are neglecting here many technical details about how to get an instance of a Service, but for this discussion they aren't important.

Another problem pertains to dynamic class loading via the `ClassLoader` facility. Each class loader introduces a separate namespace for classes. This approach is susceptible to all sorts of runtime problems (like getting `ClassCastException` or `ClassNotFoundException` exceptions). Even if the same class is loaded by two different class loaders, they will not be treated as the same type. However, the biggest issue is that all these mismatches happen during execution. There is no fail-fast mechanism to let you know at deployment time that something is wrong (e.g., Spring helps you in this respect). Getting errors earlier is much better, because you can easily spot the culprit. This is another characteristic of a modular support that is provided by OSGi.

A naive approach would be to make `ServiceImpl` a package private class, but that would potentially deprive other internal module classes from other packages from using it. Another equally naive tactic is to put into the javadoc comment of `ServiceImpl` class the phrase, "Please, this is only for internal use!" The assumption is that if you are honest toward your clients, and they play nice, then the problem is resolved. Unfortunately, people start to read the documentation when they hit a problem, which might be too late.

■ **Caution** Even the most honest client will start using your implementation class, if she or he finds advantageous stuff there (even at the price of using reflection to access nonpublic methods). This is especially true when the time-to-market pressure is high. Your implementation class surreptitiously becomes part of an API, like it or not. Someone might even publish an article like "Tips & Tricks of Service.jar" on some blog (not to endorse your API, but to brag about her or his ingenuity).

OSGi as a Disruptive Technology

These are the two facets of modularity (see [2]): the development and runtime models. You could engage only a development model, by relying on core facilities provided by a build tool (like Maven or Gradle), or you could also bring in a true runtime model (like OSGi). Does the runtime model just make things easier, or is it a game changer (a disruptive technological advance)? I think it is the latter. OSGi is not only enabling ecosystems of modules, but has a profound effect on the way you think about design, too. For example, if you try to "cheat" by using non-API classes in some of your modules, then the OSGi runtime enforcement rules will clearly reveal all such laziness.

Let me take a detour, and compare problem-solving approaches in functional programming and nonfunctional programming worlds (structured programming, OOP, etc.). The well-known divide and conquer rule revolves around breaking a larger problem into subproblems, solving the subproblems, and merging the results back to produce the final outcome. However, the subproblem might equally fit into this template, just on a smaller scale. Therefore, many of you would now think about recursion, and you would be right. But wait! They have told you that you should ban recursion, as it is expensive. Whoever told you such a bluff was surely not originating from a functional programming world! Expense is not even the biggest issue here. The problem is that recursion is simply unnatural in nonfunctional languages. On the other hand, there are some computer science problems whose formulation until now only exist in recursive form[9] (e.g., the famous coin change problem).

To give you a glance at how functional programming is a paradigm shift, let us implement a function to return all subsets of a set. Don't start coding yet (prune away all those for loops from your head). Just stop, and think! I have a set. Cool. I want all subsets of it. Even cooler! What if I know how to find all subsets of a smaller set? Does this help? Look at the following step-by-step algorithm:

1. Take out the first element from the input set, and name it `first-of-s`.

2. Produce all subsets of a smaller set (pretend that you know how to deal with a smaller problem), and name it `smaller-subsets`.

---

[9]Sure, you can always simulate recursion using a stack, but that is like simulating OOP in C (e.g., you will have to fiddle with virtual method tables and function pointers to get polymorphism, or you could just leverage GLib).

3.   Attach first-of-s to all subsets of a smaller set. Guess what? You have just
     produced all subsets of the input set (the outer append in the following listing
     glues together all subordinate subsets from each recursive stage).

What do you know for sure? Well, all subsets of an empty set are empty sets (this is the exit condition).
This pure fact is all that you need. Now, just translate the preceding algorithm into a form a machine can
understand. Functional programming helps you to perform this task in a most straightforward manner. Here
is the Racket module subsets.rkt implementing the idea:

```scheme
#lang scheme

(provide subsets)

(define (subsets s)
  (if (null? s)
      (list '())
      (let ((first-of-s (list (car s)))
            (smaller-subsets (subsets (cdr s))))
        (append smaller-subsets
                (map (lambda (t) (append first-of-s t))
                     smaller-subsets)))))

; Test case to demonstrate how this works.
(subsets '(1 2 3))
;(() (3) (2) (2 3) (1) (1 3) (1 2) (1 2 3))
```

Is this a profoundly new way of approaching a problem? I think, so. The same is true for modularity and
OSGi. I want to emphasize that modularity brought in the same fundamentally different way to reason about
the structure of a system as the previously presented divide and conquer strategy. In that sense, they are
comparable. OSGi is here for you to be able to think in modules and their APIs in the most natural way. Even
though a development model might craft a modular design, only the runtime model will make it a reality.
Dynamisms in handling modules directly affect your APIs. We will see an example of this later on.

We have seen that the divide and conquer rule was a natural fit for a functional programming style.
This is exactly what OSGi achieves regarding modular patterns. They become an integral part of a software
engineer's toolset for designing a modular system.

OSGi in Action

The previous section highlighted an important difference between logical and physical design. What looks
logically sound might be physically problematic. Logical and physical design complement each other,
and modularity is here to address the latter.[10] We strive to achieve reuse, as this is a key enabler of higher
productivity. Reuse comes with the problem of shipping the shared artifacts. The unit of shipment is also the
unit of reuse, so how we package things directly affects the reuse rate.

Besides reuse, we must take care about use, too. There is nothing more frustrating than having
ultraflexible and reusable parts that are a nightmare to use. Balancing reuse and use is simply an art.
However, both reuse and use depend on APIs. Shielding implementation details is one sure way to craft
reusable and usable APIs at the same time.

---

[10]This is not true in general, as modularity considerably influences logical design, too. For example, if you notice that a
logical package is split across multiple modules, you need to revisit your logical design to avoid this situation. Also, if
you notice a circular dependency between your modules, then you will surely need to refactor your logical design to
escape circularity in module relationships. In the end, your logical design always benefits from modularity.

Another pertinent segment facilitated by modularity is *environmental awareness*. A logical world might completely eschew the environment (except modeling its important details through abstractions). On the contrary, a physical world cannot exist without it. How to externally configure our modules to fit into the target environment is something only relevant for a physical design. Thus, modularity brings in a completely new API for configuration purposes.

The ease with which you can utilize a modular design is directly proportional to the capabilities of your modular framework. The runtime model of modularity drives the life cycle aspects of your modules during execution. The next section presents a working modular Java solution to calculate integrals (we continue our journey from Chapter 1).

■ **Caution**   Responsibility without control is a recipe for failure. If you cannot enforce visibility rules in a module, then an API will start taking on an amoeba shape (entropy will prevail). Modularity is a mechanism to leverage control over your modules and their APIs.

Modular Integral Calculation

We implement the case study from Chapter 1 using Apache Felix Service Component Runtime (Felix SCR; http://felix.apache.org) as a reference implementation of the OSGi Declarative Services specification (see [7]). This will be a perfect opportunity for you to experience a *declarative API* in practice. Relying on Felix SCR will shield our modules from the specifics of the OSGi platform, keeping them independent of the OSGi API. Achieving container independence is very important, as we avoid a danger of polluting our API with technology-related details. This could seriously hinder future reuse options. Java EE tied beans too much to the platform, hence they were not reusable outside of it. This is not a desirable direction to follow.

■ **Note**   Relying on industry standards is very important. It's a proven strategy in various engineering domains, and should be a norm in the software engineering, too. It saves your investment in a technology, and reduces the learning curve for others joining your project or using your artifacts. OSGi provides many conventional APIs relevant from the perspective of runtime management of applications and services, and relying on these aids with maintenance. You should always try to avoid proprietary solutions when there is an already established standard.

■ **Tip**   Before proceeding with the text, study the Apache Felix SCR tutorial (http://felix.apache.org/ documentation/subprojects/apache-felix-service-component-runtime.html).

Felix also helps in configuring our modules as well as wiring them together (similar to how other dependency injection frameworks assist us, like Spring, Google Guice, etc.). This again simplifies our APIs, as we don't need to concoct custom factory-based instantiations.

In this example, we separate the client and provider APIs and put them into separate modules. Separating abstractions from their implementations will enable us to alter the implementations during runtime (OSGi allows you to dynamically switch modules without a system restart). Moreover, by using separate API bundles we can explicitly version them independently from their implementations. This has a tremendous positive effect on controlling an API's evolution. This agreeably complies with this quote:

Identifying the seams in a system involves identifying clear lines of demarcation in your architecture. On either side of those lines, you'll find components that may change independently, without affecting the components on the other side, as long as the components on both sides conform to the contract specified by that interface.

— Grady Booch, James Rumbaugh, and Ivar Jacobson, *The UML User Guide, Second Edition*[11]

These delineation lines, what are so explicitly pushed forward by modules, are the most sensitive parts of the architecture. A change inside a module is confined by that module's scope. A non-backward-compatible change in the published API of a module could instigate a ripple effect in the system. One way to effectively control API changes is to version them by packing API abstractions into a dedicated module. The drawback is a proliferation of more fine-grained modules in the system, but the benefit ordinarily outweighs the extra cost. This underpins the adage that more flexibility entails more complexity, so achieving the right balance is not an easy endeavor.

Figure 2-5 shows the UML component diagram of modules comprising this demo. We see that module relationships are acyclic, and the provider interface (API) module has no outgoing dependencies (the client module also serves as an adapter between client and provider APIs). The provider API is at module level 1 (you might want to read [2] about the *Levelized Module* pattern, and other modular patterns). Assigning levels is beneficial both from the build (the pattern driving the build is called *Levelized Build*) and module startup perspective (modules should be started up based on their level in an ascending order). Providers are separated from a client and each other via APIs. Each module is an independent entity.

The Architecture of the System

The system is defined as a Maven multimodule project. Each Maven module is responsible for implementing an OSGi bundle. Bundle is the term for a module in OSGi. It is essentially a jar file with an associated OSGi manifest file. The Maven build process follows the Levelized Build process. Essentially, the build performs a topological sort on the graph with vertexes being modules, and edge dependencies between them. The Levelized Build principle is to build modules according to their level so that all dependencies are satisfied. Such a leveled approach protects modules from inadvertently referencing each other (so easy to do when the whole codebase is a huge logical monolith), as an unwanted dependency will produce a build error. Again, this is something that modularity brings into the foreground.

The following list includes all the bundles that make up this project:

- *provider-api*: Contains the API artifacts relevant for providers. The source code is actually the same as Version III from Chapter 1 (with some slight changes, like, putting everything into a nondefault package, renaming `Integral` to `IntegralSPI`, etc.). This is the simplest bundle you can imagine in OSGi.

- *client-api*: This specifies the API for users of the integral framework. It also serves as an adapter to translate a user's request into a form understandable by providers. This bundle is an OSGi µService.

- *provider-directsummation*: This implements the direct summation integral method. This is also an example of an OSGI µService.

- *demo*: This is an OSGi component, a consumer of a service. It shows how to use the client API.

---

[11]See [11].

The other two missing providers are left as an exercise (see the exercises at the end of this chapter), although they are represented in Figure 2-5.

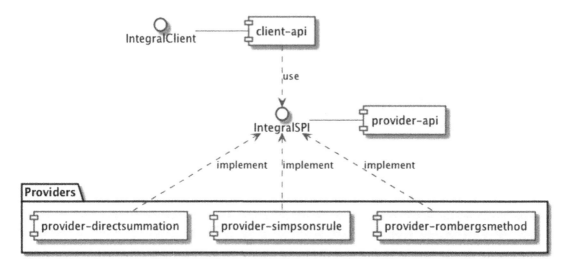

Figure 2-5. *The modules and their relationships in the system (without the demo bundle). We see that the* client-api *uses the API of providers to invoke them. However, it references only the provider API without pointing to any implementing service.*

The Provider API

It is instructive for us to look into the pom.xml build file. The details highlighted in the following listing are all you need to know if you would like to use basic OSGi bundles (just to protect the visibility aspects of a jar file). This is a perfect example of an incremental API of OSGi. Simple and common things are simple, and more advanced features require more OSGi knowledge. Therefore, you might start using OSGi right away in your projects, and later advance as required. Even these "simple" improvements mean a lot from an API's perspective. Applying information hiding immediately gives you full control over your jar files.

```xml
<?xml version="1.0"?>
<project
    xsi:schemaLocation="http://maven.apache.org/POM/4.0.0 http://maven.apache.org/xsd/maven-
    4.0.0.xsd"
    xmlns="http://maven.apache.org/POM/4.0.0" xmlns:xsi="http://www.w3.org/2001/XMLSchema-
    instance">
    <modelVersion>4.0.0</modelVersion>
    <parent>
        <groupId>rs.exproit</groupId>
        <artifactId>modular-integral</artifactId>
        <version>1.0.0</version>
    </parent>
    <artifactId>provider-api</artifactId>
    <version>1.0.0</version>
    <name>Provider API</name>
    <description>
        The bundle that encompasses the common API for integral providers.
    </description>
```

```xml
<packaging>bundle</packaging>
<build>
    <plugins>
        <plugin>
            <groupId>org.apache.felix</groupId>
            <artifactId>maven-bundle-plugin</artifactId>
            <version>3.2.0</version>
            <extensions>true</extensions>
            <configuration>
                <instructions>
                    <Bundle-SymbolicName>

                        ${project.groupId}.${project.parent.artifactId}.${project.
                        artifactId}
                    </Bundle-SymbolicName>
                </instructions>
            </configuration>
        </plugin>
    </plugins>
</build>
</project>
```

All the work is done by the Felix's Maven Bundle plug-in (for full details, visit `http://felix.apache.org/documentation/subprojects/apache-felix-maven-bundle-plugin-bnd.html`). The sections of `pom.xml` shown in bold are the interesting parts. The packaging should be `bundle`. This is one of the packaging options of the previously mentioned plug-in. The plug-in will create a standard jar file with an associated OSGi manifest file (when you invoke `mvn package`). All the rest in your project should be the same as in the case of a classical Java project.

Inside the configuration section of the plug-in, you can define various instructions (most have a decent default value). I recommend you redefine the `Bundle-SymbolicName` for a multimodule project, as shown earlier. The `Export-Package` tells what constitutes the published API of this bundle. By default, all packages and classes not containing `impl` are exported (this works for us here, so `Export-Package` is omitted). The resulting OSGi manifest file is shown next (it abbreviated a bit for clarity). Again, pay attention to the sections shown in bold.

```
Manifest-Version: 1.0
Bundle-Description: The bundle that encompasses the common API for integral providers.
Bundle-DocURL: www.exproit.rs
Bundle-ManifestVersion: 2
Bundle-Name: Provider API
Bundle-SymbolicName: rs.exproit.modular-integral.provider-api
Bundle-Vendor: Expro I.T. Consulting
Bundle-Version: 1.0.0
Created-By: Apache Maven Bundle Plugin
Export-Package: rs.exproit.modular_integral.provider.api;version="1.0.0"
Require-Capability: osgi.ee;filter:="(&(osgi.ee=JavaSE)(version=1.8))"
Tool: Bnd-3.2.0.201605172007
```

Notice that the exported package section clearly demarcates the version number. Moreover, the required capability of this bundle includes the demand for Java SE 8. At any rate, the generated jar file inside the `target` folder is ready for installation in Felix. Later I explain how to set up1 and interact with Apache Felix. The beauty of all this is that the same jar file can be used outside of an OSGi framework. In this case, it will behave as an ordinary Java jar file.

Direct Summation Provider

This provider is an OSGI μService delivering its functionality in a dynamic fashion. The actual implementation is just a textual message on a console, printing out the input parameters. If you would like, you can replace it with a real direct summation algorithm. The service registers itself inside the OSGi *Service Registry*. This is a central place where components can pick up the desired service. Using a service registry as an extension mechanism is fully standardized. You don't need to come up with a proprietary solution.

We start in this section with the build file and finish with the actual source code at the end. In this way, although it is a bit upside down, you will better appreciate the amount of automation done for you. The following is the snippet from the pom.xml build file highlighting the new details (pay special attention to the sections shown in bold).

```
<dependencies>
    <dependency>
        <groupId>org.osgi</groupId>
        <artifactId>org.osgi.service.component.annotations</artifactId>
        <version>1.3.0</version>
        <scope>provided</scope>
    </dependency>
    <dependency>
        <groupId>rs.exproit</groupId>
        <artifactId>provider-api</artifactId>
        <version>1.0.0</version>
        <scope>provided</scope>
    </dependency>
    [...]
</dependencies>
<build>
    <plugins>
        <plugin>
            <groupId>org.apache.felix</groupId>
            <artifactId>maven-bundle-plugin</artifactId>
            <version>3.2.0</version>
            <extensions>true</extensions>
            <configuration>
                <instructions>
                    <Bundle-SymbolicName>

                        ${project.groupId}.${project.parent.artifactId}.${project.artifactId}
                    </Bundle-SymbolicName>
                    <Import-Package>
                        rs.exproit.modular_integral.provider.api
                    </Import-Package>
                </instructions>
            </configuration>
        </plugin>
    </plugins>
</build>
```

If executed as an OSGi module (as in this case study), then Apache Felix will ensure that the provider-api jar file is on the classpath. If you want to use this jar outside of an OSGi runtime system, though, you might want to alter the dependency to compile. Otherwise, the Maven plug-in for producing a fat jar file will omit this dependency.

This Maven module uses the OSGi Declarative Service's annotations, so there is a dependency on it.[12] Another dependency is on the provider API (notice that the scope is set to provided). This entails a clear order in the build process. Finally, the Import-Package instruction uniquely defines what this module requires from the other bundles.[13] This is a signal to the OSGi framework to ensure that there is an available module that exports the required package. Otherwise, an error is generated. This is that fail-fast deploy time mechanism. The generated manifest file is shown here.

```
Manifest-Version: 1.0
Bnd-LastModified: 1469791780001
Build-Jdk: 1.8.0_101
Built-By: evarga
Bundle-Description: A concrete implementation of the Direct Summation
provider.
Bundle-DocURL: www.exproit.rs
Bundle-ManifestVersion: 2
Bundle-Name: Provider - Direct Summation
Bundle-SymbolicName: rs.exproit.modular-integral.provider-directsummation
Bundle-Vendor: Expro I.T. Consulting
Bundle-Version: 1.0.0
Created-By: Apache Maven Bundle Plugin
Import-Package: rs.exproit.modular_integral.provider.api;version="[1.0,2)"
Provide-Capability: osgi.service;objectClass:List<String>="rs.exproit.
modular_integral.provider.api.IntegralSPI"
Require-Capability: osgi.ee;filter:="(&(osgi.ee=JavaSE)(version=1.8))"
Service-Component: OSGI-INF/rs.exproit.modular_integral.provider.impl.
directsummation.DirectSummationProvider.xml
Tool: Bnd-3.2.0.201605172007
```

Watch out for the compatible version numbers this module assumes regarding the provider API, which is an interval [1.0.0, 2) (for a rigorous analysis of OSGi range dependency concerns, see http://wiki.apidesign.org/wiki/RangeDependenciesAnalysed). This means all versions up to 2.x should be backward compatible (version 2.x is allowed to introduce a backward-incompatible change). Nothing is exported, as the implementation package contains impl in its name. The referenced XML file is a descriptor generated by the Maven Bundle plug-in, the content of which is shown here.

```
<?xml version="1.0" encoding="UTF-8"?>
<component
  name="rs.exproit.modular_integral.provider.impl.directsummation.DirectSummationProvider">
  <implementation

    class="rs.exproit.modular_integral.provider.impl.directsummation.
    DirectSummationProvider"/>
  <service>
    <provide interface="rs.exproit.modular_integral.provider.api.IntegralSPI"/>
  </service>
</component>
```

---

[12]Don't use Felix SCR's annotations, as they are obsolete (including the Felix SCR Maven plug-in).
[13]In our case, the bnd tool will infer the imports for us, so the pom.xml could be even smaller. I have put it here to showcase the usage of the Import-Package instruction. The only situation when explicit imports are useful is the desire to leave out many parts from a huge OSGi bundle.

The section shown in bold part tells OSGi that this is a service that implements the denoted interface. In other words, it provides an implementation for this API. The source code of this provider is really lean (the keywords are not shown in bold to underline only the OSGi-specific details).

```java
package rs.exproit.modular_integral.provider.impl.directsummation;

import java.util.function.Function;

import org.osgi.service.component.annotations.Component;

import rs.exproit.modular_integral.provider.api.DirectSummation;
import rs.exproit.modular_integral.provider.api.IntegralPortfolio;
import rs.exproit.modular_integral.provider.api.IntegralSPI;

/**
 * A concrete implementation of the Direct Summation provider.
 *
 * @author Ervin Varga
 * @since 1.0
 */
@Component
public final class DirectSummationProvider implements IntegralSPI {
    @Override
    public double calculate(Function<Double, Double> f, double a, double b,
            IntegralPortfolio spec) {
        if (b <= a || spec == null || f == null) {
            throw new IllegalArgumentException("Invalid input arguments");
        }

        // Dummy implementation, you may want to replace this with real one.
        final DirectSummation ds = (DirectSummation) spec;
        System.out.println("Received: a=" + a + ", b=" + b + ", dx=" + ds.getDx());
        return 1.0;
    }

    @Override
    public Class<? extends IntegralPortfolio> getPortfolioType() {
        return DirectSummation.class;
    }
}
```

To transform this class into an OSGi service, you just need to include that single annotation; the rest happens automatically. This is the power of declarative programming and annotations. The plug-in will detect that this class implements an interface, hence it will become a service. Otherwise, it is treated as an immediate component. Of course, you can embellish the Component annotations with properties if you don't want to use the default values. However, we are keeping everything here as simple as possible to avoid too much detraction. Another detail to observe is the getPortfolioType method. This is used by the client API service to find a proper provider.

The Client API

This is the service that consumers of this project will use. It exposes an interface containing utility methods for users. The client API lets users focus on their tasks without worrying about how things in the background are set up. Internal APIs are the "glue" that connects the client and provider parts. Moreover, as users only use the exposed interface, it can evolve in a backward-compatible manner. This works, because the client API bundle is a versioned artifact. A user can attach to the version that she or he would like to use (see [9] for a brief overview of OSGi bundle resolution rules), and leave all the rest to OSGi. Here you find version 1.0.0 of the client API.

```java
package rs.exproit.modular_integral.client.api;

import java.util.function.Function;

/**
 * This is the client API consumed by users of this project.
 *
 * @author Ervin Varga
 * @since 1.0
 */
public interface IntegralClient {
    /**
     * Calculates the definite integral of a function between the limits a and b
     * using the direct summation method.
     *
     * @param f the integrand.
     * @param a the lower bound of the limit.
     * @param b the upper bound of the limit.
     * @param dx a small step size for iterating over the specified interval.
     * @return the numerical approximation of the definite integral.
     * @throws IllegalArgumentException if b <= a or dx <= 0 or f is null.
     * @throws IllegalStateException if there is no provider implementing this method.
     */
    double directSummation(Function<Double,Double> f, double a, double b, double dx);
}
```

Without OSGi this should probably be a final class, to allow smooth evolution of the API. The client bridge implements this interface inside a separate implementation package. The code for the service is shown next (the keywords are not shown in bold to underline only the new OSGi-specific details).

```java
package rs.exproit.modular_integral.client.impl;

import java.util.List;
import java.util.function.Function;

import org.osgi.service.component.annotations.Component;
import org.osgi.service.component.annotations.Reference;
import org.osgi.service.component.annotations.ReferenceCardinality;
import org.osgi.service.component.annotations.ReferencePolicy;
```

```
import rs.exproit.modular_integral.client.api.IntegralClient;
import rs.exproit.modular_integral.provider.api.DirectSummation;
import rs.exproit.modular_integral.provider.api.IntegralPortfolio;
import rs.exproit.modular_integral.provider.api.IntegralSPI;

/**
 * Implements the API for clients, and serves as a bridge toward provider API.
 * It tracks provider services, and allows clients to call into them.
 *
 * @author Ervin Varga
 * @since 1.0
 */
@Component
public final class IntegralClientBridge implements IntegralClient {
    /**
     * List of service objects.
     *
     * This field is managed by the Felix SCR and updated
     * with the current set of available integral provider services.
     * At least one integral provider service is required.
     */
    @Reference(policy=ReferencePolicy.DYNAMIC, cardinality=ReferenceCardinality.AT_LEAST_ONE)
    private volatile List<IntegralSPI> providerList;

    @Override
    public double directSummation(Function<Double,Double> f, double a, double b, double dx)
{
        if (b <= a || dx <= 0.0 || f == null) {
            throw new IllegalArgumentException("Invalid input arguments");
        }

        final IntegralSPI provider = findProvider(DirectSummation.class);
        if (provider != null) {
            return provider.calculate(f, a, b, new DirectSummation(dx));
        } else {
            throw new IllegalStateException("Cannot find a provider for this method");
        }
    }

    /**
     * Searches active providers to find the desired one.
     *
     * @param portfolioType the class of the target portfolio type.
     * @return a reference to the proper provider, or {@code null}.
     */
    private IntegralSPI findProvider(Class<? extends IntegralPortfolio> portfolioType) {
        // Put the current set of services in a local field, as the field providerList
        // might be modified concurrently.
        final List<IntegralSPI> providerListCopy = providerList;
```

```
        if (providerListCopy != null) {
            for (IntegralSPI provider : providerListCopy) {
                if (provider.getPortfolioType().isAssignableFrom(portfolioType)) {
                    return provider;
                }
            }
        }
        return null;
    }
}
```

OSGi Declarative Services automates all tedious and error-prone service dependency handling. The Felix SCR dynamically manages the list of available provider services and updates the field annotated with Reference. This is all you need to do to use OSGi service discovery. The type of service is determined by the type of the interface. In our case, the field providerList will contain references to all services providing an implementation of IntegralSPI.

The method findProvider searches active providers to find the desired one. Of course, performing this search, on each call to calculate an integral, would be overkill in a real service. You might want to optimize it to cache results into a hash map (take care to be properly notified by OSGi after each change in the providerList).

Demo

This OSGi bundle is an immediate component; that is, the consumer of a service. It gets instantiated with a proper client API service. The source code is shown here (the keywords are not shown in bold to underline only the new OSGi-specific details).

```
package rs.exproit.modular_integral.demo;

import org.osgi.service.component.annotations.Activate;
import org.osgi.service.component.annotations.Component;
import org.osgi.service.component.annotations.Reference;

import rs.exproit.modular_integral.client.api.IntegralClient;

/**
 * A very simple demo showing how to use the client API.
 *
 * @author Ervin Varga
 * @since 1.0
 */
@Component
public final class App {
    @Reference
    private volatile IntegralClient client;

    // You should not follow this rather trivial approach to run your
    // logic from the activate method.
    @Activate
    void calculateIntegral() {
        try {
            System.out.println(
```

```
                 "Calculating integral: " + client.directSummation(x -> 1.0, 1.0, 2.0, 0.1));
      } catch (IllegalStateException ex) {
          System.err.println("The requested provider isn't active.");
      }
   }
}
```

OSGi sees that the Component annotation is attached to a class not implementing an interface. This classifies it as a component instead of a service.

Summary

This chapter established a common ground and set expectations regarding modularity and its impact on APIs and software architecture in general. We have seen that taking into account physical aspects of deployment complements the logical design in a powerful way. You saw two modular frameworks in action: the built-in Racket module framework for a functional programming language, and OSGi for Java 8 for an OOP language (more precisely, multiparadigm). At any rate, the principles are the same. You need a forceful modular framework to leverage the potentials of modularity. We need modular design to create maintainable APIs around extensibility mechanisms delivered by a modular framework. Similarly, we require APIs to get the best from modularity.

SET UP, INSTALL, AND RUN THE DEMO

Getting Familiar with the Apache Felix Framework

Apache Felix is the kernel implementing the OSGi specification. Apache Karaf (http://karaf.apache.org) is a full-blown server built on top of Apache Felix. The features provided by Apache Karaf are surely required by a true enterprise modular application. We focus here on setting up Apache Felix to run our modular integral project, but I really suggest you to examine Karaf, too.

First, you need to download and install the Apache Felix framework (I've used version 5.4.0) as instructed at http://felix.apache.org/documentation/subprojects/apache-felix-framework/apache-felix-framework-usage-documentation.html. If Felix starts up properly, then exit Felix by typing Ctrl+C in the console. Download the following subprojects (only the jars) from http://felix.apache.org/downloads.cgi:

- Configuration Admin

- Metatype

- SCR (Declarative Services)

Move all these subproject jar files into <Felix installation root>/bundle directory. Now, start up Felix again. After typing help in the console, you should see commands prefixed with scr. No error message should pop up during startup. You now have a properly running Apache Felix with SCR support.

The next step is creating all bundles comprising our modular integral project. Open a command shell window, and change the working directory to chapter2/java/modular-integral folder. Type mvn clean package. All bundles should be now situated inside the corresponding target folder (e.g., provider-api/target/ provider-api-1.0.0.jar.

Now, consult the Apache Felix user manual to install and start these bundles in the order in which they are built. If you have successfully done everything, you should see the following output in the console:

```
Received: a=1.0, b=2.0, dx=0.1
Calculating integral: 1.0
```

Congratulations!

IMPLEMENT THE REMAINING TWO PROVIDERS

Practicing OSGi with Apache Felix SCR

Using the code base of this project, implement the remaining two integral providers. The implementation should follow the direct summation provider. Install the providers into Apache Felix. You will also need to extend the client API bundle.

Analyze how much effort you would need without a sophisticated OSGi runtime model.

CHURCH ENCODING MODULE

Data in Lambda Notation[14]

Assume you are given the church-encoding.rkt module (the listing is shown next). This module exposes the first three Church numerals (zero, one, and two), the function to increment a Church numeral, and the function to sum up two Church numerals. All these arithmetic functions return a Church numeral, which is a function. Therefore, all numbers are functions, and arithmetical computations are performed on these "numbers."

```
#lang scheme

(require "function-composition.rkt")

(provide zero)
(provide one)
(provide two)
(provide inc)
(provide sum)

(define zero
  (lambda (f) identity))
```

---

[14]Cobol programmer (business oriented): "Data?" Basic programmer ("let for loop live forever" oriented): "There, look!" Java 8 programmer (nothing surprises her or him, who has seen every possible paradigm on Earth): "No, dude, that is Lieutenant Commander Data from Star Trek." Turns back and throws a ReflectiveOperationException exception.

```
(define one
  (lambda (f) (lambda (m) (f m))))
(define two
  (lambda (f) (compose f f)))
(define (inc n)
  (lambda (f) (compose f (n f))))
(define (sum n m)
  (lambda (f) (compose (n f) (m f))))

; Some test cases to make this more intuitive.
; This is an auxiliary function to be used as input for numerals.
(define (dec x) (- x 1))

((zero dec) 1)
; This is 1, as we have applied zero times the dec function on 1.
((one dec) 1)
; This is 0, as we have once applied the dec function on 1.
((two dec) 1)
; This is -1, as we have twice applied the dec function on 1.
(((inc two) dec) 1)
; This is -2, as we have applied three times (one more than two) the dec function on 1.
(((sum one two) dec) 1)
; This is -2, as we have applied three times (one + two) the dec function on 1.
```

These test cases are not real unit tests. You might want to convert these into Racket's unit tests as an additional exercise. Take a look at the following documentation for more details: http://docs.racket-lang.org/rackunit/.

Users have requested that you extend the API of this module with an additional function to convert an ordinary numeral (integer) into the corresponding Church numeral. In other words, they would like to be able to encode an integer using Church encoding. The function should be named as encode and accept as an argument an integer i. (Hint: You might find the repeated function handy.) If you are stuck, look at the accompanying source code of this book for a solution. At any rate, the next expression should return –3: (((encode 4) dec) 1).

After completing this exercise, notice that the external function-composition.rkt module is 100% utilized. This is the best testimony of the module's high cohesion, reusability level, and usefulness. As an additional exercise, convert this Racket module into Java 8 using its lambda functions.

References

1. Parnas, D. L. "On the Criteria to Be Used in Decomposing Systems into Modules." *Communications of the ACM* 15 (12): 1053–58, 1972. doi:10.1145/361598.361623

2. Knoernschild, Kirk. *Java Application Architecture: Modularity Patterns with Examples Using OSGi.* Reading, MA: Addison-Wesley Professional, 2012.

3. Cockburn, Alistair. *Writing Effective Use Cases.* Reading, MA: Addison-Wesley, 2001.

4. Dooley, John. *Software Development and Professional Practice.* New York: Apress, 2011.

5. Olszak, Andrzej, and Jaroslav Tulach. *Software Modularity: Paradoxes, Principles, and Architectures.* http://www.slideshare.net/AndrzejOlszak/javaone12-software-modularity-paradoxes-principles-and-architectures

6. McConnell, Steve. *Code Complete: A Practical Handbook of Software Construction, Second Edition.* Redmond, WA: Microsoft Press, 2004.

7. Archer, Simon, Paul VanderLei, and Jeff McAffer. *OSGi and Equinox.* Reading, MA: Addison-Wesley, 2010.

8. Pólya, György. *How to Solve It.* Princeton, NJ: Princeton University Press, 1945.

9. Posta, Christian. "Understanding how OSGI bundles get resolved part I." http://blog.christianposta.com/osgi/understanding-how-osgi-bundles-get-resolved-part-i/

10. Abelson, Harold, Gerald Jay Sussman, and Julie Sussman. *Structure and Interpretation of Computer Programs, Second Edition.* Cambridge, MA: MIT Press, 1996.

11. Grady Booch, James Rumbaugh, and Ivar Jacobson, The Unified Modeling Language User Guide, Second *Edition.* Reading, MA: Addison-Wesley Professional, 2005.

CHAPTER 3

■ ■ ■

Designing Classes for Reuse

Software reuse is the major topic in software engineering, because without efficient reuse we cannot be productive. Reuse is reified in various forms across many dimensions. We can reuse code (by importing a class or module into our code base), code and design (by using a full-fledged framework), applications or services (e.g., by creating mashups combining different services into a unified portal), and so on. Software processes are also amenable for reuse, as are requirements and conceptual domain models. Moreover, we might want to reuse existent stuff, or we could also opt to build artifacts for reuse. The topic is really broad. Therefore, we limit ourselves here purely to aspects of reuse pertaining to OO systems, specifically focusing on APIs. In other words, we analyze how APIs can help or hinder efficient reuse.

■ **Note** *Copy-paste* isn't reuse,[1] although it does deceptively look like it is. Each time you clone a source code, you increase the code base that you need to maintain. Over time, this can easily get out of control, especially when a future modification has to be carried out in all copies. The problem is that you usually don't even know the locations of those copies.

Reuse is important for both production and test code. Despite differences in their purposes they do share many quality expectations. Test code should be explicit and comprehensible, so you might want to achieve a proper level of reuse with the available testing frameworks, and avoid redundancy. However, you always need to have the right attitude toward compatibility of the API. If there is a test that used to work, then you (ad absurdum) don't have a bug, but an API feature. The same code as in your test could have been written by a user of your API. If you treat compatibility seriously, then you can't change the test, even if you now think it is broken or isn't in a perfect shape. This might induce the demand to copy-paste the original test to absolutely shield it from later modifications. Therefore, attaining the Don't Repeat Yourself (DRY) principle is definitely desirable, but you must not approach it as a dogma (this applies to all principles).

We saw in the previous chapter that an API is made up of suitable abstractions. This set of abstractions (API) dictates the level of reuse, as they constrain what we can do with everything else behind an API. Each abstraction, as its name implies, is at some intellectual distance from a real-world entity. The reuse is effective and economical when the average delta between intellectual distances is small. If our expectations about distances in a given context are matched with those encompassed by an API, we can fruitfully reuse

---

[1]I witnessed situations as a consultant in companies where managers even advocated copy-paste, using the excuse that with copies there is no need to worry about design trade-offs associated with common code base. Although it is true that each copy can be independently shaped, the price is extraordinary. This approach leads to a maintenance nightmare. When you start copy-pasting the same code all over the place, you are responsible for keeping those clones in a good shape. Copy-paste isn't a scalable approach. It might be treated as a reuse for a one-shot action, but not as a general technique for large code bases. Every action hampering evolution is a recipe for a failure, and must be avoided.

© Ervin Varga 2016
E. Varga, *Creating Maintainable APIs*, DOI 10.1007/978-1-4842-2196-9_3

the artifacts represented by that API. Otherwise, we have to fight against the emerged impedance mismatch issue. One effective way to control and categorize these distances is the application of a *stratified* design, or layered approach. Each layer is supposed to contain things at a similar abstraction level. In this setup, we can purposefully choose the layer onto which to build our own products.

Proper handling of intellectual distances aids cohesion and provides consistency at a client programmer's side. The following list briefly summarizes additional principles and techniques (besides encapsulation and information hiding) governing proper reuse (I suggest you read [1] for a superb overview regarding design and reuse in general).

- *Law of Demeter (altered a bit to fit APIs):* We can apply this law on our distances to judge the reusability of an API. For example, adding a control parameter (inducing a control coupling between entities) to a method signature is problematic, and thwarts reuse. Such a parameter introduces a so-called control coupling between entities. The main issue is that reuse cannot happen without diving deeper into the implementation details of a class. We have to know what is happening inside to control its behavior outside. The Law of Demeter would kick in, saying that we should only "talk" up to some distance from the API. Anything further than that isn't allowed (implementation details of methods are too far). Using a Strategy or State pattern is a different story.[2] The latter operates on an API level, whereas the former (control parameter) works at the implementation level. In this context, it is obvious that indiscriminate getters and setters are evil, as emphasized by Allen Holub [1].

- *Liskov substitution principle:* Anytime you enter a dangerous zone to break it, then you should stop and rethink what you're trying to achieve. One such zone is an overriding of methods carrying implementation. This means that you're breaking the Law of Demeter for APIs and looking behind the method's signature (specifying the *What?* part). A Template pattern is again a different matter. The template method is abstract;[3] hence you are specializing the behavior of the class by just "talking" to the API.

- *Programming into/in a language:* You should apply the Law of Demeter for APIs when programming into a language, resisting the temptation to program in a language. There is a direct relationship between the expressiveness of the programming language and an API crafted using that language. Nonetheless, it isn't advisable to fly above the skies, by pretending that you speak a better language, to come up with a more sophisticated API. If you try to mimic an object-oriented API in a standard C program (I'm not thinking here about GLib or ObjectiveC), then you will surely confuse many C developers. Your API must naturally fit inside the paradigms of the target programming language; that is, the distance in style between your API and the one advocated by the language must be short. Therefore, programming into a language must be a controlled activity. Otherwise, reusing your API would be cumbersome.

---

[2]When you have a control coupling, you inherently peek into the implementation (somebody can observe and depend on it). With a Strategy or State pattern the variances are embodied inside an API and are well encapsulated. It is important to eschew exposing undesirable control coupling via an API.

[3]The term *abstract* here is language neutral. This just signals that the behavior described by the template method is expected to vary in subclasses. In Java that method would be designated as `abstract`, but in other languages (like SmallTalk) they could remain "normal." In some setups, an abstract method might even throw an error when invoked directly.

- *Provide an API:* This rule might sound a bit harebrained, but it is crucial for reuse. As a software engineer, you are responsible for both proper and improper reuse of your stuff. You surely want to disallow the latter by letting an API proactively ensure adequate reuse. The best way to achieve this is to clearly separate the abstract definition of an API from its actual implementation; that is, ensure coding against interfaces. With an appropriate API you prevent a client from sweeping in extra assumptions outside of the API's boundaries, thus protecting both a client and yourself against entropy. In this respect, the extends Java keyword is a misnomer. It isn't that extending a class is bad per se, but that it is a signal that you're probably letting volatile assumptions creep into your solution space. Of course, using the extends keyword with interfaces is a different matter. It is related to type extension rather than implementation inheritance (a usual case with classes).

In the rest of this chapter we introduce two fictional case studies. Both of them are going to simulate what typically happens in the software industry. These case studies complement an approach from [1], where patterns are presented in the light of real code. In this book, we simulate how that real code is born in the first place.

Case Study: Client of Reuse

In our first case study we are going to demonstrate the hurdles a client might encounter when trying to reuse artifacts from a framework. The assignment is to implement a graphical user interface (GUI) combo box showing items in sorted order. Java already provides a mature, stable GUI framework called Swing. If you've not worked with Swing before, then you might read [2] before proceeding.

Imagine that this same task (realizing a sorted combo box) is given to a more experienced software engineer in each version; that is, Version I is performed by a novice, Version II by a junior, and so forth. Also, assume that the task is part of a maintenance effort, and not some greenfield project. These presuppositions truly reflect what is happening in corporations (software maintenance is habitually considered mundane work, not at all attractive to hot shots). So, let us start our journey.

Version I

A combo box is represented as the JComboBox class, which extends the JComponent class (both of them are members of the javax.swing package); that is, it is treated as a component. Looking at the description of the JComboBox class (it is part of the JDK's API documentation), the novice has concluded that this task is a piece of cake. He just needs to extend the public nonfinal JComboBox class, and create a new public class JSortedComboBox. Besides providing constructors, the novice also must override two public nonfinal methods: addItem and insertItemAt. The happiness was at a level of ecstasy, and the novice even started to dream about a promotion.

Here is the full source code[4] of the new class. I'm following the strategy from [1] to give you complete visibility into the source code.

```
package rs.exproit.swing;

import java.util.Arrays;
import java.util.Collections;
import java.util.Vector;
```

---

[4]Source syntax coloring is omitted in this chapter to present code in a way you will encounter in the industry. Sometimes you will need to browse legacy code in a field using a rudimentary editor.

```java
import javax.swing.ComboBoxModel;
import javax.swing.JComboBox;

@SuppressWarnings("serial")
public class JSortedComboBox<E extends Comparable<E>> extends JComboBox<E> {
    public JSortedComboBox() {}

    public JSortedComboBox(ComboBoxModel<E> aModel) {
        this(toVector(aModel));
    }

    public JSortedComboBox(E[] items) {
        super(sort(items.clone()));
    }

    @SuppressWarnings("unchecked")
    public JSortedComboBox(Vector<E> items) {
        super(sort((Vector<E>) items.clone()));
    }

    /**
     * Adds an item to this combo box, while keeping its sorted order.
     *
     * @param item the item to be added to this combo box.
     */
    @Override
    public void addItem(E item) {
        final int insertionPoint = binarySearch(item);

        if (insertionPoint >= getItemCount()) {
            super.addItem(item);
        } else {
            super.insertItemAt(item, insertionPoint);
        }
    }

    private int binarySearch(E item) {
        int low = 0;
        int high = getItemCount() - 1;
        int insertionPoint = -1;

        while (low <= high) {
            int mid = (low + high) >>> 1;
            E midVal = getItemAt(mid);

            if (midVal.compareTo(item) < 0) {
                low = mid + 1;
            } else if (midVal.compareTo(item) > 0) {
                high = mid - 1;
            } else {
                insertionPoint = mid;
```

```
                break;
            }
        }

        if (insertionPoint == -1) {
            insertionPoint = low;
        }
        return insertionPoint;
    }

    /**
     * Adds an item to this combo box, while keeping its sorted order.
     *
     * @param item the item to be added to this combo box.
     * @param index this is ignored, as it is meaningless.
     */
    @Override
    public void insertItemAt(E item, int index) {
        addItem(item);
    }

    private static <E extends Comparable<E>> Vector<E> toVector(ComboBoxModel<E> aModel) {
        final Vector<E> items = new Vector<>(aModel.getSize());

        for (int i = 0; i < aModel.getSize(); i++) {
            items.add(aModel.getElementAt(i));
        }
        return items;
    }

    private static <E extends Comparable<E>> E[] sort(E[] items) {
        Arrays.sort(items);
        return items;
    }

    private static <E extends Comparable<E>> Vector<E> sort(Vector<E> items) {
        Collections.sort(items);
        return items;
    }
}
```

The unit test is provided next (the company where the novice works leverages a well-established software process, and test-driven development [TDD][5] is an integral part of it).

```
package rs.exproit.swing;

import static org.junit.Assert.*;

import java.util.Arrays;
```

_____

[5]TDD will be the principal topic in the next chapter.

```java
import java.util.Vector;

import javax.swing.DefaultComboBoxModel;

import org.junit.Before;
import org.junit.Test;

public class JSortedComboBoxTest {
    private final static String[] testItems = new String[] {"A", "Y", "X", "D", "C"};
    private final static String[] testItemsCopy = testItems.clone();

    @Before
    public void assureTestItemsAreIntact() {
        assertArrayEquals("Original array modified in some of the tests",
                testItemsCopy, testItems);
    }

    @Test
    public final void testNoArgConstructor() {
        final JSortedComboBox<String> cbox = new JSortedComboBox<>();
        assertNotNull(cbox);
    }

    @Test
    public final void testConstructorWithModel() {
        final DefaultComboBoxModel<String> model = new DefaultComboBoxModel<>(testItems);
        final JSortedComboBox<String> cbox = new JSortedComboBox<>(model);

        verifySortedOrder(cbox);
    }

    @Test
    public final void testConstructorWithArray() {
        final JSortedComboBox<String> cbox = new JSortedComboBox<>(testItems);

        verifySortedOrder(cbox);
    }

    @Test
    public final void testConstructorWithVector() {
        final Vector<String> items = new Vector<>();
        items.addAll(Arrays.asList(testItems));
        final JSortedComboBox<String> cbox = new JSortedComboBox<>(items);

        verifySortedOrder(cbox);
    }

    @Test
    public final void testAddingItems() {
        final JSortedComboBox<String> cbox = new JSortedComboBox<>();
        for (String item : testItems) {
            cbox.addItem(item);
        }
```

```
        verifySortedOrder(cbox);
    }

    @Test
    public final void testInsertingItems() {
        final JSortedComboBox<String> cbox = new JSortedComboBox<>();
        for (String item : testItems) {
            cbox.insertItemAt(item, 0);
        }

        verifySortedOrder(cbox);
    }

    private void verifySortedOrder(JSortedComboBox<String> cbox) {
        assertEquals("A", cbox.getItemAt(0));
        assertEquals("C", cbox.getItemAt(1));
        assertEquals("D", cbox.getItemAt(2));
        assertEquals("X", cbox.getItemAt(3));
        assertEquals("Y", cbox.getItemAt(4));
    }
}
```

Superficially everything is just perfect. The new class smoothly fits into Swing, and there were no serious hacks. The test coverage is satisfactory, all tests are passing, and the sorted combo box performs as requested. The code follows the company's coding style. The novice has pushed back the changes into the version control system and published the jar file into the company's repository manager (e.g., Artifactory). Done!

The novice has shown a great attention to details. For example, the input data structures (see the constructors) were cloned to keep them intact (this was even tested). The only murky point is the conversion of a combo box model into a sorted vector. However, the novice knew nothing about Swing models, and so improvised a bit (a typical maneuver under pressure, which is another characteristic of a software maintenance work).

All in all, what happened in this version is exactly what developers are taught in various courses, and what book authors like to lament about. Follow the rules, don't hack, cover your code with tests, document it properly, keep it tidy, and you're good.

Version II

Soon after the publication of Version I a true scandal has broken out! Seniors have complained that the solution is outrageous. It breaks every possible principle of OO design; most important, it abuses implementation inheritance (consult [1] for more details). Moreover, nobody wanted to change the current code base, which relied on a pure JComboBox class with various models. They demanded a Swing-compliant result. The novice was puzzled, as according to him, that is exactly what had been provided.

Version I demonstrates one of the consequences of a slack API. The poor novice trusted that Swing would give some guidance.[6] Nothing warned the novice that he was strolling on the wrong path. The methods addItem and insertItemAt should have been final (better yet, they shouldn't even exist), hence undoubtedly signaling that the solution is lurking somewhere else.

---

[6]Swing is just too open, because it was designed to be like that. Even if you close your API in the first version, though, after a while, you will get duplications. There will be more ways to achieve the same thing (the old one and the new one). You can deprecate the old version (if it has some issues), but that is the most that can be done as a remedy.

51

■ **Note**   As you move to *system boundary* frameworks (like Swing), they tend to be more flexible to cover a broader number of possible use cases. Such an increase in flexibility is followed by a same increase in complexity. Part of that complexity stems from the lack of guidance from an API.

The novice's boss has reassigned the task to a more experienced software engineer (let's call her the junior). The junior was aware that Swing components are built around the *Model-View-Controller* (MVC) pattern. Everything that is presented inside a combo box (its content) is handled by the matching model class. The default model for combo boxes is the DefaultComboBoxModel class (if you create a new JComboBox object, it comes preinstalled with this default model). At any rate, to have a combo box with sorted items, the junior has concluded that she needs to implement a custom model. It is easy, she reasoned, as most of the code can be transferred from the JSortedComboBox class into the new SortedComboBoxModel class, which will extend the DefaultComboBoxModel. Basically, the methods addItem and insertItemAt should be renamed addElement and insertElementAt, respectively. Here is the source code of this new class:

```java
package rs.exproit.swing;

import java.util.Arrays;
import java.util.Collections;
import java.util.Vector;

import javax.swing.DefaultComboBoxModel;

@SuppressWarnings("serial")
public class SortedComboBoxModel<E extends Comparable<E>> extends DefaultComboBoxModel<E> {
    public SortedComboBoxModel() {}

    public SortedComboBoxModel(E[] items) {
        super(sort(items.clone()));
    }

    @SuppressWarnings("unchecked")
    public SortedComboBoxModel(Vector<E> items) {
        super(sort((Vector<E>) items.clone()));
    }

    /**
     * Adds an item to this combo box model, while keeping its sorted order.
     *
     * @param item the item to be added to this combo box model.
     */
    @Override
    public void addElement(E item) {
        final int insertionPoint = binarySearch(item);

        if (insertionPoint >= getSize()) {
            super.addElement(item);
        } else {
            super.insertElementAt(item, insertionPoint);
        }
    }
```

```
    private int binarySearch(E item) {
        int low = 0;
        int high = getSize() - 1;
        int insertionPoint = -1;

        while (low <= high) {
            int mid = (low + high) >>> 1;
            E midVal = getElementAt(mid);

            if (midVal.compareTo(item) < 0) {
                low = mid + 1;
            } else if (midVal.compareTo(item) > 0) {
                high = mid - 1;
            } else {
                insertionPoint = mid;
                break;
            }
        }

        if (insertionPoint == -1) {
            insertionPoint = low;
        }
        return insertionPoint;
    }

    /**
     * Adds an item to this combo box model, while keeping its sorted order.
     *
     * @param item the item to be added to this combo box model.
     * @param index this is ignored, as it is meaningless.
     */
    @Override
    public void insertElementAt(E item, int index) {
        addElement(item);
    }

    private static <E extends Comparable<E>> E[] sort(E[] items) {
        Arrays.sort(items);
        return items;
    }

    private static <E extends Comparable<E>> Vector<E> sort(Vector<E> items) {
        Collections.sort(items);
        return items;
    }
}
```

The corresponding test class is listed here:

```
package rs.exproit.swing;

import static org.junit.Assert.*;
```

```java
import java.util.Arrays;
import java.util.Vector;

import org.junit.Before;
import org.junit.Test;

public class SortedComboBoxModelTest {
    private final static String[] testItems = new String[] {"A", "Y", "X", "D", "C"};
    private final static String[] testItemsCopy = testItems.clone();

    @Before
    public void assureTestItemsAreIntact() {
        assertArrayEquals("Original array modified in some of the tests",
                testItemsCopy, testItems);
    }

    @Test
    public final void testNoArgConstructor() {
        final SortedComboBoxModel<String> cbox = new SortedComboBoxModel<>();
        assertNotNull(cbox);
    }

    @Test
    public final void testConstructorWithArray() {
        final SortedComboBoxModel<String> cbox = new SortedComboBoxModel<>(testItems);

        verifySortedOrder(cbox);
    }

    @Test
    public final void testConstructorWithVector() {
        final Vector<String> items = new Vector<>();
        items.addAll(Arrays.asList(testItems));
        final SortedComboBoxModel<String> cbox = new SortedComboBoxModel<>(items);

        verifySortedOrder(cbox);
    }

    @Test
    public final void testAddingItems() {
        final SortedComboBoxModel<String> cbox = new SortedComboBoxModel<>();
        for (String item : testItems) {
            cbox.addElement(item);
        }

        verifySortedOrder(cbox);
    }

    @Test
    public final void testInsertingItems() {
        final SortedComboBoxModel<String> cbox = new SortedComboBoxModel<>();
        for (String item : testItems) {
```

```
        cbox.insertElementAt(item, 0);
    }

    verifySortedOrder(cbox);
}

private void verifySortedOrder(SortedComboBoxModel<String> cbox) {
    assertEquals("A", cbox.getElementAt(0));
    assertEquals("C", cbox.getElementAt(1));
    assertEquals("D", cbox.getElementAt(2));
    assertEquals("X", cbox.getElementAt(3));
    assertEquals("Y", cbox.getElementAt(4));
}
}
```

The junior was taught that one of the benefits of an OO technology is that you should only pay attention to the subset of the system under change. Encapsulation and information hiding will prevent ripple effects. The junior also assumed that the other unaltered classes will continue to behave as usual. Therefore, she has concluded that the job was well done, as all tests have passed regarding the new combo box model. The junior didn't care to rename the corresponding methods and variables to reflect elements instead of items. Why bother with such childish activities? The junior was fast with copy-pasting, and any slowdown was not an option.

It would be better if the junior would have added at least a warning in the documentation that the base class's contract was altered. Nevertheless, this would still be a workaround for the erroneous API design. The documentation is part of an API, and it cannot be considered less important than the code itself. They should have an equal reputation.

Version III

The seniors have complained again, albeit not that as strongly as last time. They still demanded a correct OO solution, and refrained from abusive implementation inheritance. Moreover, they were not able to control the sorting order. Items in a combo box were always sorted in type-dependent ascending order. Finally, they didn't want to have a limitation of dealing only with elements implementing Comparable.

The junior's boss was really desperate, and escalated the issue (he had no senior engineers on his team). The task was finally assigned to the most experienced software engineer in the company. The senior decided to perform a thorough analysis of the whole problem before doing any coding. He was cautious (a positive side effect of being experienced). He has reasoned as follows about the quality attributes of the next resolution:

- The JComboBox should be instantiated with a new model, and must behave as specified in its API.

- The new combo box model should remain mutable, as this was implicitly asked by everyone (to allow additions of elements during runtime).

- The sorting mechanism must be separated from a policy; that is, a Strategy pattern should be applied to define the sorting order.

- The OO principles have to be satisfied as much as possible. Of course, you might occasionally break a principle for pragmatic reasons, but you should have a good reason for doing that.

He started by depicting the Swing's combo box model class diagram, as shown in Figure 3-1. He was deeply disappointed by the image. The senior immediately realized that the clean OO solution would require more work than initially planned. Later on he will find out an even more shocking fact.

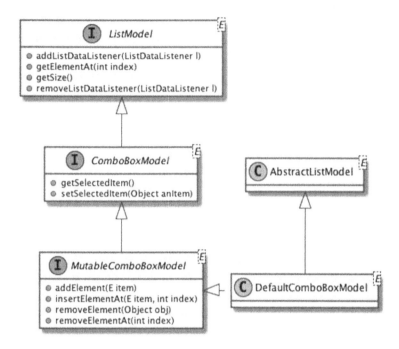

Figure 3-1. *Swing's combo box model class diagram (classes and interfaces)*

The biggest concern was the `MutableComboBoxModel` interface with those dreaded `addElement` and `insertElementAt` methods (it would be more accurate to say operations, but methods is common terminology). The problem with the `addElement` method is its public documentation (part of its API): "Adds an item at the end of the model." In a sorted combo box a newly added element could end up anywhere, so adding it at the end is meaningless. Consequently, using composition over inheritance to reuse much of the `DefaultComboBox` functionality wouldn't help much either, because the API of the new `SortedComboBox` class (implementing the previously mentioned interface) would still be wicked.

The senior's next idea (honestly, this was more of a desperate attempt instead of something you would want to follow) was to try creating a new interface called `SortedComboBoxModel`, which would look like this:

```
package rs.exproit.swing;

import javax.swing.ComboBoxModel;

/**
 * A sorted combo box model, which is assumed to be mutable.
 */
public interface SortedComboBoxModel<E> extends ComboBoxModel<E> {
    /**
     * Adds an item to the model. The implementation of this method should notify all
     * registered ListDataListeners that the element has been added.
     *
     * @param element the element to be added.
     */
    void addElement(E element);
```

```
    /**
     * Removes an element from the model. The implementation of this method should should
     * notify all registered ListDataListeners that the element has been removed.
     *
     * @param element the element to be removed.
     */
    void removeElement(E element);

    /**
     * Removes an element at a given index. The implementation of this method should
     * notify all registered ListDataListeners that the element has been removed.
     *
     * @param index the location of the element to be removed.
     */
    void removeElementAt(int index);
}
```

An astute reader (that is you) will notice that this interface fixes minor naming problems in the MutableComboBoxModel interface (items are renamed to be elements, and the removeElement method accepts an object of type E instead of Object). Nevertheless, the senior soon abandoned this outline. One reason is that it is ugly to have a mutable combo box model type without relating it to the MutableComboBoxModel. The biggest problem, though, is that the whole idea is infeasible.

The JComboBox class's addItem and insertItemAt methods behave in a pretty strange way. Here is the citation from the JDK's documentation for the addItem method (the same is true for the other one): "This method works only if the JComboBox uses a mutable data model." What a blow! Hence, if you provide a JComboBox an object of type SortedComboBox, then it will become immutable, irrespective of the fact that the matching combo box model is mutable. There is no other way than to extend the MutableComboBoxModel interface. However, in that case you will essentially end up in the same position as when directly extending the DefaultComboBox class (at least from the standpoint of the API)! Game over!

The senior has advised the management that there is no superior way than to extend the DefaultComboBox model (as in Version II) and augment it with an external comparator (see the exercises at the end of this chapter).

For a greenfield project there is a much better route. One could leverage the dependency inversion principle, and introduce a layer of abstraction over Swing (an approach used by the NetBeans Platform). This UI bridge would contain sound abstractions for dealing with any GUI framework. Any issues with the target GUI framework, like Swing, will have been handled by this new bridge layer. Unfortunately, it isn't that easy to add such abstractions to a legacy code base, and this was an assumption in this case study.

Conclusion

The most important part of any API is its set of exposed abstractions. If those abstractions are not adequate (e.g., when they are radically different from the problem domain in the given context), then nothing else matters. You can try to use interfaces instead of classes, use composition over inheritance, use aspect-oriented programming, and so on. The outcome will always be the same, as demonstrated in this case study.

The MutableComboBoxModel interface is unfortunate, as it ties the mutability aspect of a model to a concrete implementation (presumes an unordered list). The proper way would have been to simply use our SortedComboBoxModel and rename it MutableComboBoxModel. However, this cannot be done anymore without breaking backward compatibility.

The hidden dependencies, for example, between the JComboBox and MutableComboBoxModel entities, are especially cumbersome. The IDE cannot help you notice the error until it is too late, when it pops up during execution.

All in all, reusing artifacts from a framework isn't that easy, let alone crafting a brand new one.[7] The reuse potential is directly proportional to the energy invested into an API. This is reminiscent of a chess game (I was a former chess player), as depicted in Figure 3-2. If you mess up the preparation or opening phases (equivalent of an API), then the rest of the game will be a struggle for a draw. Figure 3-2 also emphasizes the holistic approach to API design, as you need to evaluate a broad spectrum of possibilities to properly judge the future vector of changes. Those are the potential directions of evolution. As in chess, you cannot play tournaments without a plan,[8] deciding what move to make solely based on the current position. Your position wouldn't be evolvable.

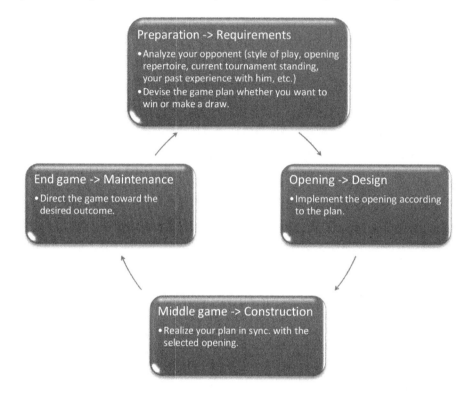

Figure 3-2. *Illustration of the life cycle of the chess game and how different phases can be mapped to software development (see [3]). In each phase you always need to watch what your opponent is doing, and make corrections accordingly (these are like constant change requests from a customer). The only huge difference is, that in software, the maintenance is really when things begin to happen (this is the longest period in the software's life cycle).*

The case study has also revealed a truth behind maintenance, and why it is so hard. Most often, all that remains is the source code (possibly with some documentation). This is nothing but a snapshot of a complex and involved mental process. It is rarely the case that anybody invests the energy to document the whole thing (there is a time when developers are capable and motivated to create high-quality documentation, as explained at http://wiki.apidesign.org/wiki/Teamwork). Sometimes, if you are lucky, you might squeeze out some information from the version control system, by looking at the history, but chances for success are rather small.

---

[7]You should avoid creating a new framework before looking around for already available options. For example, if you need an additional layer of abstraction and control over the GUI, then you might use the NetBeans platform instead of plain Swing. As an additional benefit, you would acquire a platform caring about your application's life cycle.
[8]Opening = first version of an API; chess game plan = evolution plan for the future; struggling after opening = living with design mistakes from the first version.

Case Study: Provider of Reuse

We will change roles here, and see how it looks when you would like to create an artifact for others to reuse. The intention is to showcase all the difficulties associated with creating highly reusable entities (this time we will try to make it proper on the first attempt). The task here is to implement a generic, serializable, randomized "queue" abstract data type (for a full description of the assignment, without bothering about the client part, visit http:// www.cs.princeton.edu/courses/archive/fall05/cos226/assignments/queues.html). The double-ended queue is now part of the JDK, so we will not implement that. For an introduction to algorithms, read [4].

To make this case study more interesting, we will additionally demand that our new data structure fit into the Java Collections framework. This will allow clients to reuse it in a familiar way (like they reuse the ArrayList or LinkedList classes). However, we will relax the constraint regarding Java library functions and allow ourselves to call them. After all, this chapter is about reuse.

The first decision is how to properly name our abstraction (remember that naming is one of the most crucial things to do right). It is obvious that *queue* is a loose term. Looking at the description of the Collection interface, it gives us a hint that *bags* should implement this interface directly. This is exactly what we want. Basing our abstraction on the Queue interface would be plain wrong. Therefore, our new data type will be named RandomizedBag.

Implementing the Collection interface directly is quite tedious, due to many methods. For this reason, the Collections framework provides a convenient abstract base class AbstractCollection.[9] Here is the citation from its documentation: "This class provides a skeletal implementation of the Collection interface, to minimize the effort required to implement this interface." Extending this class is okay, because we are principally using interface inheritance instead of implementation inheritance (e.g., it would be an error to extend the ArrayList class). We now just need to follow the documentation of the AbstractCollection class to comply with its API.

The next decision revolves around what to use internally for holding the elements in our collection. The best candidate is the universal ArrayList class. We use composition instead of inheritance, and check that ArrayList does implement Serializable. It turns out it does. So far, so good.

To generate random numbers, we will use the JDK's built-in Random class, which also implements Serializable (this is important, as we would like to get a deserialized object with its random number generator's state restored). However, we would like to be able to replace it with any other linear congruential random number generator. Also, we will allow a client to seed our generator to be able to reproduce a random sequence.

Finally, we want our class to be evolvable in a backward-compatible fashion. This requirement regularly has a great impact on an API. The source code of the RandomizedBag class is presented here (the most important details are shown in bold, some of them because they are wrong).

```
package rs.exproit.util;

import java.io.Serializable;
import java.util.AbstractCollection;
import java.util.ArrayList;
import java.util.Collection;
import java.util.Collections;
import java.util.Iterator;
import java.util.List;
import java.util.NoSuchElementException;
```

---

[9]It is educational to notice the different conventions between the Java Collections framework and Swing. In Swing, this kind of a convenience class has a suffix Adapter, which is totally misleading. For example, the MouseMotionAdapter's documentation states the following: "An abstract adapter class for receiving mouse motion events. The methods in this class are empty. This class exists as convenience for creating listener objects." It serves the same purpose as the AbstractCollection, but with a wrong name and an inaccurate documentation (it isn't abstract at all). It would have been more appropriate to follow the later JDK convention with the Base/Default prefix/suffix instead of Adapter.

```java
import java.util.Random;

/**
 * Implements the generic randomized "queue" ADT as described
 * <a href="http://www.cs.princeton.edu/courses/archive/fall05/cos226/assignments/queues.html">
 * here</a>.
 * The randomization process uses a linear congruential random number generator. This may be
 * configured with a seed value, to reproduce the random number sequence.
 *
 * @author Ervin Varga
 *
 * @param <E> the type of elements contained inside this bag.
 */
public final class RandomizedBag<E> extends AbstractCollection<E>
        implements Serializable {
    private static final long serialVersionUID = 1L;

    private final List<E> elems = new ArrayList<>();
    private final Random rnd;

    public RandomizedBag() {
        rnd = new Random();
    }

    public RandomizedBag(long seed) {
        rnd = new Random(seed);
    }

    public RandomizedBag(Collection<E> c) {
        this();
        addAndshuffleElementsInPlace(c);
    }

    public RandomizedBag(long seed, Collection<E> c) {
        this(seed);
        addAndshuffleElementsInPlace(c);
    }

    private void addAndshuffleElementsInPlace(Collection<E> newElems) {
        assert newElems != null;

        elems.addAll(newElems);
        Collections.shuffle(elems, rnd);
    }

    /**
     * Adds a new element to this collection. The collection permits duplicates, but doesn't
     * allow {@code null} elements.
     *
     * {@inheritDoc}
     */
```

```java
    @Override
    public boolean add(E e) {
        if (e == null) {
            throw new NullPointerException();
        }

        elems.add(e);

        // Shuffle the last added element with a random one from the queue.
        final int idx = rnd.nextInt(elems.size());
        elems.set(elems.size() - 1, elems.get(idx));
        elems.set(idx, e);
        return true;
    }

    /**
     * Deletes and returns an element from the bag, uniformly at random.
     *
     * @return the deleted element from this bag.
     * @throws NoSuchElementException if the bag is empty.
     */
    public E remove() {
        if (isEmpty()) {
            throw new NoSuchElementException("Cannot remove an element from an empty bag.");
        }

        return elems.remove(0);
    }

    public Iterator<E> iterator() {
        List<E> elemsCopy = new ArrayList<>(elems);
        Collections.shuffle(elemsCopy, rnd);
        return elemsCopy.listIterator();
    }

    @Override
    public int size() {
        return elems.size();
    }
}
```

The accompanying test case class is shown here:

```java
package rs.exproit.util;

import static org.junit.Assert.*;

import java.io.ByteArrayInputStream;
import java.io.ByteArrayOutputStream;
import java.io.ObjectInputStream;
import java.io.ObjectOutputStream;
```

```java
import java.util.ArrayList;
import java.util.List;

import static org.hamcrest.core.IsEqual.*;
import static org.hamcrest.core.IsNot.*;
import org.junit.BeforeClass;
import org.junit.Test;

public class RandomizedBagTest {
    private static final List<Integer> baseItems = new ArrayList<>();

    @BeforeClass
    public static void setupBaseItems() {
        for (int i = 0; i < 10; i++) {
            baseItems.add(i);
        }
    }

    @Test
    public void testConstructorWithoutCollection() {
        RandomizedBag<Integer> bag = new RandomizedBag<>();
        assertNotNull(bag);
        assertTrue(bag.isEmpty());
    }

    @Test
    public void testConstructorWithCollection() {
        RandomizedBag<Integer> bag = new RandomizedBag<>(baseItems);
        assertNotNull(bag);
        assertEquals(baseItems.size(), bag.size());
    }

    @Test
    public void testConstructorWithCollectionAndSeed() {
        RandomizedBag<Integer> bag1 = new RandomizedBag<>(1, baseItems);
        RandomizedBag<Integer> bag2 = new RandomizedBag<>(1, baseItems);
        Object[] bag1Content = bag1.toArray();
        Object[] bag2Content = bag2.toArray();
        assertArrayEquals(bag1Content, bag2Content);

        bag1 = new RandomizedBag<>(1, baseItems);
        bag1Content = bag1.toArray();
        bag2 = new RandomizedBag<>(2, baseItems);
        bag2Content = bag2.toArray();
        assertThat(bag1Content, not(equalTo(bag2Content)));
    }

    @Test(expected = NullPointerException.class)
    public void addNull() {
        RandomizedBag<Integer> bag = new RandomizedBag<>();
        bag.add(null);
```

```java
}

@Test(expected = NoSuchElementException.class)
public void removeFromEmptyBag() {
    RandomizedBag<Integer> bag = new RandomizedBag<>();
    bag.remove();
}

@Test
public void addElementsAndIterateOverThem() {
    RandomizedBag<Integer> bag1 = new RandomizedBag<>(3);
    for (Integer e : baseItems) {
        bag1.add(e);
    }
    Integer[] bag1Content = new Integer[baseItems.size()];
    int idx = 0;
    for (Integer e : bag1) {
        bag1Content[idx++] = e;
    }

    RandomizedBag<Integer> bag2 = new RandomizedBag<>(3);
    for (Integer e : baseItems) {
        bag2.add(e);
    }
    Integer[] bag2Content = new Integer[baseItems.size()];
    idx = 0;
    for (Integer e : bag2) {
        bag2Content[idx++] = e;
    }
    assertArrayEquals(bag1Content, bag2Content);
}

@Test
public void removeElementRandomly() {
    RandomizedBag<Integer> bag1 = new RandomizedBag<>(1, baseItems);
    RandomizedBag<Integer> bag2 = new RandomizedBag<>(1, baseItems);
    assertEquals(bag1.remove(), bag2.remove());

    bag1 = new RandomizedBag<>(1, baseItems);
    bag2 = new RandomizedBag<>(2, baseItems);
    assertNotEquals(bag1.remove(), bag2.remove());
}

@SuppressWarnings("unchecked")
@Test
public void testSerialization() throws Exception {
    RandomizedBag<Integer> bag1 = new RandomizedBag<>(1, baseItems);
    byte[] bag1Memento;
    try (
        ByteArrayOutputStream buffer = new ByteArrayOutputStream();
        ObjectOutputStream objectStream = new ObjectOutputStream(buffer);
    ) {
```

```
            objectStream.writeObject(bag1);
            bag1Memento = buffer.toByteArray();
        }

        RandomizedBag<Integer> bag2;
        try (
            ByteArrayInputStream buffer = new ByteArrayInputStream(bag1Memento);
            ObjectInputStream objectStream = new ObjectInputStream(buffer);
        ) {
            Object obj = objectStream.readObject();
            bag2 = RandomizedBag.class.cast(obj);
        }

        Object[] bag1Content = bag1.toArray();
        Object[] bag2Content = bag2.toArray();
        assertArrayEquals(bag1Content, bag2Content);
    }

    @Test
    public void verifyThatIteratorHasRemove() {
        RandomizedBag<Integer> bag1 = new RandomizedBag<>(baseItems);
        Iterator<Integer> iter = bag1.iterator();
        assertTrue(iter.hasNext());
        assertNotNull(iter.next());
        // This should not throw an exception.
        iter.remove();
    }
}
```

The RandomizedBag class is final for us to gain full control. It is better to be restrictive than to allow all sorts of customizations via extension. Clients will definitely find ways to abuse inheritance. As change requests arrive, we will learn what the weak points are. At any rate, we will be able to expand a final class in a backward-compatible manner. If nothing helps, then we can introduce a new type later, while retaining the old one for simple uses.

The previous musing supposedly goes against the Open/Closed principle. After all, by closing the class for extensibility (via extends) we actually open it up for evolution (the opposite of what this principle says). However, there is no paradox. The Open/Closed principle has two facets: implementation and API. The confusion arises when these are mixed up. By adding new methods to the final class, we are extending its API (open for extension). We aren't allowed to break the API (closed for modification of existing stuff). Java interfaces are extended differently than classes. For interfaces, the extends mechanism is the natural way to evolve.

It is tempting to be overly assertive and replace the generic parameter E with E extends Serializable. This would seriously limit the reuse possibilities, as you would suppose that all use cases will involve serialization, but this is a false assumption.

The serialVersionUID field is crucial. Once you make your class Serializable, then all the private fields become part of an API. In the future, to control the serialization format, you will need versioning. Another more advanced possibility is implementing Externalizable. The latter gives you more control of what is saved into an output stream. Of course, Externalizable comes with its own baggage of restrictions, and Java binary serialization is a bit obsolete nowadays. This is the reason XML/JSON serialization is much better.

The class internally uses an `ArrayList`. This is a fine example of a composition over inheritance. Extending the `ArrayList`, or for that matter any concrete class, would be a serious mistake. Our `RandomizedBag` can be seen as an ordinary `Collection`, which increases its reuse potentials. Moreover, it can be adorned with decorators provided by the `Collections` class (e.g., to make thread-safe or immutable variants). An additional improvement could be the replacement of public constructors with factory methods.

The private methods should be protected by assertions (they blow up in a stronger way than a code throwing ordinary exceptions), but public methods should explicitly implement the principles of defensive programming. In a production run, assertions are usually turned off.

The way the shuffling is implemented in the `add` method is important to remember, although more efficient methods are possible (for more details, refer to [4]). A naive approach to always reshuffle the complete array would be wrong and slow at the same time.

The no-arg `remove` method is new, and it isn't part of the `Collection` interface. It is okay to augment the interface with extra methods in your class as long as you fully obey the contract of that interface.

Returning a `listIterator` ensures that elements can be removed through it. If a collection is mutable, then its iterator must support element removal.

■ **Warning**   There are severe undisclosed troubles in the `RandomizedBag` class and its associated test. If you notice five serious problems, then you are an ace. Otherwise, try to figure them out yourself before reading further (especially Chapter 4).

To give you a hint of how to analyze the code, I reveal here one important concern (so you are now left with four additional issues). The private `addAndshuffleElementsInPlace` method uses an assertion to verify whether the input collection is `null` (this is how books teach you). This wouldn't be a problem by itself, if the public constructors weren't relying on this private method as a guarantee that a client hasn't provided `null`. In production, assertions are turned off. Luckily, this method has a nonintuitive side effect (in this case a positive one): Even in production it will properly signal a `NullPointerException`. Its behavior depends on the `addAll` method of `ArrayList` (it throws the previous exception if the input is `null`). Where is this functionality tested and documented? This is the biggest problem. There is no test case to check whether the constructors will throw such an exception. During maintenance, if an unsuspecting developer changes the `ArrayList` to something else, which doesn't behave as `ArrayList`, then a new bug will appear in an allegedly "correct" code. Who is to blame: the maintainer or the original irresponsible author? With a proper test this would be immediately discovered. At least there would be a clear statement how constructors should handle a `null` input. This fact would be part of an API, and not some hidden "pearl" of the software.

Summary

This chapter has reinforced the statements about the importance of proper abstractions to create reusable and maintainable APIs. The OO technology doesn't give you the ability to reuse artifacts for free. You must work hard to reach a satisfactory reuse level. Of course, once you master the secrets, then your productivity will undeniably improve. This is especially true in multiparadigm languages, like Java 8, where you can combine various paradigms to boost your expressive power.

We have also attested that each time you introduce a framework into your code base, you bring in lots of stuff. You must be aware of the framework's power and limitations. If you see that the framework's API is sloppy, then you should be remarkably vigilant. Examine lots of code, browse through the test cases (they are sometimes the best documentation[10]), and read high-quality books. I recommend you look for a book written by the author who is also the main contributor in the matching open source framework (if you are searching for purely technology-related books). Blogs are okay, but only if you have already accrued a decent knowledge and experience in the corresponding area. Forget about Wikipedia, unless you're an expert, and want to fix errors.

AUGMENT THE SORTED COMBO BOX MODEL

Practice Design Patterns

The SortedComboBoxModel model from Version II doesn't allow a client to customize the sorting behavior. This is a serious limitation. Your task is to come up with Version IV enabling a client to pass a custom Comparator (an example of the Strategy design pattern).

You should also remove an ill-advised restriction on a generic type; for example, instead of E extends Comparable<E>, it should be just E.

VERSION IV

Admire the Importance of Good API Design

There is another possibility to implement a sorted combo box without actually creating a new subclass of the combo box component or its model. Swing provides an interface called ListDataListener, and this is implemented by the JComboBox component (for more information visit https://docs. oracle.com/javase/tutorial/uiswing/events/listdatalistener.html). The DefaultComboBox has a method to register ListDataListener instances. The model's addElement method should notify all registered listeners. Those listeners might do anything, including reordering of elements (the Javadoc of the ListDataListener doesn't prevent users from doing that, nor it is prevented in the implementation).

Your task is to implement Version IV of the sorted combo box component. You would want to encapsulate the registration mechanism inside your custom listener (to accept a combo box for what it needs to handle the sorting). Notice that you will be able to find out the source of the event by calling the getSource method of the ListDataEvent object (this is passed to listeners).

This approach might be the least invasive, but it doesn't solve the main problem. You will still need to trigger the event via that addItem method. The added element could end up anywhere, so the contract is still broken.

---

[10]It is important to differentiate tests written to illustrate a use cases from those produced to reproduce bugs (usually, these tests are quite cluttered). There is a Maven plug-in that allows you to extract code snippets from use case tests (as they are tidy) and embed them into Javadoc. The plug-in is available at https://github.com/jtulach/codesnip-pet4javadoc. This relieves you from manually copy-pasting material.

References

1. Holub, Allen. Holub on Patterns: Learning Design Patterns by Looking at Code. New York: Apress, 2004.

2. "Trail: Creating a GUI with JFC/Swing." Oracle. `https://docs.oracle.com/javase/tutorial/uiswing/`

3. Varga, Ervin. "The Holistic Approach to Software Engineering." Presented at the 5th PSU-UNS International Conference on Engineering and Technology (ICET-2011), Thailand, 2011.

4. Sedgewick, Robert, and Kevin Wayne. Algorithms, Fourth Edition. Reading, MA; Addison-Wesley Professional, 2011.

CHAPTER 4

■ ■ ■

TDD as an API Design Technique

TDD is usually associated with the phrase "Write tests first, and then implement." However, this is a rather distorted and reduced view of TDD. I would say that it misses all the major points of it. TDD is a paradigm shift, a brand new way of thinking about how to specify, design, and implement a software system. It is applicable as a concept in all phases of a software's life cycle. The previously mentioned phrase is bad, as it also suggests that TDD can be used only on greenfield projects. This chapter demonstrates quite the opposite. Before proceeding, I would suggest you read an excellent treatment of TDD [1], which also introduces tools supporting TDD. This chapter essentially complements the methods presented in that book.

TDD is a powerful mental shift about asking questions. Traditional software engineering processes (not necessarily crude waterfall, but definitely formal) tend to introduce delineations between major software life cycle phases. In this manner, implementation (construction) is treated differently than requirements; that is, there are strict perceptions of domain (problem) space and solution space. Programmers, who are mainly concerned with software construction, used to move and think purely inside the solution area. Consequently, the main question they ask is "How?" The people dealing with a problem domain are taught to forget about "How?" and focus on "What?" This could lead to a serious dichotomy, as the resulting conceptual and architectural models, which were challenged by only "What?" aspects, might not fit well into the "How?" space. In other words, they might be cumbersome to implement in the target programming language and environment. On the contrary, programs crafted by following solely the "How?" concerns frequently couldn't even address the core needs of the customer. TDD is a paradigm change to cross this chasm.[1] By proactively thinking about testability of requirements, design, and code (known in the theory as *Testing V*), TDD forces all participants to ask both questions at the same time. For example, a requirement cannot be stated without a clear indication of *how* it is going to be tested during acceptance tests. This has a profound positive effect on a quality of the system requirements specification, hence on further analysis and design artifacts. In a similar manner, a code cannot be created without first answering the question "*What am I supposed to implement here; that is, what use case(s) are my code supposed to realize?*"

Another common question, what TDD puts forward to all participants, is "To whom?" There is a huge difference between a closed-form and open-form test (these terms are mine, so I apologize if they're unwieldy at this moment; I will try to explain them in a moment from the viewpoint of a programmer).

A closed-form test is written by a programmer for herself or himself in a most selfish manner. It serves to assure the programmer that the code "works." The semantic behind the word *work* is again defined by the same programmer. A closed-form test is totally confined by the programmer's view of the project. The answer to the question "To whom?" is "Only to me."

An open-form test is written by a programmer for everybody to look at. This test tries to verify that the code is following the needs of a business (it is use-case driven). The matching test is also intended to be a documentation for other programmers, who must understand what is going on (especially important during

---

[1]A similar abyss crossing movement is DevOps, where construction isn't totally isolated from deployment and operational aspects of the produced system.

the maintenance phase). An open-form test might even be specified to be readable by nontechnical people (we will see an example of this later on). By caring about what to implement (an influence of TDD) the programmer automatically starts to appreciate the demands of the project. He or she wants to implement a useful code. This change in attitude changes the way he or she specifies tests.

■ **Note** TDD brings use cases to programmers, and equips analysts and architects with pragmatism. In other words, TDD raises programmers from the muddy ground, and prevents analysts and architects from entering outer space, where Earth looks like an electrical point charge. Software modules are a common denominator for both architects and programmers, when they are confronted with an overall testability aspect of the product. In this respect, TDD fosters modularity.

Software testing is a quality control technique (with limited efficacy). TDD is a quality assurance technique with a high impact on the overall quality of a software product. Thinking about testability produces better design, which supports software development and evolution. Moreover, higher quality tests boost the quality control efficiency of bare testing, thus lowering the chance that undetected bugs will end up in a release.

The next list enumerates the primary benefits of using TDD (the list isn't ordered by any means, so all bullet points are equally important).

- Produces a battery of high-quality tests (we assume that these are all automated) for detecting bugs as well as helping maintenance activities (these happen throughout the software's life cycle, not just in its maintenance and evolution phase). Constant refactoring cannot happen without frequent regression testing. As new features are added, without doing perfective maintenance in parallel, they will make the code more complex. Uncontrolled complexity hampers further evolution.

- Produces a better design by advocating loose coupling and high cohesion (strongly coupled and low cohesive units are hard to test). The desire to break dependencies to control peer classes (to mock them out) frequently introduces new abstractions (dependency inversion in action). TDD drives you to think about design principles and patterns and apply them judiciously in your code.

- Subjugates entropy and acts as a powerful risk mitigation technique (you reduce the probability of a catastrophic failure in production). Exposing code to tests early abolishes surprises in later phases of development. TDD is very similar to measurements in quantum physics. A quantum state collapses into a deterministic one as soon as you apply a measurement to it. When you execute tests, you perform such "quantum" measurements over the code. Each uncovered bug disappears (collapses) after a fix, so you reduce the footage of the unknown bug haze in a product.

- Helps make clean and tidy APIs. An API is a window through which all communications happen with the matching software entity (let us presume a class now). TDD nudges you think about behavioral aspects of the system and the types of interactions involving your class. In every such interaction, an instance of the class plays a specific role, and these roles should be embodied in its API.

The RandomizedBag class wasn't created with TDD in mind (see Chapter 3). In the rest of this chapter, we explain the consequences of not following TDD and present the reworked version of the RandomizedBag class driven by tests. All this is done via various case studies.

Case Study: TDD Doesn't Replace OOD Principles

Suppose TDD is performed by the rookie, who knows nothing about the standard OOD principles, but has read about "write tests first, and then implement" wisdom in a multitude of blog posts (this is all our rookie knows about TDD, as is the case with many bloggers, too). This rooker has also been commanded to apply TDD blindly in the company, where he is employed. Let us simulate what typically happens in this situation, for the same task of creating a randomized "queue" class. Also, let's forget about our previous attempt with RandomizedBag, and let the rookie start from scratch; of course (for rookies), let's start with a wrong class name (a typical blunder coming along with bad design choices). Therefore, the rookie has started with the following test case for testing the two mandatory constructors that have to be provided according to the Collection interface's specification.

```java
package rs.exproit.util;

import static org.junit.Assert.*;

import java.util.LinkedList;
import java.util.List;
import org.junit.BeforeClass;
import org.junit.Test;

public class RandomizedQueueTest {
    private static final List<Integer> baseItems = new LinkedList<>();

    @BeforeClass
    public static void setupBaseItems() {
        for (int i = 0; i < 10; i++) {
            baseItems.add(i);
        }
    }

    @Test
    public void testConstructorWithoutCollection() {
        RandomizedQueue<Integer> queue = new RandomizedQueue<>();
        assertNotNull(queue);
        assertTrue(queue.isEmpty());
    }

    @Test
    public void testConstructorWithCollection() {
        RandomizedQueue<Integer> queue = new RandomizedQueue<>(baseItems);
        assertNotNull(queue);
        assertEquals(baseItems.size(), queue.size());
    }
}
```

The new data type was named RandomizedQueue because the rookie has chosen to extend it from the LinkedList class. He figured that it already delivers 90% of the implementation, so it would be a good choice as the parent class. The two constructors were added to this child class to come up with the first version. Here is the listing (the Javadoc comments are omitted for brevity).

```
package rs.exproit.util;

import java.util.Collection;
import java.util.Collections;
import java.util.LinkedList;
import java.util.Random;

@SuppressWarnings("serial")
public final class RandomizedQueue<E> extends LinkedList<E> {

    public RandomizedQueue() {
    }

    public RandomizedQueue(Collection<E> c) {
        super(c);
        Collections.shuffle(this);
    }
}
```

All of the test passed. The LinkedList class implements Serializable, and the warning about the missing serialVersionUID[2] was silenced with the @SuppressWarnings("serial") annotation (beginners are especially rapid on muting warnings). Nonetheless, the rookie was not satisfied with the test case, as he was not sure whether the given collection was really shuffled or not. The test case was extended in the following manner (the parts shown in bold are the most interesting ones).

```
package rs.exproit.util;

import static org.junit.Assert.*;

import java.util.Collection;
import java.util.Collections;
import java.util.LinkedList;
import java.util.List;
import java.util.Random;

import org.junit.BeforeClass;
import org.junit.Test;

public class RandomizedQueueTest {
    @SuppressWarnings("serial")
    private static class MyRandomizedQueue extends RandomizedQueue<Integer> {
        public MyRandomizedQueue() {}

        public MyRandomizedQueue(Collection<Integer> c) {
            super(c);
        }
```

---

[2]This is one of the *lint* checks performed by the Java compiler. For an excellent overview of the possible options, you might want to read the JavaWorld article "javac's -Xlint Options," which is available at http://www.javaworld.com/article/2073587/javac-s--xlint-options.html.

```
    @Override
    public Random createRandom() {
        return new Random(1L);
    }
};

private static final List<Integer> baseItems = new LinkedList<>();
private static final List<Integer> shuffledBaseItems = new LinkedList<>();
private static final Random rnd = new Random(1L);

@BeforeClass
public static void setupBaseItems() {
    for (int i = 0; i < 10; i++) {
        baseItems.add(i);
        shuffledBaseItems.add(i);
    }
    Collections.shuffle(shuffledBaseItems, rnd);
}

@Test
public void testConstructorWithoutCollection() {
    RandomizedQueue<Integer> queue = new MyRandomizedQueue();
    assertNotNull(queue);
    assertTrue(queue.isEmpty());
}

@Test
public void testConstructorWithCollection() {
    RandomizedQueue<Integer> queue = new MyRandomizedQueue(baseItems);
    assertNotNull(queue);
    assertEquals(baseItems.size(), queue.size());
    assertArrayEquals(shuffledBaseItems.toArray(), queue.toArray());
}
}
```

The corresponding new version of the target class is given next (notice the parts shown in bold).

```
package rs.exproit.util;

import java.util.Collection;
import java.util.Collections;
import java.util.LinkedList;
import java.util.Random;

@SuppressWarnings("serial")
public class RandomizedQueue<E> extends LinkedList<E> {
    private Random rnd;

    public RandomizedQueue() {
        rnd = createRandom();
    }
```

```
public RandomizedQueue(Collection<E> c) {
    super(c);
    rnd = createRandom();
    Collections.shuffle(this, rnd);
}

public Random createRandom() {
    return new Random();
}

public void setRandom(Random rnd) {
    this.rnd = rnd;
}
}
```

The rookie has rightly concluded, that without controlling the random number generator it is impossible to test the RandomizedQueue class. He has stumbled across the *Factory Method* design pattern, and the solution was at his fingertips. He was so happy, because using design patterns is just cool (he has heard about patterns, when senior engineers talked about them in the company's café)! So, the rookie introduced a createRandom factory method that was aimed to be overridden by classes not satisfied with the default generator. He also figured, to make the class even more flexible, that a setter method would be handy, too. He also removed the final modifier on the class because it was an obstacle for implementing the factory method (he even wondered why anybody would use such an annoying final on the class).[3]

The rookie has announced to his boss that the implementation will be ready in a minute. After all, the hardest parts are already solved. The remaining add method is a piece of cake. His boss was also pleased, and added, "I've told you that TDD is good!"

Conclusion

If you think that I have embellished the example, believe me that I didn't. As a consultant, I've seen much worse production code (let alone code written by some of my students). Nevertheless, the case study shows what happens when TDD is applied out of context. The biggest issue is that people afterward conclude that the problem is with the TDD, and not the preconditions regarding its usage. These are some of the most salient problems in the preceding solution:

1. Extending the RandomizedQueue class from the LinkedList one is a brutal abuse of implementation inheritance. You might find examples of this even in the JDK: Stack extends Vector, Properties extends Hashtable, and so on. Try to enumerate how many ways you can thwart the RandomizedQueue class's integrity by using methods inherited from the LinkedList class.

2. Giving away the Random class is a brutal violation of the encapsulation and information hiding principles. Classes cannot be made flexible and reusable by just deciding to give away all of their internal details. Look at the API of the preceding RandomizedQueue class. It's awful.

---

[3]Adding an instrumentation API for testing purposes is a sound practice, but it should never weaken the main API. The aim is to increase testability without giving up on information hiding, encapsulation, or both (e.g., it isn't advisable to remove a private modifier just to make something testable). Otherwise, this instrumentation API is a standard practice in electronics, where you have so-called reference points in circuitry. If you make measurements with an oscilloscope on test points, then you can compare the measured signals to the expected ones. Any mismatch is an indication of an error. At any rate, if your test needs "privileged" access to the code, then you might leverage a library to help you with this (e.g., take a look at https://code.google.com/archive/p/privilegedaccessor/).

3. The motivation to introduce a factory method by the rookie is shocking (together with the act of removing the `final` modifier). A factory method should never break encapsulation and information hiding, and is aimed to return an instance implementing an abstraction, the concrete class of which is unknown or hidden. The factory method here is used to configure the internal `Random` instance. What a misapplication!

4. You should never call a nonfinal method from the constructor. Clients might override it, and make some forbidden actions on a half-baked instance. This has caused a famous threading bug in the JDK's `SwingWorker` class. If you do need to call such a method from one of your constructors, then take care to document it properly, including all potential consequences.

■ **Note**   TDD requires a holistic approach to software engineering. It is not a replacement for all solid principles of OOD and OOP (including SOLID itself[4]), but is rather their supplement. Lack of a proper OOD knowledge and experience considerably diminishes the effects of TDD.

You should avoid the pitfall of writing tests first, and then just greedily trying to find ways to pass them. After all, if you know your tests, then it is easy to pass them without implementing anything useful. Sometimes, this is exacerbated with code coverage tools and a frantic desire to achieve 100% coverage. This all happens when TDD is deeply misunderstood. The next case study highlights these problems.

Case Study: Tests Are Rubbish Without TDD

Let us revisit again our class from Chapter 3. As hinted there, the `RandomizedBagTest` test class is troublesome. After this section you might even say that it is rubbish (to phrase it politely). Can you believe that it will pass 100% (generate a bunch of false positives) for the next version of the randomized bag type (it is appropriately called `RandomizedBagRubbish`)?

```
package rs.exproit.util;

import java.io.Serializable;
import java.util.AbstractCollection;
import java.util.ArrayList;
import java.util.Collection;
import java.util.Collections;
import java.util.Iterator;
import java.util.List;
import java.util.NoSuchElementException;
import java.util.Random;

@SuppressWarnings("serial")
public final class RandomizedBagRubbish<E> extends AbstractCollection<E>
        implements Serializable {
    private final List<E> elems = new ArrayList<>();
```

---

[4]The word *solid* is an adjective, whereas SOLID as an acronym introduced by M. Feathers for the five most important OOD principles of Robert C. Martin: single responsibility, open-closed, Liskov substitution, interface segregation, and dependency inversion.

```java
    public RandomizedBagRubbish() {
    }

    public RandomizedBagRubbish(long seed) {
    }

    public RandomizedBagRubbish(Collection<E> c) {
        elems.addAll(c);
    }

    public RandomizedBagRubbish(long seed, Collection<E> c) {
        this(c);
        Collections.shuffle(elems, new Random(seed));
    }

    @Override
    public boolean add(E e) {
        if (e == null) {
            throw new NullPointerException();
        }

        elems.add(e);
        return true;
    }

    public E remove() {
        if (isEmpty()) {
            throw new NoSuchElementException("Cannot remove an element from an empty bag.");
        }

        return elems.remove(0);
    }

    public Iterator<E> iterator() {
        return elems.listIterator();
    }

    @Override
    public int size() {
        return elems.size();
    }
}
```

As you might notice, this class barely does anything more than implement a minimalistic collection. The only moment when shuffling is performed (it is shown in bold) is in the constructor accepting a collection with an initial seed value. What happened, taking into account the fact that RandomizedBagTest covered the whole original code base? Well, this is a consequence of having tests that are not written using TDD. It is not surprising, then, that the class under test might contain dozens of bugs, but none of them will be found during testing. Without applying a true TDD you will just fool yourself that "Write tests first, and then implement" is your motto toward a triumph.

At the heart of any OO system is the graph of collaborating objects talking to each other. In every such instance of a communication, participants take specific roles. These roles are associated with well-defined behaviors. You might want to assure in your tests that the APIs cover these scenarios, and objects behave properly. In other words, your tests must reflect the use cases; that is, give answers to all sorts of "What?" questions. For example, you might find in the original test case the test with the name of verifyThatIteratorHasRemove. What is the purpose of this test? Is it really the case that somebody is interested in that an iterator has a remove? Isn't it better to ask whether the RandomizedBag provides an iterator through which elements could be removed? The difference in how you formulate your questions, and accordingly your tests, is profound. That is what TDD is about!

Without acquiring the fundamentals of TDD, programmers habitually write tests just to bulldozer over all the paths of execution of a code, like warthogs. When they reach coverage above 90% (you can find suggestions about how much tests are enough at https://openide.netbeans.org/tutorial/test-patterns.html#enough), then they stop. This is an abomination. The RandomizedBagTest from Chapter 3 is a perfect example how the outcome looks by following this "variant" of TDD.

Case Study: Retrofitting Tests to Follow TDD

In this case study we will fix the problems in the RandomizedBagTest test class as well as the target class (it contains a serious bug). This study proves that TDD is applicable in all phases of a software's life cycle. TDD is a paradigm, and as such has no physical limits. You just need to tune your mind to ask proper questions, and follow your knowledge and experience to come up with correct answers. Here is the new version of the test class (I've retained its name).

```java
package rs.exproit.util;

import static org.junit.Assert.*;
import static org.hamcrest.CoreMatchers.*;
import java.io.*;
import java.util.*;
import org.junit.*;

public class RandomizedBagTest {
    private static final long SEED_ONE = 1L;
    private static final List<Integer> baseItems = new ArrayList<>();
    private static final List<Integer> baseItemsCopy = new ArrayList<>();
    private static final List<Integer> shuffledBaseItemsWithSeedOne = new ArrayList<>();

    @BeforeClass
    public static void setupBaseItems() {
        for (int i = 0; i < 10; i++) {
            baseItems.add(i);
            baseItemsCopy.add(i);
        }
        shuffledBaseItemsWithSeedOne.addAll(Arrays.asList(6, 8, 0, 2, 5, 7, 1, 4, 9, 3));
    }

    @Before
    public void verifyThatBaseItemsAreIntact() {
        assertEquals("base items should be intact", baseItemsCopy, baseItems);
    }
```

```java
@Test(expected = NullPointerException.class)
public void tryToCreateABagWithNullInputCollection() {
    new RandomizedBag<>(null);
}

@Test(expected = NullPointerException.class)
public void tryToCreateABagWithNullInputCollectionAndAPredefinedSeed() {
    new RandomizedBag<>(SEED_ONE, null);
}

@Test
public void createAnEmptyBag() {
    RandomizedBag<Integer> bag = new RandomizedBag<>();
    assertNotNull("bag should exist", bag);
    assertTrue("bag should be empty", bag.isEmpty());
}

@Test
public void createAnEmptyBagWithAPredefinedSeed() {
    RandomizedBag<Integer> bag = new RandomizedBag<>(SEED_ONE);
    assertNotNull("bag should exist", bag);
    assertTrue("bag should be empty", bag.isEmpty());
}

@Test
public void createANonEmptyBag() {
    RandomizedBag<Integer> bag = new RandomizedBag<>(baseItems);
    assertNotNull("bag should exist", bag);
    assertEquals("bag's size equals collection's size", baseItems.size(), bag.size());
    assertTrue("bag contains all items", bag.containsAll(baseItems));
    assertThat("bag should be shuffled",
            baseItems.toArray(), is(not(equalTo(bag.toArray()))));
}

@Test
public void createANonEmptyBagWithAPredefinedSeed() {
    RandomizedBag<Integer> bag = new RandomizedBag<>(SEED_ONE, baseItems);
    assertNotNull("bag should exist", bag);
    assertEquals("bag's size equals collection's size", baseItems.size(), bag.size());
    assertThat("bag should be shuffled with a given seed",
            shuffledBaseItemsWithSeedOne.toArray(), is(equalTo(bag.toArray())));
}

@Test(expected = NullPointerException.class)
public void tryToAddANullItem() {
    RandomizedBag<Integer> bag = new RandomizedBag<>();
    bag.add(null);
}

@Test(expected = NoSuchElementException.class)
public void tryToRemoveFromAnEmptyBag() {
```

```java
    RandomizedBag<Integer> bag = new RandomizedBag<>();
    bag.remove();
}

@Test
public void addItemsToABag() {
    RandomizedBag<Integer> bag = new RandomizedBag<>();
    for (Integer e : baseItems) {
        bag.add(e);
    }
    assertEquals("bag's size equals collection's size", baseItems.size(), bag.size());
    assertTrue("bag contains all items", bag.containsAll(baseItems));
    assertThat("bag should be shuffled",
            baseItems.toArray(), is(not(equalTo(bag.toArray()))));
}

@Test
public void removeItemsFromABag() {
    RandomizedBag<Integer> bag = new RandomizedBag<>(SEED_ONE, baseItems);
    for (Integer e : shuffledBaseItemsWithSeedOne) {
        assertEquals("bag's head should follow the shuffling", e, bag.remove());
    }
}

@Test
public void saveAndReadFromAnObjectStreamUsingStandardSerialization() throws Exception {
    RandomizedBag<Integer> originalBag = new RandomizedBag<>(SEED_ONE, baseItems);
    RandomizedBag<Integer> streamBag = readFromStream(saveIntoStream(originalBag));
    assertArrayEquals("deserialized bag should equal the original",
            originalBag.toArray(), streamBag.toArray());
}

@SuppressWarnings("unchecked")
private RandomizedBag<Integer> readFromStream(byte[] bagMemento)
        throws ClassNotFoundException, IOException {
    try (
        ByteArrayInputStream buffer = new ByteArrayInputStream(bagMemento);
        ObjectInputStream objectStream = new ObjectInputStream(buffer);
    ) {
        Object obj = objectStream.readObject();
        return RandomizedBag.class.cast(obj);
    }
}

private byte[] saveIntoStream(RandomizedBag<? extends Serializable> bag)
        throws IOException {
    byte[] bagMemento;
    try (
        ByteArrayOutputStream buffer = new ByteArrayOutputStream();
        ObjectOutputStream objectStream = new ObjectOutputStream(buffer);
    ) {
```

```java
            objectStream.writeObject(bag);
            bagMemento = buffer.toByteArray();
        }
        return bagMemento;
    }


    @Test
    public void iterateOverItemsOfABag() {
        RandomizedBag<Integer> bag = new RandomizedBag<>(SEED_ONE, baseItems);
        Iterator<Integer> bagIterator = bag.iterator();

        for (int i = 0; i < shuffledBaseItemsWithSeedOne.size(); i++) {
            assertEquals("bag's iterator should follow the shuffling",
                    shuffledBaseItemsWithSeedOne.get(i), bagIterator.next());
        }
    }


    @Test(expected = IllegalStateException.class)
    public void tryToRemoveAnItemFromABagViaItsIteratorWithoutFirstGettingTheNextItem() {
        RandomizedBag<Integer> bag = new RandomizedBag<>();
        Iterator<Integer> bagIterator = bag.iterator();
        bagIterator.remove();
    }


    @Test
    public void removeItemsFromABagViaItsIterator() {
        RandomizedBag<Integer> bag = new RandomizedBag<>(SEED_ONE, baseItems);
        Iterator<Integer> bagIterator = bag.iterator();

        bagIterator.next();
        bagIterator.remove();
        assertEquals("bag's size should be reduced after remove",
                baseItems.size() - 1, bag.size());
        for (int i = 1; i < shuffledBaseItemsWithSeedOne.size(); i++) {
            assertEquals("bag's iterator should follow the shuffling",
                    shuffledBaseItemsWithSeedOne.get(i), bagIterator.next());
        }
    }
}
```

This test fails with the original `RandomizedBag` class. It turns out that the `iterator` method was improperly implemented. It returned a `listIterator` instance over a copy of the internal data store instead of the data store itself. There was no way to remove an element through this iterator. Moreover, it reshuffled the items unnecessarily. This new test will also fail with the `RandomizedBagRubbish` class, hence avoid producing false positives. You should notice how the names of tests now truly reflect the various behaviors for what clients might be interested in. Some names are really long, but in tests this is okay. After all, you will not need to type them more than once. The fixed `iterator` method is shown here.

```java
public Iterator<E> iterator() {
    return elems.listIterator();
}
```

Case Study: Introduction to BDD

Behavior-driven development (BDD) is really just a variant of TDD. BDD is associated with higher level tests (integration and end-to-end tests). There are two approaches to writing them:

- Use JUnit directly, and introduce *Hamcrest* custom matchers and factory methods to create tests (possibly with mock objects to control dependencies), which are readable even by nontechnical people. A superb tutorial for this style is found in [1].

- Use a higher level tool to create BDD tests. We will demonstrate this tactic using Cucumber for Java (`https://cucumber.io`). In Cucumber, you specify a test using a formatted English text. This is executed by matching segments of that text via regular expressions. Each matched expression triggers an appropriate action implemented in a target programming language. All actions are run under JUnit, as Cucumber provides its own test runner.

BDD is useful for introducing your APIs to a broader audience, to allow them to reason about the APIs' applicability at a system level. The way the BDD test is specified is understandable to even nontechnical people, so they can also actively participate in specifying the API's behavior. Sometimes the API is very close to end users (like in this case study), and the tests must follow that elevated level of abstraction.

We implement here a small client application using our fixed `RandomizedBag` class. The client application will read in k unique strings from a command line (forming a set), and print out k subsets of them in a random order. We have already seen how to produce subsets of a set, this time we will implement it in Java (see the accompanying source code of the book for the class `PowerSet` and its test class `PowerSetTest`). Of course, we will start first with a test case, watch it fail, and after providing a correct implementation, see it in green. We will repeat this loop couple of times (to save space I will just show an end result of each artifact). The next listings show our first test specification in plain English as well as the accompanying Java code implementing custom test steps.

```
@ClientApplicationTest
Feature: Generating Subsets Using a Command Line Interface
  I want to generate subsets of a set (given as sequence of unique strings
  on a command line) and print them out in random order.
  The number of subsets printed must equal the input length (the number of unique strings).

  Background: A Running Client Application
    Given the client application is running

  Scenario: Missing Input
    When I do not provide input
    Then the application should show an error

  Scenario Outline: Creating Subsets
    When I read an input: <inputSet>
    Then the response should contain: <outputCardinality> subsets
    And the subsets should be in random order
    And the subsets should be members of the power set

  Examples:
    | inputSet | outputCardinality |
    | A B      | 2                 |
    | A        | 1                 |
    | A B C    | 3                 |
```

I recommend you use an appropriate plug-in for your IDE to edit a Cucumber specification file. The extension of the file is features. I've marked with bold the keywords for what you need to provide step definitions (the text following the corresponding keyword is also part of the step definition). Each scenario describes one particular user story (a concrete occurrence of an interaction with the application). The outline scenario is a template, which receives data from examples (see the Examples table earlier). Scenarios are grouped into a feature. I recommend you spend some time giving your feature a good title and description. The background is a generic precondition that is applied at the beginning of each scenario (remember that an outline scenario will produce as many scenarios as there are rows in the Examples table).

The main advantage of using Cucumber tests is its comprehensibility even for nontechnical people. They can just read a plain English text, and understand what is going on. All the gory details are hidden inside the step definitions. There is no better way to showcase the capabilities of your APIs.

The next step is to prepare the scaffolding for running Cucumber tests inside JUnit. You will need to add the following dependencies to your pom.xml file (besides the JUnit jar file itself):

```
<dependency>
    <groupId>info.cukes</groupId>
    <artifactId>cucumber-java</artifactId>
    <version>1.2.4</version>
    <scope>test</scope>
</dependency>
<dependency>
    <groupId>info.cukes</groupId>
    <artifactId>cucumber-junit</artifactId>
    <version>1.2.4</version>
    <scope>test</scope>
</dependency>
```

Because this client application uses the RandomizedBag class, you will also need to install its jar file into your local Maven repository (just run mvn clean install from the chapter4/java/randomized-queue-correct-impl folder), and add the dependency to it. After this you can create a simple test class to drive the Cucumber session (it could also contain auxiliary tests to try out particular edge cases, like in our case later). Here is the code.

```
package rs.exproit.client.cucumber;

import org.junit.runner.RunWith;

import cucumber.api.CucumberOptions;
import cucumber.api.junit.Cucumber;

@RunWith(Cucumber.class)
@CucumberOptions(
    monochrome = true,
    plugin = {"pretty", "json:target/cucumber.json", "rerun:target/rerun.txt"},
    dryRun = false
)
public class ClientApplicationTest {
    @Test(expected = NullPointerException.class)
    public void illegalStartupWithANullInputArgument() {
        ClientApplication.main(null);
    }
}
```

I suggest you set monochrome to true, otherwise you will get some strange characters in your IDE's console. Now, you are ready to implement the step definitions. These are shown next (the parts shown in bold are especially important).

```java
package rs.exproit.client.cucumber;

import static org.junit.Assert.*;
import java.util.Arrays;
import java.util.Collection;
import java.util.HashSet;
import java.util.Iterator;
import java.util.Set;

import cucumber.api.java.Before;
import cucumber.api.java.en.And;
import cucumber.api.java.en.Given;
import cucumber.api.java.en.Then;
import cucumber.api.java.en.When;
import rs.exproit.client.ClientApplication;
import rs.exproit.client.PowerSet;

public final class GeneratingSubsetsStepdefs {
    private Exception lastThrownException;
    private Set<Set<String>> lastGeneratedPowerSet;

    @Before("@ClientApplicationTest")
    public void cleanupBeforeScenario() {
        lastThrownException = null;
        lastGeneratedPowerSet = null;
    }

    @Given("^the client application is running$")
    public void the_client_application_is_running() {
        // Do nothing here, as our client application is trivial.
    }

    @When("^I do not provide input$")
    public void i_do_not_provide_input() {
        try {
            ClientApplication.main(new String[0]);
        } catch (IllegalArgumentException e) {
            lastThrownException = e;
        }
    }

    @Then("^the application should show an error$")
    public void the_application_should_show_an_error() {
        assertNotNull("application should generate an exception", lastThrownException);
        assertTrue("the exception should be for illegal arguments",
                lastThrownException instanceof IllegalArgumentException);
    }
```

```java
private static Collection<Set<String>> lastGeneratedRandomOutput;

public static final class TestOutputBuilder implements
        ClientApplication.OutputBuilder<String> {
    @Override
    public void startOutput() {
        lastGeneratedRandomOutput = new HashSet<>();
    }

    @Override
    public void addContent(Set<String> subset) {
        lastGeneratedRandomOutput.add(subset);
    }

    @Override
    public String finalizeOutput() {
        return lastGeneratedRandomOutput.toString();
    }
}

@When("^I read an input: (.+)$")
public void i_read_an_input(String inputSeq) {
    String[] args = inputSeq.split("\\s+");
    lastGeneratedPowerSet = new PowerSet(new HashSet<>(Arrays.asList(args))).subsets();
    ClientApplication.setOutputBuilder(TestOutputBuilder.class);
    ClientApplication.main(args);
}

@Then("^the response should contain: (\\d+) subsets$")
public void the_response_should_contain(int outputCardinality) {
    assertEquals(outputCardinality, lastGeneratedRandomOutput.size());
}

@And("^the subsets should be in random order$")
public void the_subsets_should_be_in_random_order() {
    // For a very small power set it might be the case that the shuffled
    // set is the same as the original.
    if (lastGeneratedPowerSet.size() > 4) {
        boolean allSame = true;
        Iterator<Set<String>> powerSetIter = lastGeneratedPowerSet.iterator();
        Iterator<Set<String>> randomOutputIter = lastGeneratedRandomOutput.iterator();

        while (randomOutputIter.hasNext()) {
            allSame = randomOutputIter.next().equals(powerSetIter.next());
        }
        assertFalse(allSame);
    }
}

@And("^the subsets should be members of the power set$")
public void the_subsets_should_be_members_of_the_power_set() {
```

```
            assertTrue(lastGeneratedPowerSet.containsAll(lastGeneratedRandomOutput));
    }
}
```

Our feature is tagged with @ClientApplicationTest, so that we may refer to it from the Before annotation. Tagging features is handy to introduce feature-specific hooks into the process. For larger test bases you can group common step definitions and reuse them from feature-specific ones.

The step definition to test whether the output is shown in a random order is rather trivial. To judge how well the specimen follows a particular distribution (in our case uniform) you would need a more stringent statistical test, but this is outside the scope of this book. If you are interested, you can explore the possibilities by using a good statistics book.

```
package rs.exproit.client;

import java.util.Arrays;
import java.util.HashSet;
import java.util.Set;

import rs.exproit.util.RandomizedBag;

/**
 * This client application reads in k unique strings from a command line (forming a set),
 * and prints out k subsets of them in a random order.
 *
 * @author Ervin Varga
 * @since 1.0
 */
public final class ClientApplication {
    /**
     * This is an API to build the output, which is based on the Builder pattern.
     *
     * @param <T> the type of output to generate.
     */
    public interface OutputBuilder<T> {
        void startOutput();
        void addContent(Set<String> subset);
        T finalizeOutput();
    }

    private static final class ConsoleOutputBuilder implements OutputBuilder<String> {
        private final StringBuilder buffer = new StringBuilder();

        @Override
        public void startOutput() {
            buffer.append("Selected subsets of an input set in random order:\n");
        }

        @Override
        public void addContent(Set<String> subset) {
            buffer.append(subset.toString());
            buffer.append('\n');
        }
```

```java
    @Override
    public String finalizeOutput() {
        return buffer.toString();
    }
};

private static Class<? extends OutputBuilder<?>> activeOutputBuilder =
        ConsoleOutputBuilder.class;
private static final ClientApplication app = new ClientApplication();

/**
 * Sets the active output builder for this application.
 *
 * @param newOutputBuilder a class definition of the new output builder.
 */
public static <T> void setOutputBuilder(
        Class<? extends OutputBuilder<T>> newOutputBuilder) {
    activeOutputBuilder = newOutputBuilder;
}

private Set<Set<String>> producePowerSet(String[] inputSeq) {
    assert inputSeq != null && !(inputSeq.length == 0);
    Set<String> inputSet = new HashSet<>(Arrays.asList(inputSeq));
    return new PowerSet(inputSet).subsets();
}

private RandomizedBag<Set<String>> randomizePowerSet(Set<Set<String>> powerSet) {
    assert powerSet != null;
    return new RandomizedBag<Set<String>>(powerSet);
}

@SuppressWarnings("unchecked")
private String generateConsoleOutput(String[] inputSeq) {
    assert inputSeq != null && !(inputSeq.length == 0);
    RandomizedBag<Set<String>> rndPowerSet = randomizePowerSet(producePowerSet(inputSeq));
    try {
        OutputBuilder<String> output =
                (OutputBuilder<String>) activeOutputBuilder.newInstance();
        output.startOutput();
        for (int i = 0; i < inputSeq.length; i++) {
            output.addContent(rndPowerSet.remove());
        }
        return output.finalizeOutput();
    } catch (Exception e) {
        return e.toString();
    }
}

/**
 * Main entry point of this client application.
 *
```

```
 * @param args the strings forming an input set. They should be separated by space.
 * @throws NullPointerException if the input parameter is {@code null}.
 * @throws IllegalArgumentException if the input argument list is empty.
 */
public static void main(String[] args) {
    if (args == null) {
        throw new NullPointerException("The input argument cannot be null");
    }

    if (args.length == 0) {
        throw new IllegalArgumentException("The input argument list cannot be empty");
    }

    System.out.println(app.generateConsoleOutput(args));
    }
}
```

This case study has revealed the importance of using adequate tools for the task at hand. BDD is valuable to exercise your artifacts in the context of the overall application. As you work with higher level tests, you should expect to have nontechnical people on board. For them, showing the test specification in plain English is surely more plausible than through "raw" Java code.

Case Study: TDD for APIs Is a Complex Topic

We are not done yet with our RandomizedBag class, at least not if we want to publish it as a generic abstract data type. So far, and this is showcased in the previous client application, we have been the master of use cases; that is, we knew in advance all the different ways our abstraction is going to be leveraged. In some way, we had an opportunity to optimize for only those possibilities. However, this isn't the case when you publish an API for general use. You cannot know in advance how it will be (ab)used. In this sense, designing maintainable APIs is like coming up with a new security solution. The hardest part in security engineering is to enumerate all possible ways a malicious person (or a software acting on her or his behalf) might try to penetrate a system.

The latest version of the RandomizedBag class's API isn't ready for publication for the following reasons:

- It doesn't obey the Collection interface contract 100% (we are assuming here Java 8). This might come as a surprise to you, but this is only because this fact hasn't been important for us, yet. However, it might be for some user. It is better to be precise from the very beginning than to start lazy and accumulate problems over time. One viable approach is to show as little as possible at the start. So, when problems (missing features) accumulate over time, then we can resolve them using our API evolution plan. Again, it is crucial to have a plan.

- We haven't included in our build process any way to trace changes from the perspective of backward compatibility. We cannot compare the base API with subsequent releases and judge whether are we moving in the right direction. You see, we are just asking the right question: What technique should I use to ensure that method signatures in the API are compatible with the base snapshot? This is TDD in action.

- We haven't included any statistical analyzer in our build process. We will do it soon. It is mandatory to use proper tools, which could help avoid embarrassing errors.

- The serialization support is really amateurish. We will improve this. This is going to affect the API, too.

- We haven't provided any hints about performance of our data type. We will fix this, too. The performance statement will become part of an API. If you look at classes from JFC, they all do contain such guarantees (usually in Big-O notation).

Now, if you managed to detect all these issues (as announced in the previous chapter), including the bug in the original RandomizedBag class, you are a guru. Let's start handling these bullet points one by one.

The Subtleties of the Spliterator API

If you haven't heard about the Spliterator interface, then you should read the JDK API documentation before proceeding. It has quite an extensive treatment of this interface. The RandomizedBag class inherits it from the AbstractCollection. The default implementation is really just for testing purposes, and definitely not for a production release. Besides performance issues, it isn't even appropriate for our class. If we try to directly give back a Spliterator instance from the embedded ArrayList object, we will again encounter a similar glitch. It doesn't apply out of the box for the RandomizedBag class.

The RandomizedBag class doesn't guarantee any ordering in its returned iterator. Therefore, we cannot use the one we would receive from the ArrayList, as it is ordered. On the other hand, we disallow null elements in our collection. Therefore, we must signal this characteristic in our Spliterator. Again, ArrayList doesn't do this, as you can put null into an ArrayList object. All in all, we must return a custom Spliterator to comply with the Collection API.

Checking for API Incompatibilities Between Different Versions

We will use the tool SigTest with an associated Maven plug-in to check for incompatible changes (for more information visit http://wiki.netbeans.org/SigTest). It basically solves all our needs. The idea is to make a base signature file for version 1.0.0, and check subsequent releases against this one (or some other). You could try to experiment with the tool on your own, by making changes and see what it will report (don't forget to alter the version number after each release).

Here is the snippet showing what needs to be added into the pom.xml file to create the signature snapshot for the initial version:

```
<plugin>
    <groupId>org.netbeans.tools</groupId>
    <artifactId>sigtest-maven-plugin</artifactId>
    <version>1.0</version>
    <executions>
        <execution>
            <goals>
                <goal>generate</goal>
            </goals>
        </execution>
    </executions>
    <configuration>
        <packages>rs.exproit.util</packages>
    </configuration>
</plugin>
```

After executing mvn clean install it will produce the signature file and install it inside your local Maven repository (you might even want to publish it together with your jar file in a public Maven repo).

Postprocessor as a Rescue for Bugs

We will include in our build the FindBugs analyzer for Java (see `http://findbugs.sourceforge.net`). It comes with a Maven plug-in. It is amazing how many bugs can be discovered in this effortless fashion. There is no justification to omit a tool when there is one on the market (especially when it is open source). Here is the snippet that has to be included in the `pom.xml` file (note the parts shown in bold).

```
<reporting>
    <plugins>
        <plugin>
            <groupId>org.codehaus.mojo</groupId>
            <artifactId>findbugs-maven-plugin</artifactId>
            <version>3.0.4</version>
            <configuration>
                <effort>Max</effort>
                <threshold>Low</threshold>
            </configuration>
        </plugin>
    </plugins>
</reporting>
```

You just need to execute `mvn site`, and the project report will be ready for you as part of the Maven-generated site documentation.

Better Serialization Support

Just dumping everything into an object stream isn't a smart solution for serialization. We will enhance the `RandomizedBag` class to use the `Externalizable` API. Besides improved performance, this will really give us full control over what is put, read into, and from a stream.

Performance Guarantees Are Mandatory

We simply cannot publish a new ADT without saying anything about the performance guarantees, at least, expressed using the Big-O notation (see the `ArrayList` documentation for an example of how it is done in the JDK). The `RandomizedBag` class should execute all operations approximately in a *constant amortized time* (remove requires a linear time). Talking in terms of this is usually enough and feasible (naturally, we cannot say anything about exact runtime values of methods). The amortized time is calculated over a sequence of N operations. If we start from an empty bag, and execute N add/remove/size/iterator operations, then it should scale in $O(N)$ steps. In other words, each action will take $O(1)$ time to execute on average. Sometimes an add operation will take more time (e.g., the garbage collector kicks in), but over a long period of time, we might say that it has an $O(1)$ time dependence. We insert this guarantee in our API.

Again, if you want to make strong performance guarantees, then you will need to implement the internal storage yourself. Nevertheless, you should always watch out what you state in your API.

The Reworked Version Ready for Publication

Here is the reworked `RandomizedBag` class (note the sections shown in).

```
package rs.exproit.util;
```

```java
import java.io.*;
import java.util.*;

/**
 * Implements the generic randomized "queue" ADT as described
 * <a href="http://www.cs.princeton.edu/courses/archive/fall05/cos226/assignments/queues.
   html">
 * here</a>.
 * The randomization process uses a linear congruential random number generator. This may be
 * configured with a seed value, to reproduce the random number sequence.
 *
 * All operations are executed approximatively in a constant amortized time
 * (remove requires a linear time).
 *
 * @author Ervin Varga
 *
 * @param <E> the type of elements contained inside this bag.
 */
public final class RandomizedBag<E> extends AbstractCollection<E>
        implements Externalizable {
    private static final String serialVersion = "1.0";

    private final List<E> elems = new ArrayList<>();
    private Random rnd;

    public RandomizedBag() {
        rnd = new Random();
    }

    public RandomizedBag(long seed) {
        rnd = new Random(seed);
    }

    public RandomizedBag(Collection<E> c) {
        this();
        if (c == null) {
            throw new NullPointerException();
        }
        addAndshuffleElementsInPlace(c);
    }

    public RandomizedBag(long seed, Collection<E> c) {
        this(seed);
        if (c == null) {
            throw new NullPointerException();
        }
        addAndshuffleElementsInPlace(c);
    }

    private void addAndshuffleElementsInPlace(Collection<E> newElems) {
        assert newElems != null;
        addAll(newElems);
```

```
}

/**
 * Adds a new element to this collection. The collection permits duplicates, but doesn't
 * allow {@code null} elements.
 *
 * {@inheritDoc}
 */
@Override
public boolean add(E e) {
    if (e == null) {
        throw new NullPointerException();
    }

    elems.add(e);

    // Shuffle the last added element with a random one from the queue.
    final int idx = rnd.nextInt(elems.size());
    elems.set(elems.size() - 1, elems.get(idx));
    elems.set(idx, e);
    return true;
}

/**
 * Deletes and returns an element from the bag, uniformly at random.
 *
 * @return the deleted element from this bag.
 * @throws NoSuchElementException if the bag is empty.
 */
public E remove() {
    if (isEmpty()) {
        throw new NoSuchElementException("Cannot remove an element from an empty bag.");
    }

    return elems.remove(0);
}

public Iterator<E> iterator() {
    return elems.listIterator();
}

@Override
public Spliterator<E> spliterator() {
    return Spliterators.spliterator(elems,
            Spliterator.SIZED | Spliterator.SUBSIZED | Spliterator.NONNULL);
}

@Override
public int size() {
    return elems.size();
}
```

```java
@Override
public void writeExternal(ObjectOutput out) throws IOException {
    out.writeUTF(serialVersion);
    // Save the whole state of our random number generator (peeking into it via
    // reflection to get the seed isn't advised at all).
    out.writeObject(rnd);
    // Write out all the contained items.
    out.writeInt(size());
    for (E item : this) {
        out.writeObject(item);
    }
}

@SuppressWarnings("unchecked")
@Override
public void readExternal(ObjectInput in) throws IOException, ClassNotFoundException {
    // Currently, we ignore the serial version number, but in the future it will be
    // important.
    in.readUTF();
    // Restore the random number generator.
    rnd = (Random) in.readObject();
    // Read in all the saved items.
    int numItems = in.readInt();
    for (int i = 0; i < numItems; i++) {
        Object item = in.readObject();
        elems.add((E) item);
    }
}
}
```

The refactored original tests all pass. It was expanded with the following test.

```java
@Test
public void iterateOverItemsOfABagInParallel() {
    RandomizedBag<Integer> bag = new RandomizedBag<>(SEED_ONE, baseItems);
    Spliterator<Integer> spliter = bag.spliterator();

    assertNotNull("should have a spliterator", spliter);
    assertTrue("should be SIZED", spliter.hasCharacteristics(Spliterator.SIZED));
    assertTrue("should be SUBSIZED", spliter.hasCharacteristics(Spliterator.SUBSIZED));
    assertTrue("should be NONNULL", spliter.hasCharacteristics(Spliterator.NONNULL));
    assertEquals("should have a proper size estimate", bag.size(), spliter.estimateSize());

    Spliterator<Integer> partition = spliter.trySplit();
    assertTrue("partition should be bigger or equal than half size of the original",
            partition.estimateSize() >= bag.size() / 2);
}
```

The refactored test suite also contains the following two test cases to explicitly test for `null` during construction:

- `tryToCreateABagWithNullInputCollection`
- `tryToCreateABagWithNullInputCollectionAndAPredefinedSeed`

These are necessary, as the new version of our bag doesn't piggyback anymore on the `ArrayList` `addAll` method to test for `null`. We have already seen in Chapter 3 why such a practice is terribly wrong.

FindBugs were not able to find any issues. We cannot spot any obvious problems, either (we could improve the class by replacing the constructors with factory methods). Nevertheless, after you publish your work, users will report bugs. They will ask for improvements. The evolution will start when development is done, and it's the longest period in a software's life cycle. How long this will last depends foremost on the maintainability of your APIs.

Summary

TDD has a tremendous positive impact on the quality of software (including its APIs). It is a game changer regarding how you approach design in general. Those who design a system also have to design test cases for it. This is an amazing observation. In some way, it even goes up to Karl Popper's falsifiability principle (read more about it at `http://plato.stanford.edu/entries/popper/`), which states that those who design a system or theory also need to say when it will not work or will become invalid.

We have witnessed through these case studies what happens without TDD, and how it helps improve the solution, once properly applied in concert with other standard OO practices. Of course, one chapter can only scratch the surface of TDD. Nevertheless, I hope that you've grasped its main tenets. The most important thing is to start using it as soon as possible. Just look back, and notice how many aspects were considered during the implementation of the `RandomizedBag` class. The tests are longer than the target class. Imagine how hard is to come up with a decent solution without driving your tests as TDD dictates.

EXTEND THE CLIENT APPLICATION

Learn How to Drive GUI Tests

The client would like to change the UI to a Swing-based graphical one. The wire frame of the new GUI is presented in Figure 4-1. You need to apply TDD to implement this change request.

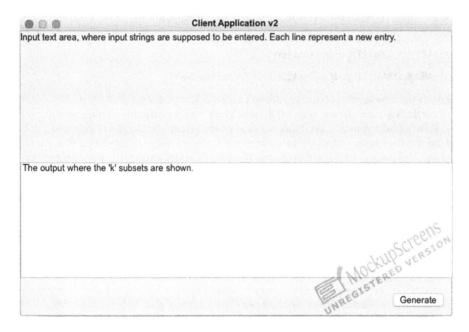

Figure 4-1. *A wire frame showig a tentative GUI for the new version of the client application (the screen was made using the commercial MockupScreens tool; see* http://www.mockupscreens.com). *Such mockups are really useful to discuss the various UI choices in a rapid manner.*

Driving the end-to-end tests through a GUI is nearly impossible without a sophisticated tool. The JDK has a built-in `java.awt.Robot` class to help you in this endeavor. Here is the citation from its documentation: "This class is used to generate native system input events for the purposes of test automation, self-running demos, and other applications where control of the mouse and keyboard is needed. The primary purpose of Robot is to facilitate automated testing of Java platform implementations."

However, using the `Robot` class directly is still hard. If you use *DukeScript*, then you could use an equivalent "clicking" driver (see https://dukescript.com/update/2015/12/23/webdriver-release.html). [1] uses *Window Licker*, contains a good overview of its capabilities, and provides lots of examples. Another viable option is to use the open source *Marathon* framework (https://marathontesting.com).

Finally, you might want to switch a viewpoint, and solve the GUI testing by harnessing another architectural style. If you haven't heard about the Model-View-ViewModel (MVVM) concept, then you should read the article about combining MVVM with TDD by using DukeScript (the blog is available at https://dukescript.com/best/practices/2015/02/16/tdd-with-dukescript.html).

BETTER WAY TO SERIALIZE AN OBJECT

Practice the writeObject/readObject Methods

Our last bag implementation relies on the `Externalizable` mechanism to serialize itself. However, `Externalizable` restricts you in the following ways:

- There needs to be a public default constructor.

- The read/write methods are public (very bad for an API), so everyone can call them.

To improve control over what is being written and read you might consider the `readObject`/`writeObject` methods of the standard serialization facility (see the JDK for more information). This can give you absolute control without those limitations associated with the `Externalizable` API.

References

1.   Freeman, Steve, and Nat Pryce. *Growing Object-Oriented Software, Guided by Tests.* Reading MA: Addison-Wesley Professional, 2009.

2.   Watkins, John, and Simon Mills. *Testing IT: An Off-the-Shelf Software Testing Process, Second Edition.* Cambridge, UK: Cambridge University Press, 2011.

CHAPTER 5

■ ■ ■

Identifying Resources

A *resource* is the central element in resource-oriented architectures (ROAs), and a system built around the REpresentational State Transfer (REST) architectural style is a member of ROA. There are many ingredients to REST. As is the case with recipes, you could end up with an unpalatable meal using the same ingredients as for a truly tasty one. It all depends on the chef. The same is true with REST. There is a huge misconception that by using HTTP, sending back and forth XML/JSON documents, and using URLs to mark endpoints of an API is what counts toward being RESTful (the major three constituents associated with REST in marketing campaigns). Many development tools are built around this fallacy. REST is an instance of a profound paradigm shift pertaining to network-based architectures. It isn't about HTTP per se,[1] although HTTP is a preferable choice due to its widespread use in WWW (an inspirational example of a successful large-scale distributed system). Again, the software engineer's knowledge and experience determines whether the outcome will be a truly RESTful solution or some botched "variant" of it.

A resource is an abstraction, and as such inherits all of its properties (see Chapter 2). In a RESTful world, a resource's main purpose is to tame complexity by shielding clients from knowing anything about processes implementing it. This is in contrast with a remote procedure call (RPC) approach (SOAP/HTTP is its Web variant), where clients are driving processes via RPCs. A resource could be anything you care about (document, business process, problem domain concept, another resource, etc.).

A resource is the mechanism by which you organize information sharing between the server responsible for a particular set of resources and clients interested in those resources. A resource is publicly exposed via its representation, and exchanging different representations of a resource (this is that information-sharing part) between a client and a server is what drives state changes in a RESTful system. On the contrary, in the case of an RPC, a client sends actions instead of new representations toward the server to propel changes. This has a huge effect on an API. In a RESTful case, a client sends an altered representation to tell the server about the preferred state of the system. This might trigger a chain of events on the server side to carry out the necessary state change(s). In RPC, a client explicitly tells the server what to do to arrive at a desired state of the system (making calls in the wrong order could cause an illegal state exception, so the client does need to maintain a sort of shared state with the server[2]). Therefore, a REST communication tends to be high-grained, whereas an RPC anticipates greater chattiness.[3] Furthermore, when a client is constantly interested in a very small subset of a resource's representation, the borderline between RESTful and RPC approaches is starting to blur.

---

[1]Embedded systems can be built using the same REST principles without using HTTP. There is a standard called Constrained Application Protocol (CoAP) defined in RFC 7252 (see http://coap.technology and [1]) for devices with low capacity. CoAP delivers a non-HTTP REST model for such small devices.

[2]This might occur in RESTful services, too. For example, with security (based on obtaining a token), making a secure call without having the right token produces an exception. Web sites and browsers sometimes exchange shared state with cookies.

[3]With HTTP 2.0, even REST services will be able to allow efficient, fine-grained communication patterns. It is a binary protocol, uses header compression (only differences are passed along), and implements an efficient pipelining mechanism. HTTP 2.0 has the notion of a *stream*, which is a bidirectional virtual channel in a connection. Streams carry frames (a unit of data), and multiple frames constitute a logical request and response message. Frames can be interleaved in a connection. HTTP 2.0 doesn't have the *head-of-line* blocking problem.

© Ervin Varga 2016
E. Varga, *Creating Maintainable APIs*, DOI 10.1007/978-1-4842-2196-9_5

It is very easy to start a RESTful frenzy, by trying to make every service RESTful (this tendency is heavily driven by the market, as being RESTful is nowadays a matter of prestige). REST isn't a silver bullet, though, so you should be careful. Be aware that a REST service is usually more expensive than its RPC equivalent (you might take a look at Apache Thrift for building RPC services; for more details visit `https://thrift.apache.org`). I recommend you prefer RPC services for internal use, unless you have clear arguments against this.

The following are the most salient traits of a resource inside a REST-based system.

- *It is a representable stateful abstraction with a clear purpose and role(s)*: A resource might not physically exist, but should have a well-defined function in a given context (dictated by the matching use cases of a system). A resource could play various roles in different usage scenarios. Each role might entail a specific representation, and this is the way a resource's role is materialized from the viewpoint of its clients. The state of the resource is kept on the server, and state transitions are initiated by altering and exchanging representations.

- *It is uniquely identified*: Every resource must be uniquely identified using a URL (this identifier should preferably remain stable[4]). A client doesn't "see" the resource directly, but its representation. Therefore, a representation must be retrievable and the identifier must be resolvable. Sometimes, there is a 1:1 mapping between a resource and its representation. It could also happen that various representations are associated with different URLs. The uniqueness of all these URLs is the sole responsibility of the server; that is, the provider of the resource and its representations. There is no central authority to decide what URLs are attached to resources. To guarantee uniqueness, the server's domain name (this is allocated by a central authority) is usually part of a resource's URL. At any rate, even if a resource alters its state, that resource's URL should remain intact.

- *It can easily migrate in a distributed system*: Migrating code in a heterogeneous distributed system is quite a challenging task. All sorts of complications could hinder the endeavor, depending on the type of process-to-resource[5] bindings. In a REST system, a client is completely shielded from processes. A resource is just an abstraction with a well-specified address. A client doesn't care who implements that resource. If hitting a new URL would enable a smooth operation of a client, then that is what migration is all about from a client's perspective. The only remaining issue is to inform clients about that new URL (luckily, this is already part of an HTTP, and you will see examples of it later on). The biggest difference between a REST and RPC system regarding code migration revolves around self-descriptive representations and stateless communication. These are the two most important constraints imposed by a REST style. A client holding such a self-describing representation could use it with a migrated service, as nothing would have happened. There is no need to worry about the server's state, nor provide extra contextual data. We will see that those previously mentioned characteristics also enable efficient caching of responses.

---

[4]It is possible to use persistent URLs (PURLs), which is another indirection mechanism for Web resources (for more information, visit `https://purl.org`). This might give protection against domain name changes. Another more advanced possibility is to publish an OWL (see `https://www.w3.org/OWL/`) document with the following content (it is presented here in N-Triples format):

```
@prefix owl: <http://www.w3.org/2002/07/owl#> .
```

```
<old URL> owl:sameAs <new URL>
```

[5]Don't mix the meaning of a resource here with our REST notion of a resource (a fine proof that most words in software engineering are pretty overloaded). The resources in this context are low-level system resources, like files, sockets, devices, and so on. Most often a process (as an executable code) cannot be migrated without migrating all referenced resources. It is easy to copy over a static file, but not that easy to transfer the state of the memory.

- *It can be combined and augmented in a decentralized manner:* A resource hosted by one server may be extended by another resource in a fully decentralized manner. Dynamically linking resources and establishing various relationships between them is simply a game changer. All this could happen without the awareness of the source server. Interlinking resources on an Internet scale essentially boils down to referencing them via URLs. It's that simple! Moreover, the relationships themselves may be promoted into resources if they comprise part of a shareable information space.

■ **Tip**   I highly suggest you watch the brief webinars mentioned in [2] and [5] about building modern REST-based services. You can also learn more about this topic from [1] and [4].

Case Study: Problem Reports Microservice

The aim of this case study is to showcase the use case (behavior–centric) API design methodology resulting in a set of resources and their representations. It is important to emphasize that we will only perform design work here (the whole process is iterative, but we will proceed in a linear fashion to save space, and to be able to present it in a book). In some sense, resources will bubble up as a consequence of this design effort, or surface as an implementation detail. Nevertheless, they are part of the design process, as clients are going to retrieve and manipulate them via their representations. Knowing about these resources and their roles is therefore crucial.

Our HTTP REST microservice for problem reports should accept problem descriptions from clients and store them in local storage. The concept of a *microservice* is related to a set of architectural features on top of SOA, portraying the service as a self-contained, independently deployable unit (a kind of a service we intend to build). The service needs to provide a capability to list reported problems and search them using various criteria. The reports should be correlated with each other, if possible. The service should support both XML and JSON payloads. The basic media types advertised by the service have to be `application/xml` and `application/json`. This is the bare minimum for the first version of this service.

The service is aimed at extending the abilities of an existing Web production system, which already uses these base XML and JSON media types. This is a fine example, when the choice of a media type is fixed in the requirements. I don't typically recommend the bare `application/xml` and `application/json` media types, as they result in another fiat (proprietary) standard defying the principles of *Web of Data* (interlinked and interoperable services). We thoroughly examine the JSON API (as a superb choice for a hypermedia-driven media type) later in this book.

Discovering and Describing Resources

At this stage we will try to enroll the different resources (more precisely, their representations) handled by the service, including transitions between them. All this should happen in the context of the use cases; that is, driven by the goals of external clients of this service. In Chapter 7, we expand the list of goals to allow clients to learn *affordances* (see [3] for a definition of this term) regarding resources. This list enumerates the main goals, and Figure 5-1 shows the UML use case diagram for our service.

- List all reported problems.

- Search (filter) the reported problems to get a reduced list (e.g., to retrieve related problems).

- Create a new problem report by sending in all data.

- Delete a problem report from the system.

- Update an existing problem report.

- Retrieve favorite reports (presented in Chapter 8).

99

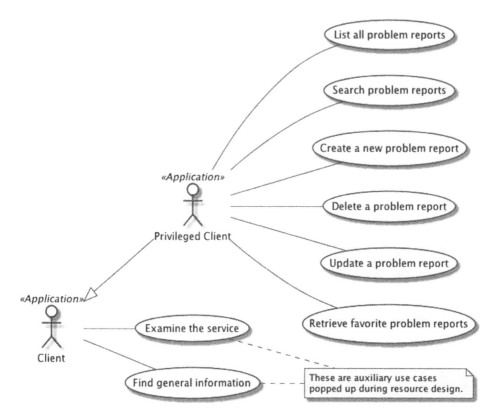

Figure 5-1. *The UML use case diagram showing clients and their associations with major use cases. The nonprivileged client can browse what the service offers (visiting the Home and About pages), but cannot access the problem reports (implementing the security aspects is covered in Chapter 9). We see here an inheritance relationship between actors. The privileged client is also a client, and thus can also access those ancillary use cases. Usually the associations are bidirectional, which is a natural situation on the programmable Web.*

This list of goals resembles the typical create/read/update/delete (CRUD) operations over resources. In the classical approach of a REST service design, the focus would be only on problem domain resources and their associated operations. However, our focus is on behavior and transitions between resource states embodied in various representations. Using this technique, we discover resources that might not even appear as such in the traditional approach. Figure 5-2 shows the static resource model.

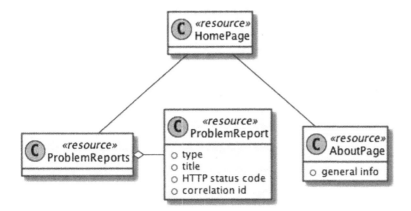

Figure 5-2. *The UML class diagram showing the static relationships between resources. An association between two entities means a link from one resource representation to the other. For example, a client can reach the about page from the home page, and vice versa.*

Figure 5-2 depicts two resources not mentioned this far: HomePage and AboutPage. These are preparing the terrain for a true hypermedia-driven REST service, which is finalized in the next chapter. At any rate, the home page represents the starting point for a client. The URL associated with this page is sometimes called the billboard URL (as this is usually advertised on panels). The about page is the conventional place for presenting some general information about the service.

The ProblemReports resource is just a collection of individual ProblemReport instances. Each instance groups together attributes describing a single problem. Most fields are self-explanatory, except for the correlation id, which is used to relate problems. Namely, in the microservices architectural style, the emphasis is on collaboration among services. Each occurrence of a collaboration may be designated by an identifier (frequently, this id is created at the beginning of a sequence of actions related to a particular business use case). As services call each other they also have to pass along this correlation identifier (Chapter 16 includes an example of how this same principle can be used to group log entries). Problems are always reported with this id. The overall benefit is that by looking at the whole group of related problem reports, we can get better insight into error propagation patterns across the system.

The static picture isn't satisfactory to build a modern Level 3 REST service (see [2] for details about the RMM classification). We also need to showcase the transitions between resource states. Figure 5-3 illustrates the dynamic resource model.

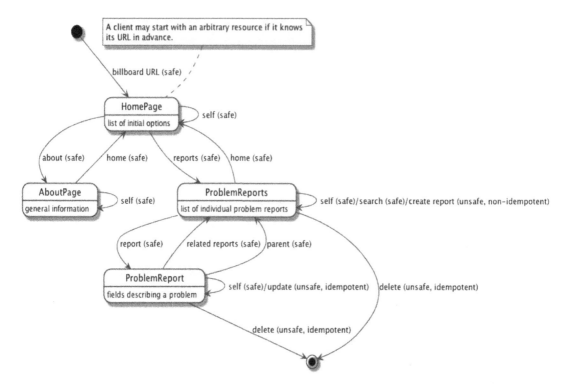

Figure 5-3. *The state diagram depicting state transitions of resources. Transitions are marked with qualifiers* safe, unsafe, idempotent, *and* non-idempotent.

A safe transition doesn't change the matching resource's state, whereas an idempotent operation can be repeated multiple times with the same outcome (e.g., deleting the same resource multiple times cannot do any harm). We see in Chapter 7 how these transitions are mapped onto actions. Figure 5-3 shows all possible transitions and ways in which resources are interlinked. This is reminiscent of screen-flow diagrams showcasing the dynamics of the UI. At any rate, we have identified our major resources, and now we need to see how to properly describe them. The initial list of attributes was just a hint.

Rapid Application Development (RAD) Tactic

The name reconciliation stage (see the next section of the text) of the REST API design is the most neglected one in practice (even Figure 5-3 and dynamic modeling is skipped altogether). The traditional approach is satisfied by having discovered the ProblemReports and ProblemReport entities. The implementation immediately starts, as nobody sees any reason to lose more precious time. The domain objects are annotated, and development tools (including IDEs) generate all the RESTful parts. The outcome is an API exposing the complete internal storage model of a system, creating a rigid and brittle solution. The clients are usually programmed in a similar fashion, hard-coding all the relationships and affordances in advance. Let me demonstrate this tactic by using the Restlet Studio (https://restlet.com) to implement this service. If all this sounds familiar to you, then an acronym like *HATEOAS* is probably scary at this moment, but there is nothing to "hate" about it.

Figure 5-4 shows a screenshot of the Restlet Studio with the finalized API definition for this service. It took me about 20 minutes to complete everything, including comments. The Restlet Studio has autogenerated both the server and client skeletons for Node (you could also choose to produce Java code). Also, I've exported the matching RAML file. All this can be found in the accompanying source code (see the chapter5/node folder). The autogenerated material even contains readme files to give instructions how to start up the server and use the client skeleton. After you start up the server with node index.js, then you will be able to hit the built-in Swagger UI at http://localhost:8081/docs. Figure 5-5 shows how it looks. It is a live documentation ready to exercise your service.

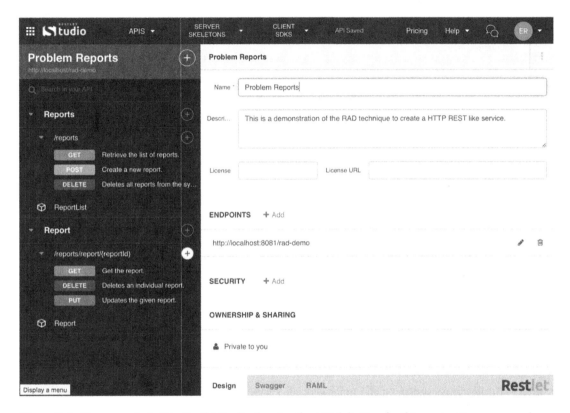

Figure 5-4. *The screenshot of the Restlet Studio showing the API definition for this service. You can reproduce the design steps by importing the RAML file, which is included in the source code for this book (the file is located inside the chapter5/node directory). Restlet Studio is free while working with one API at a time.*

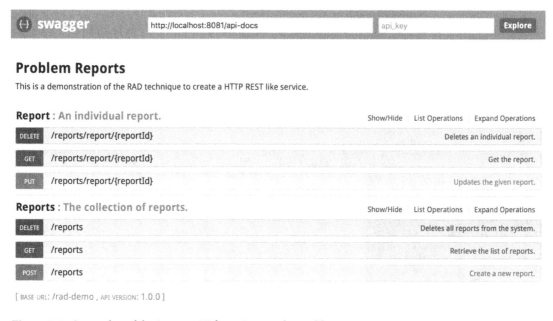

Figure 5-5. Screenshot of the Swagger UI for trying out the Problem Reports microservice.c

All this might sound fantastic, but there is one "small" problem: The implemented service has minimal connection with the actual REST philosophy. If you look into the autogenerated code, you will notice that everything is hard-coded. Once developers start adding more features to these server and client skeletons, nobody will be able to touch the API anymore without breaking backward compatibility.

There is another problematic factor in Figure 5-4. The URL designating an individual report is specified via the URI Template (defined in RFC 6570) /reports/report/{reportId}. Figure 5-2 doesn't suggest such a firm containment. By encoding structural relationships between resources (in our case between a report list and a report) inside URLs, those relationships are cemented once and for all. Honestly, the list of reports is more an auxiliary collection resource than a genuine business entity.

■ **Note** The Restlet ecosystem (Studio, framework, etc.) is very powerful. However, when using such a powerful tool you must always recall Voltaire's famous adage: "With great power comes great responsibility." The preceding example demonstrated what happens due to a total lack of responsibility. We revisit this API tool support in Chapter 9 with greater attention to correctness.

Name Reconciliation

If you skip name reconciliation and just take into account the dynamic model (including directions laid out in Chapter 6), then you would still miss the doctrines of the *Linked Data* movement. Your API will become a semantic island, incomprehensible outside of corporate boundaries. You will also need to craft custom code to process your resources, as only you can understand the meaning of the fields. Much of this can be changed by reusing terms already defined in public vocabularies (ontologies) as well as by looking after more suitable media types (in our case we have to stick to the basic application/xml and application/json types).

You should bookmark the following sources while engaging in API design:

- IANA registered link relation types (`http://www.iana.org/assignments/link-relations`). For example, it already contains the term `about`, which is exactly what we need to link the home and about pages together.

- Schema.org (`http://schema.org`) vocabulary. It is filled with dozens of predefined structured contents. For example, there is a definition of an AboutPage (`http://schema.org/AboutPage`). For our purposes, we might just reuse a single field for the general information called text (`http://schema.org/text`). There is no need to concoct fields like `genInfo`, `aboutContent`, and so on.

- Application-Level Profile Semantics (ALPS; `http://alps.io`). The mission of ALPS is described on its site: "ALPS profile documents describe hypermedia interfaces (data elements and state transitions) that are helpful when implementing a service and when implementing client applications that will access services."

- Activity Streams (`http://activitystrea.ms`). This has a very useful set of definitions, and we will use it to define the list of reports.

- The FOAF Project (`http://www.foaf-project.org`). We will use it for the home transition, and it will appear again in Chapter 16.

- IANA registered media types (`http://www.iana.org/assignments/media-types`). A media type isn't strictly speaking an ontology, but it does specify terms and rules related to the given representation format (we will see a very sophisticated specimen later). If there is a domain-specific media type, then it should be considered part of the solution. Even if you cannot use it directly, it might contain hints helping you considerably. For example, by browsing through the registered types you might stumble across `application/problem+json` and `application/problem+xml`.[6] They are both elaborated on in RFC 7807 (`https://tools.ietf.org/html/rfc7807`). After peeking into it we can conclude that it talks about individual problem reports, the kind of thing we must define. This is huge progress, as it solves most of our dilemmas regarding fields. RFC 7807 also contains suggestions for how to extend the initial set of problem report fields. The best would be to just use it as it is, but we will need to find a side route.

Table 5-1 contains the mappings of terms from Figure 5-3 onto known published names (the name of a data field is usually called a *semantic descriptor*). During this translation, resource names can also change. Moreover, we will translate the names of state transitions, too (they will become registered link relation types). Currently, we are just dealing with API design; in Chapter 7 we focus on encoding actions. This entails creating proper representations for our resources, together with definitions of profiles (semantic attachments referencing public ontologies; that is, giving proper context for all our terms). This struggle of referencing known terms is trying to mitigate the semantic gap problem inherent in current distributed systems. We cannot solve it fully, in the sense of having autonomous software agents acting on behalf of humans in all possible scenarios, but at least we can close some cracks.

---

[6]When you return a media type in a response, then the response must fully follow that type. You cannot mix multiple types and just signal one of them. This is the reason it is a better strategy to choose a flexible, well-established hypermedia media type as a base (like JSON API), and customize it using a profile (e.g., by leveraging JSON-LD as presented in Chapter 7).

Table 5-1. *Mapping of Custom Terms onto Known Names and Types (Many of Them Are Already in a Proper Form)*

Resource	Transition	Context	Standard Name/Type
	about	IANA Link Relations	about
	Billboard URL	FOAF	homepage
	home	FOAF	homepage
AboutPage		Schema.org	AboutPage
HomePage		Schema.org	WebPage
	reports	IANA Link Relations	contents
	report	Activity Streams	Collection#items
	parent	IANA Link Relations	collection
	related reports	IANA Link Relations	related
	Self	IANA Link Relations	self
	Search	IANA Link Relations	search
	Update	IANA Link Relations	edit + HTTP PUT
	Delete	IANA Link Relations	edit + HTTP DELETE
	create report	IANA Link Relations	edit + HTTP POST
ProblemReports		Activity Streams	Collection
ProblemReport		IANA Media Type	problem (as per RFC 7807) + correlationId

The `ProblemReport` resource will contain fields from the `problem` class, and we will basically serve it as plain `application/xml` or `application/json`. This is not an optimal way to do things, but at least we can refer to RFC 7807 for the full description. Once we get a chance to deliver the proper media type, we will not need to alter anything in the code or the representation. At any rate, what we definitely need to provide is an explanation for that extra `correlationId` field.

Sometimes the mapping is ambiguous. For example, the `Collection` term can be reused from Activity Streams (as in our case), or from Hydra (see `http://www.hydra-cg.com/spec/latest/core/#collections`). Even with these issues, it is still better to reference already published nomenclatures than to invent new ones.

Summary

This chapter has presented the strict API design work for a RESTful service via a small case study. We expand on this example in Chapter 7 by adding hypermedia controls. The API design must be motivated by use cases and requires dedication. Using shortcuts offered by tools is a suspicious long-term strategy.

It might turn out, that some state isn't encompassed by an API. For example, if some portion of a client's application state (defines where the client is currently positioned inside a Web service graph) is also important for the server, then it might be better to transform it into a resource state. This would trigger the creation of a new resource. In a REST API, additions are pretty well tolerated from the standpoint of backward compatibility. Therefore, you might be reluctant to include everything in an API (it isn't like ordinary Java interfaces, where additions are troublesome).

GENERAL INFORMATION ABOUT THE HOST

Getting Used to RFCs

The Web host metadata is sometimes served by servers according to the rules specified in RFC 6415 (`https://tools.ietf.org/html/rfc6415`). Analyze this RFC, and augment our example service's API to allow clients to retrieve such metadata from the *Well Known* URL (a client has to issue an HTTP GET request on `/.well-known/host-meta` or `/.well-known/host-meta.json`, depending on whether it wants an XML or JSON response).

Think about the AboutPage resource. Wouldn't it be better to include it as part of the host metadata instead of serving it from the home page?

As an additional exercise, take a look at the process of registering a Well-Known URI (`https://tools.ietf.org/html/rfc5785`).

CREATE A CUSTOM PROFILE

Acquire Experience with Ontologies

In Chapter 7 we will produce a custom profile for our service, referencing standard names depicted in Table 5-1. We will do it for the JSON format using JSON-LD.

Your task is to try specifying a similar profile using ALPS for XML. You can read the following document, which contains couple of ALPS profile examples: `http://alps.io/spec/alps-to-html/`. Notice how ALPS nicely differentiates between semantic descriptors and affordances (transitions).

References

1. Ruby, Sam, Mike Amundsen, and Leonard Richardson. *RESTful Web APIs.* Sebastopol, CA: O'Reilly Media, 2013.

2. Amundsen, Mike. *REST, Hypermedia, and the Semantic Gap.* Sebastopol, CA: O'Reilly Media, 2015.

3. Norman, Don. "Affordances and Design." 2004. `http://www.jnd.org/dn.mss/affordances_and_desi.html`

4. Sletten, Brian. *Resource-Oriented Architecture Patterns for Webs of Data.* San Rafael, CA: Morgan & Claypool, 2013.

5. Amundsen, Mike. *API Design Methodology.* Sebastopol, CA: O'Reilly Media, 2014.

■ ■ ■

CHAPTER 6

Versioning REST APIs

In an ideal world, we wouldn't need explicit version numbers (or any version identifiers for that matter) in our REST APIs. If you think that such a world doesn't exist, well, it is all around us. It is the Web! Our web browsers can handle all sorts of web sites, usually without significant problems (we assume that our modern browser understands different dialects of HTML, and the site is not specifically targeted for another browser). Part of the magic stems from hypermedia controls embedded in an HTML content. Take a look at the source HTML (try to load some complex web page into your browser, and ask it to show the page source), and you will encounter all sorts of links to other web pages, various forms for uploading data, as well as forms for performing custom searches, and so on. All this Web content processing happens without a need to upgrade the browser when a site changes its content, or when you visit a brand new web page. Moreover, you don't need to remember anything except the entry point URL (usually just a domain name without any version number). All the rest inside your browser is driven by hypermedia controls (in Chapter 7 we analyze how to create similar programmable web APIs).

Of course, we must admit that our browser has a powerful companion: us. Therefore, the content parsing subject is a human being and not a machine. The biggest problem with machines today is their inability to cross semantic chasms. For a machine, a word means nothing, unless it is instructed to obey specific rules regarding that word. A traditional approach of REST API implementation, as demonstrated in Chapter 5, tries to fix everything. All the details regarding the API are kept in a human-readable documentation. This embodies protocol details as well as the meaning of all data structures. Even machine-readable material is deceptive, as it is just a blueprint for code generators, or a helper for UI front ends to exercise various endpoints of an API. Fixing everything can speed up the initial development, but is an API maintenance nightmare. For this sort of API, no versioning strategy can buttress its evolution.

However, if we can "teach" software to recognize some generic control commands, then it might be able to autonomously figure out the structure of an API. Obviously, such an API should try to avoid reliance on non-computer-processable documentation. Hypermedia controls (as we have mentioned them in relation to HTML) could help a lot. They enable the server to signal back to a client what affordances are allowed at any given moment regarding the data passed down the line. In this sense, we don't need to fix in advance the overall structural dependencies between entities (as we did in that /reports/report/{reportId} URL), nor predefine all possible interactions. Nonetheless, we might still have a situation in which a client can recognize a new element in the data space, but has no clue how to proceed. This issue is especially reinforced when those newly added elements start to be mandatory. Old clients wouldn't be able to properly communicate with a new server, and will probably get 4xx errors. We also need to stress that even if someone can conceive a supersmart client boosted by artifical intelligence (AI), it isn't realistic to have them in production yet. These are the principal reasons we need versioning, as we cannot totally bridge the semantic gap.

The Main Traits of REST API Versioning

REST APIs differ from modular OO APIs regarding versioning. In Java, you can publish a new jar file using an ordinary version number (e.g., following the semantic versioning scheme), and it becomes the responsibility of the dependency manager tool to handle the versions properly. In Maven, it is simply enough to reference a specific version of a jar file, and all the rest happens automatically[1] (you can also publish artifacts in a similar fashion). All in all, there is no design work associated with version numbers. In REST APIs you have to decide the location of version numbers, hence the versioning strategy does affect the API.

The major drawback of this extra flexibility (obviously too much freedom isn't always beneficial) is the lack of common consensus on how to annotate a REST API with a version number. Again, nobody in the Java world worries about this, as everything is more or less standardized by the dependency manager (most Java software uses Maven's scheme). There are many proposals, and an organization implementing the REST service has to choose among them. The main problem is that once you implement a concrete strategy it is a non-backward-compatible change to abruptly switch to another one (it is possible to use multiple versioning schemes in parallel, but that is an agony). It isn't surprising that frequently the versioning resolution is postponed until the last moment.[2] Sometimes delaying a decision might help, but it is usually hard to tell in advance how the chosen approach will work out in the future.[3]

There is, however, a definite advantage of REST APIs over their OO counterparts in regard to versioning. For example, in Java there is no way for a framework to redirect old clients to a new version in some standard fashion. Such redirection isn't a first-class citizen, although there are some approaches mimicking this (see `http://wiki.apidesign.org/wiki/Visitor`). The connection between a client and a provider is rigid from the viewpoint of software versioning. In HTTP REST APIs the situation is much better, as the HTTP protocol includes couple of procedures for telling clients how to upgrade.

To better understand the various versioning options, it is beneficial to highlight the principal sections of a REST API that could change in the future, and hence require versioning.

- *Resource identifiers (URLs) encompassed by an API:* These are the regular URLs, which denote endpoints of a REST API.

- *State transitions as well as media-type-related aspects dictating the application and protocol semantics between a client and a server.* The protocol changes might also include a switch from HTTP version number 1.1 to 2.0 (we will see how this might be negotiated between parties). We assume that the underlying Transmission Control Protocol (TCP) network protocol will remain fixed.

- *Message payloads exchanged between parties:* For example, adding a new required field into a resource's representation (we assume that a client will still work properly if an optional field is added to the representation) is surely a backward-incompatible change.

---

[1]Maven efficiently handles dependencies for the compilation phase, but the runtime might be different (via the `provided` and `system` scopes). For example, in the case of OSGi, just plain Maven versioning might not be enough.

[2]I've also seen quite an "extreme" approach in the industry, where the first version of the service is released without any versioning at all (a common mistake in any API). For example, even OSGi gurus (who are very scrupulous about versioning) have made the same mistake (see `http://wiki.apidesign.org/wiki/PropertyFiles`). At first glance, this might sound ingenious, but under the hood it silently acknowledges the URL versioning scheme. At any rate, I recommend you make a firm decision about versioning before releasing the first production system. The versioning scheme must be part of an API from the very beginning.

[3]This conundrum is similar to the situation regarding what kind of authentication to use in a REST service. General advice is to start with OAuth in mind as early as possible, because switching an authentication scheme isn't a straightforward process (in addition, it is an incompatible change for a production system).

■ **Note** In a layered architecture there might be various intermediaries between a client and a server (e.g., various proxies, gateways, etc.). These could affect the functional compatibility of the whole distributed system after being updated or upgraded, but we will omit such effects from our analysis.

Altering the Resource URLs

The most common convention[4] (also supported by many tools) is to specify the version number inside a URL by applying, for example, the URI template: `http(s)://<host>/api/{versionIdentifier}`. Usually the version identifier is of the form vX (e.g., v1, v2, etc.).[5] The outcome is a partitioned set of URLs, where each set designates a particular version of the API. A similar result could be achieved by using subdomains (instead of `example.com/api/v1`, we would have `api-v1.example.com`), query parameters, or custom HTTP headers. Partitioning completely isolates version-specific application and protocol semantics from each other. Clients might deliberately choose the desired version, and work solely with resource representations associated with that version.

Another less common approach is to embed hypermedia links in the home (start) page, and let a client choose the appropriate link. RFC 5829 (`https://tools.ietf.org/html/rfc5829`) defines link relation types dealing with version history. The server may deliver the home page with default content (related to the latest version), and provide inside the `Link` HTTP response header the version-history "pointer." This allows navigation through other versions of the home page (the last versions would be explicitly denoted using the `latest-version` relation type). Effectively, a client could start with any supported version of the home page, hence any version of the system. Of course, such version history could be attached to any resource, not just the home page. The benefit of this technique is that it relies on a documented process, and there is no need to come up with a proprietary solution. Moreover, accessing a complete version history, a client can figure out what versions are supported by the server, without a trial-and-error tactic (e.g., an old client hitting v1 might get an error from a server already on version v5). The downside is that a client will have to make some additional roundtrips with the server to reach the desired version.

The previous proposal has many variations. For example, the version history might be part of the home page with embedded version-specific links. An older client, which doesn't understand the new version, would only follow the link for the version it can manage. This is somehow similar to the approach of encoding a version number inside a System property on the JVM platform. A software component, which doesn't know anything about a new version, would never be configured with nor reference future System property values. Furthermore, a server might prefer an older default version of the service (instead of sticking to the latest one). At any rate, the previous approach can only work with clients aware of the version history. Otherwise, they would break when trying to parse the content related to the latest version of the system (unless the changes are backward compatible).

In all these cases, the version identifier should denote a full system generation.[6] In other words, in the version template vX, the number X should play the role of the major version number in the semantic versioning scheme (see `http://semver.org`). Incompatible changes are forbidden without modifying X. We will see in Chapter 7 that hypermedia-driven REST APIs rarely need to alter the version number.

---

[4]In case of Java, this would be similar to releasing a new version of an API inside a different package. That is a brute force coexistence (see `http://wiki.apidesign.org/wiki/Co-existence`), but is probably better than perpetrating incompatible changes.

[5]Sometimes you will bump into dates instead of familiar version identifiers. For a REST API it is more natural to have version identifiers, as mentioned in this book. However, Semantic Web documents are better controlled via dates, as the Semantic Web technology primarily deals with vocabularies and descriptions rather than service implementations.

[6]This is an interesting question in modular design, too. Should we version each module independently, or rather mark the whole release with a single version? The answer depends on the use case: If you want to plug a module into some version of the product, then it is easier to have a uniform version number for all the modules. However, if you are building reusable modules, which are also leveraged inside an application, then it is better to have a separate version for each of them.

API Keys as a Way to Control Versioning

Modern REST APIs employ the concept of an API key to identify the caller of the service. This identification is most often related to authentication and authorization purposes for a system to see what data and actions are allowed for the matching client. The API key is generated by a server, and is an opaque binary token (the client cannot interpret it). Usually it is a pair of tokens, with public and private parts. You can look into Amazon Web Services documentation for more details, which uses the term *Access Keys* to allow programmatic usage of its services. This is available at `http://docs.aws.amazon.com/IAM/latest/UserGuide/id_credentials_access-keys.html`.

The API key is passed inside the URL each time a client issues an HTTP request. The path parameter is frequently named key, and the request looks like this: `http(s)://<host>/api/<some endpoint>?key=<API key>`. However, nothing prevents a server from partitioning the API key space based on versions. The client would indicate explicitly what version of an API key it needs from a server during registration. The generated API key would incorporate all the necessary version information. As long as the client will use that specific API key, all requests will refer to that concrete version of the system. Henceforth, API keys could save URLs from pollution regarding version identifiers.

The Importance of Stable UR[IL]s

There is a general consensus that *cool URIs* (see [1] for details) should be simple, stable, and manageable (this is associated with a need to version them). Confusion arises among developers when URIs are mixed up with URLs, and resources are substituted for their representations.

URI is an abbreviation for uniform resource identifier (see RFC 3986 at `https://tools.ietf.org/html/rfc3986`), and URL stands for uniform resource locator.[7] All URLs are also URIs, but the opposite isn't true. URIs are used to identify *real-world objects*, the kind of things that don't even need to exist as software entities (e.g., a person, business concept, physical object, etc.). URLs identify things that can be located and retrieved on the Web. In other words, URLs implicitly contain protocol details, as without a proper protocol nothing can be downloaded from a server. In a RESTful world, we mostly deal with URLs.

A URL in the REST realm is a bit of a misnomer. It would be more appropriate to call it a uniform representation locator. Nevertheless, to fully understand what should be cool (a URI or URL), and what should remain stable (resource or representation locators), we will take a small detour into the domain of the *Semantic Web*. Figure 6-1 shows the relationships between the URI for a real-world entity (abstract resource), the URL for a REST entity (information resource), and the URL for a representation. The whole discussion is simplified to make it more appealing for a broader audience (I hope it isn't oversimplified), and accommodated to programmable Web (the original Semantic Web documents are referring to the Web in general). As an additional constraint, we require that a client should be able to retrieve from the Web at least a description for any abstract resource (let us assume that those descriptions are offered as RDF documents).

---

[7]The uniform resource name (URN), which was used for a stable name, is deprecated in favor of the URI.

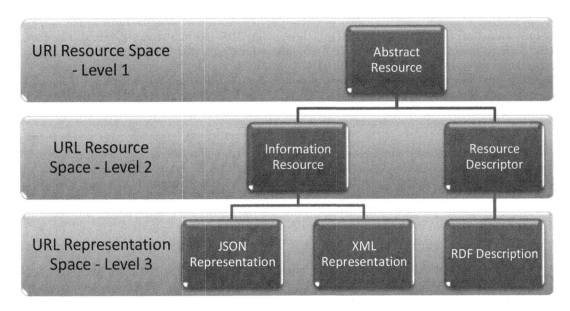

Figure 6-1. *The different reincarnations of a resource inside the global Web. In a RESTful purview only URL representation space is "delivering" content to clients. As we move toward higher hierarchical levels, the stability of UR[IL]s turns out to be more important.*

Let me refer to our example REST service (see Chapter 5) to make this elaboration tangible. The service's name was *ProblemReports*, and we will pretend that our domain is example.org (you can visit http://example.org to get some details about its purpose). The service itself, from an organization's viewpoint, is an abstract asset. Nevertheless, it is identifiable, and an organization can talk about it, offer it for sale (in case it is a commercial product), and so on. Its URI is http://example.org/asset/2016/01#ProblemReports.[8] What should happen when a client hits this URI? Recall that we have demanded live URIs.

First, we need to clarify how this URI is reconciled by an HTTP server. Our URI is a so-called *Hash URI* (very popular in the Semantic Web realm), as it contains the # symbol. According to the HTTP convention, everything on the right side of the hash mark is simply pruned away. Therefore, from the HTTP server's viewpoint, our URI is resolved to http://example.org/asset/2016/01. This means that any description document served "from" this URI will have to contain all entities mentioned with a hash mark (one of them is our ProblemReports term). This strategy is useful when the matching description document isn't too big; otherwise, the abstract URI space has to be further partitioned.

There are many options, but we will proceed using the HTTP 303 redirect approach with content negotiation. A client has to specify what content it requires, so the media type can be used as a general switch toward the matching representation. Here is a client's corresponding HTTP request:

```
GET /asset/2016/01#ProblemReports HTTP/1.1
Host: example.org
Accept:text/turtle, text/html;q=0.8
Accept-Language: en
```

---

[8]Stay away from premature conclusions whether this URI is also a URL. Having http inside it doesn't inevitably mean it is a URL. You need to be able to resolve that address, and get back an apt representation to qualify it as a URL. The HTTP 404 Not Found response isn't a viable representation, though.

A client has expressed that it has a slight preference for RDF description using the Turtle format (http://www.w3.org/TR/turtle/) over an HTML variant using RDFa (see https://rdfa.info). This means it is more interested in to machine process the description rather than to view it in a human-readable form. The language parameter is especially relevant for the latter case. At any rate, the server can figure out what the client wants, and will respond in the following manner (the URL below is just an example):

```
HTTP/1.1 303 See Other
Location: http://example.org/data/2016/01/OfferedServices
```

The server has responded with a redirection instruction, as it couldn't deliver the abstract notion of the service from the original address. Fragment identifiers might avoid 303 redirections and the need to poke around with the Access-Control-Allow-Origin HTTP response header. The idea is pertaining to the assumption that such URIs cannot point to concrete stuff, as fragments are removed by the server. However, this triggers a paradox, by which UR[IL]s shouldn't be treated in a special fashion, although we have just treated them as such. Moreover, the original assumption doesn't even hold. For example, a browser would scroll the content to match the exact section of a web page if it contains headings and you reference one of them.

At any rate, the client now has to issue a new request, using the address from the Location header:

```
GET /data/2016/10/OfferedServices HTTP/1.1
Host: example.org
Accept:text/turtle, text/html;q=0.8
Accept-Language: en
```

This time the server can return the matching representation (it has managed to fulfill the client's desire for a machine-plausible RDF document):

```
HTTP/1.1 200 OK
Content-Type: text/turtle
Content-Language: en
Content-Location: http://example.org/data/2016/01/OfferedServices.en.turtle

@base <http://example.org/asset/2016/01/> .
@prefix rdf: <http://www.w3.org/1999/02/22-rdf-syntax-ns#> .
@prefix rdfs: <http://www.w3.org/2000/01/rdf-schema#> .
@prefix foaf: <http://xmlns.com/foaf/0.1/> .

<#ProblemReports>
    a foaf:Project ;    # This designates products under development, as they're still
projects.
    foaf:name "Problem Reports Service" ;
    foaf:homepage <http://example.org/api/ProblemReports> .
    # Other Turtle (subject, predicate, object) triples about this service.
```

The Content-Location header should point to the concrete document hosted by the server. The RDF description documents are regularly static files, as they don't change often. If the client would directly use the http://example.org/data/2016/01/OfferedServices.en.turtle URL, then the server would also signal back the canonical URL toward the base descriptor resource. Such a canonical URL would be provided in the Link HTTP response header as follows:

```
Link: <http://example.org/data/2016/01/OfferedServices>; rel="canonical"
```

The home page URL denotes the entry point resource for the service (it omits the version identifier, so it refers to the default version). This is where a client should start the navigation (this is the Billboard URL). The representation of the home page should be again chosen by specifying the media type (in our case `application/xml` or `application/json`). You shouldn't put any implementation details into a resource URL (belonging to Level 2). That would make it fragile, in the same way as when you directly reference a class's field instead of its method. Representation URLs are allowed to have all sorts of appendixes, as they are related to implementation. Once again, clients should negotiate them based on a media type.

The home page resource (more precisely its representation) should refer to its RDF description via the `alternate` link relation type (the link could be provided via the `Link` header). This is the mechanism to interconnect a resource with its formal description. We should also state that the resource reifies its abstract description. In the next chapter, we see how media types are expanded with profiles, which are also semantic descriptions.

Figure 6-2 shows the RDF graph resulting from the previous service description in Turtle (the graph was autogenerated by the tool EasyRDF available at `http://www.easyrdf.org`).

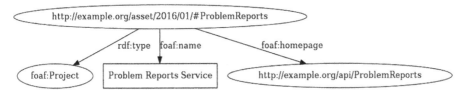

Figure 6-2. *The visual representation of the RDF statements written down in Turtle format*

■ **Tip** A handy way for a company to advertise its products with live demos is to publish the top abstract service (resource) URI.[9] Clients interested in machine-processing the offerings would only retrieve the corresponding RDF descriptions. Otherwise, they could ask for the entry point location. The server could generate a time-limited API key and return it together with the home page representation. The API key could also encompass the latest version identifier for the service.

The next two techniques, versioning of media types and profiles, are intended to preserve the stability of URIs. I mention them here as they are tightly related to URIs. For example, a profile itself can be versioned using a versioned URL. We talk more about profiles in the next chapter.

---

[9]Instead of a URI, a company could also use a more generic internationalized resource identifier (IRI), defined in RFC 3987 (see `https://tools.ietf.org/html/rfc3987`). Furthermore, by exposing a SPARQL endpoint (usually at the relative URL of `/sparql`), anyone could issue `DESCRIBE <Company's IRI>` to get RDF descriptions about that resource. You can read more about the SPARQL protocol and query language at `http://www.w3.org/TR/sparql11-protocol/` and `http://www.w3.org/TR/sparql11-query/`, respectively. It is even possible to translate terms (implement the dictionary from Chapter 16) by using the CONSTRUCT instruction.

Versioning of Media Types

The media type is dictating some parts of the application and protocol semantics (we will see in later chapters how a media type can be very powerful in this respect). The idea is to leverage the HTTP content negotiation mechanism to select the required version of the system. There are two possibilities:

- Create your own domain-specific media type with versioning support.
- Use an existing media type with versioning support.

The second option is only viable if you happen to stick to a media type that already has versioning. Obviously, you cannot just pick an arbitrary media type, because it has such versioning aid. The problem is that a very limited number of media types already include the version number. On the other hand, the first option isn't scalable, and should be avoided.

Introducing a domain-specific media type is only feasible if it really embodies a large part of the application and protocol semantics. In this case, it should be generalized, and published for the others to reuse. A client using your custom media type (indicated via the vnd. prefix) would define the HTTP Accept request header as follows:

```
Accept: application/vnd.my-media-type?version=X
```

The biggest challenge is how to evolve the media type in a controlled manner. You should keep in mind that it does comprise part of your API. If it starts to pull in too many API aspects, then you will need to version it. Suddenly you will end up having an overloaded version designator. All in all, a much more scalable approach is to use a well-established base media type and customize it via profiles.

■ **Warning**   If you use any sort of media type-based versioning, your server must set the Vary HTTP response header (don't use the wildcard shortcut). This is a signal to any intermediaries (proxies, gateways, etc.) that the same URL might return different responses based on the Accept header (in this case, a pure URL-based caching will not work).

Versioning of Profiles

A profile might segregate the chunks of application semantics that might break clients if they change. The media type would comprise those parts, which may be driven by hypermedia, and could vary dynamically. A client can designate the desired profile using the profile link relation type (it is specified inside the Link header). It is also possible to use content negotiation, if the media type supports the profile section (in this case the previous warning also applies). The nice thing is that you can provide multiple versions of your API in parallel, by letting clients choose among available profiles.

Switching API Versions

After some period, you'll inevitably come to the stage when a brand new version of the API is the only choice. Naturally, you cannot just make a switch in one swoop, even if the period for which you've guaranteed to provide support has expired. Breaking existing clients isn't a prudent strategy. The best option is to keep multiple versions of your API in parallel for some time (after an expiration of the previous version). The good news is that HTTP REST APIs are quite tolerable to this setup. The procedure might look like this.

1. Advertise to clients that the current API will cease to exist, and give a firm shutdown date. Stop issuing API keys (if applicable) for this version for new clients (this is another benefit of using API keys for versioning purposes).

2. Deploy a new version of your API in parallel to the current one. This could work out smoothly if you proactively included versioning support in your API from the very beginning.

3. During the transition period, always include the `successor-version` link relation type in responses hitting the old version. This is a reminder for old clients that a new version is available.

4. After reaching the end date, your server should respond to old API requests with the status code of `410 Gone`. The `Link` header should contain the link relation type `latest-version` pointing to the actual version of the system.

Upgrading the HTTP Version

As HTTP 2.0 gains momentum, we might expect in the future that servers will stop supporting the current 1.1 version (this will not happen soon, as the story with IPv6 shows). HTTP already includes rules for a client and a server to negotiate the desired HTTP version. The next steps demonstrate how this might happen (for a thorough treatment, refer to RFC 7540 at `https://tools.ietf.org/html/rfc7540`).

1. A client sends a connection upgrade request using HTTP 1.1 by setting the following headers:

   `Connection: Upgrade, ...`

   `Upgrade: h2c`

2. If the upgrade is possible, then the server responds with the status code of `101 Switching Protocols`. It will immediately start speaking HTTP 2.0 with the given client. Otherwise, the server will ignore the upgrade request, and continue to speak with the old version.

Summary

We have seen various ways to put evolution of a REST API under our control. It isn't possible to change things without taking into account their possible impacts on existing clients. The only way to control this process is to leverage versioning. This chapter has introduced different options to version REST APIs. There is no single best answer to this conundrum. Each choice has its benefits and drawbacks. By knowing the implications of each variant, though, you will be in a better position to select the optimal strategy. At any rate, if you can solve versioning without frequently altering the URLs, then it is definitely a positive result. In the next chapter, we focus our attention on hypermedia and how it might help us in crafting REST APIs with a high tolerance to change.

USER-FRIENDLY SEMANTIC WEB DOCUMENTS

Getting Acquainted with RDFa

Currently, we have only one description of the service in Turtle format. It isn't quite good for people to consume, and most browsers don't understand the `text/turtle` format. Luckily, there is an HTML format with embedded RDF.

Translate the Turtle format into RDFa, and devise a strategy for clients to negotiate the new format starting with the abstract service URI.

Reference

1. Sauermann, Leo, and Richard Cyganiak. "Cool URIs for the Semantic Web." December 2008, W3C Note. `https://www.w3.org/TR/cooluris`

CHAPTER 7

■ ■ ■

Encoding Actions on Resources

In Chapters 5 and 6 we dealt mainly with the design aspects of our REST API. In this chapter we partially implement the example service for you to see things in action (some parts will be left as an exercise). We use Spring HATEOAS (a subproject of the famous Java framework Spring available at `http://projects.spring.io/spring-hateoas/`) to realize our hypermedia-driven service, as well as JSON-LD (`http://json-ld.org`) to attach an ontology. Because we are building an HTTP REST API, we will inherit features from HTTP (like the uniform interface concept).

It is important to understand the role of HTTP and what it brings into the picture. First, HTTP as a protocol is well established, and is the main web protocol of the. From the viewpoint of a programmable Web, it establishes a uniform interface made up of the following major parts: URLs, methods (verbs), request and response headers, and response status codes (you might want to consult [1] for a good overview of these). HTTP offers the next standardized methods advantageous from an API's viewpoint: GET, POST, PUT, DELETE, PATCH, HEAD, and OPTIONS (this last one is a bit obsolete due to hypermedia controls inside a representation).[1] The uniform interface relieves clients from learning fundamentally new ways of handling resources. Everything happens via URLs (these are identifiers and handles of resources at the same time) and HTTP regular methods (see the sidebar "Identifier vs. Handle" later in this chapter for more details about them).

Superficially, the richness of an interaction between a client and a server is far bigger than what is possible to describe with only these methods. Thus, it appears that we need many more methods to define an API (something similar to what we are used to doing in an RPC-based API). However, it turns out that this isn't the case; that is, the previously enrolled methods are quite enough. The trick lies in the fact that the richness of the communication is encompassed inside the variety of resources and their representations. In classical (Level 2) REST APIs, much of the knowledge about resources, their representations, and the allowable actions on them are fixed and burned inside the code. The rules governing the resource manipulations are mostly documented in human-readable form. The idea behind the hypermedia-driven REST API is to get rid of these predetermined assumptions as much as possible, thus reducing the amount of documentation. This has a profound effect on clients and a server. They can evolve independently, as future changes will be communicated toward clients in a dynamic fashion.

---

[1]The OPTIONS can be used by a client to figure out the affordances regarding a particular resource. The response would be a set of HTTP methods (GET, PUT, etc.). In a Level 3 REST API the server sends this information proactively using hypermedia controls. Therefore, the client isn't any more motivated to issue OPTIONS, nor in doubt about what is affordable with a resource (you can read more about this HTTP header at `http://zacstewart.com/2012/04/14/http-options-method.html`).

© Ervin Varga 2016

E. Varga, *Creating Maintainable APIs*, DOI 10.1007/978-1-4842-2196-9_7

IDENTIFIER VS. HANDLE

The Similarities and Differences between These Terms

The identifier is just a mechanism to point to something. It could even be a purely abstract thing. The handle is an asset by which you can manipulate a resource. Think about an ordinary file. It has a full path (identifier), but to alter the file you need to open it first. The operating system (OS) would return a file handle (honestly, this is again a kind of an OS-specific identifier), by which you can operate on a file. In REST, these two things are melded, and you have a URL that both identifies a resource and serves as its handle.

Another analogy is the URL (identifier) and URLConnection (handle) classes in Java. We have already mentioned that every URL is also a URI. Interestingly this isn't reflected in the class hierarchy in JDK. The URL class has no relationship with the URI class. They are totally separate entities having the root Object class as their common parent. This is definitely an API design flaw. The variety of hypermedia controls built into the corresponding resource representation are dictated by the chosen media type. This is why it is crucial to select a proper media type, as it has a huge impact on the capabilities of your API. There is a formal classification regarding the level of hypermedia support in a media type aptly named the H factor (see http://amundsen.com/hypermedia/hfactor/ and [1] for a brief introduction). It is interesting to note that HTML embodies quite a large set of hypermedia factors (it isn't surprising then, that our browsers can handle so many different web pages without any problems). The quote that follows nicely conveys the idea behind the hypermedia, and why it is important for us to incorporate as many machine-processable elements in REST APIs as possible.

When I say hypertext, I mean the simultaneous presentation of information and controls such that the information becomes the affordance through which the user (or automaton) obtains choices and selects actions. Hypermedia is just an expansion on what text means to include temporal anchors within a media stream; most researchers have dropped the distinction. Hypertext does not need to be HTML on a browser. Machines can follow links when they understand the data format and relationship types.

—Roy T. Fielding, http://roy.gbiv.com/untangled/2008/rest-apis-must-be-hypertext-driven

■ **Warning** As an API designer, you must know from where things have emanated; that is, you have to be aware of the history. You shouldn't repeat the QWERTY keyboard mistake in a RESTful manner! Traditionally, HTML didn't buttress the CR H factor (you cannot specify the desired response type for GET links). Therefore, developers introduced a workaround by placing response type suffixes to URLs (e.g., http://example.com/mySite/resource.json or http://example.com/mySite/resource.xml). This isn't a settlement; this is a pure hack. You should use HTTP content negotiation to choose the preferred media type. If you have to make dirty stunts, then at least be aware of why you do it.

A REST service is meant to be part of a larger distributed system, and for practical purposes (to make the client's life easier) it is beneficial to formulate actions to be idempotent. This makes distributed failure handling much easier, as a client can just repeat its previous action (until getting a response, or after hitting the maximum number of retries) without any undesirable side effects. Generally, GET, PUT, and DELETE are idempotent (GET must also be safe). The PATCH request can be made idempotent by using HTTP's conditional processing. POST is by definition an unsafe and nonidempotent operation. HEAD and OPTIONS are also safe, but aren't used very often.

Implementing the Core Features

We first set up a Spring HATEOAS Maven project (to set up a new project just follow the instructions from the guide at `https://spring.io/guides/gs/rest-hateoas/`) and implement the resources. We have already decided that the entry point URL for our service will be `http://example.org/api/ProblemReports` (in our case, the host will be `localhost:8080` as we don't own the `example.org` domain). The semantic descriptors (field names inside the document) will be those described in Chapter 5. The only new detail is the encoding of links. Spring HATEOAS gives nice support for creating links and associating them with Spring MVC controllers.

Selecting a media type is an implementation detail, and should precede any actual coding. In our case, it was baked in as part of the requirements specification (usually this isn't the case). Nevertheless, we will see that even into a basic JSON/XML message payload we can incorporate lots of hypermedia controls, thanks to the existence of the standardized link relation types. This will also allow us to confer our vocabulary (expressed in JSON-LD) in an unobtrusive fashion. The links will be contained inside the `links` property. Each individual link will have a name as given in Table 5-1 (see Chapter 5).

Our goal here is to convey the benefits of having hypermedia controls in representations as well as to showcase the importance of choosing the right frameworks. Part IV of the book is devoted to JSON API, and will show you a more complex example with a real database in the background. You might want to compare this solution to the one from Chapter 17 to see the importance of selecting a powerful, well-established base media type (nowadays, there are couple of them competing in the field of JSON). As an added benefit, you will have an opportunity to choose among many frameworks for jump-starting your implementation efforts. The current version of Spring HATEOAS (at the time of this writing it was 0.20.0) has built-in support for Hypertext Application Language (HAL; `http://stateless.co/hal_specification.html`) and Atom Syndication Format (Atom; `https://tools.ietf.org/html/rfc4287`).

Interaction of Resources via Hypermedia Controls

The home page should respond to an HTTP `GET` request, and return an HTTP status code 200 `OK` together with the representation of the `HomePage` resource inside the body of the message. We might expect the following content (the output is beautified here, but in reality you wouldn't pass around extra white space).

```
{
  "name":"Problem Reports service's home page",
  "links":[
    {
      "rel":"self",
      "href":"http://localhost:8080/api/ProblemReports/"
    },
    {
      "rel":"about",
      "href":"http://localhost:8080/api/ProblemReports/About"
    },
    {
      "rel":"contents",
      "href":"http://localhost:8080/api/ProblemReports/Reports"
    }
  ]
}
```

The HomePage is of the type schema.org/WebPage, so it has the name property (this is all now implicit, but later on we will use JSON-LD to make these facts explicit). The links section contains IANA registered links to the about page, home page itself (a self-referencing link[2]) and to the contents of the service (the list of reported problems). Notice that you don't need to additionally explain the meaning of these links, as they are all standardized by IANA. Moreover, this nicely illustrates why URL design isn't that important. When you designate the URL with an about link, it doesn't really matter how you have structured it.

By following the about link, the client should arrive at the AboutPage resource. Again, it is assumed that the server will return an HTTP status code of 200 OK for the GET request. The response body should look like this.

```
{
  "name": "About the Problem Reports service",
  "about": "Stores problem reports registered in a system",
  "text": "The example micro-service for chapter 7.",
  "links":[
    {
      "rel":"self",
      "href":"http://localhost:8080/api/ProblemReports/About"
    },
    {
      "rel":"http://xmlns.com/foaf/spec/#term_homepage",
      "href":"http://localhost:8080/api/ProblemReports"
    }
  ]
}
```

The AboutPage is of the type schema.org/AboutPage (a subclass of the WebPage) so it has the name, about, and text properties. It also has a link to the home page using the homepage term from FOAF (it uses link expansion to reference the term, as it isn't registered with IANA).

Skeleton of the Service

In Spring HATEOAS you model a resource representation by introducing the matching resource representation class. It is beneficial to extend the ResourceSupport class, as it implements the necessary methods to handle links (allows you to add instances of the Link class, and performs the rendering as shown before). Spring uses the Jackson library to do JSON serialization of representations. Instructions for Jackson are incorporated via annotations. A similar remark applies for XML support using JAXB. Here is the listing for the about page resource representation class (watch out for the sections shown in bold).

```
package rs.exproit.problem_reports.resource;

import javax.xml.bind.annotation.XmlAttribute;
import javax.xml.bind.annotation.XmlRootElement;

import org.springframework.hateoas.ResourceSupport;
```

---

[2]It is also possible to use the url property of the WebPage, but it is better to be consistent across your APIs. In case you need a self-link from a representation, which isn't a WebPage per se, then you would need to come up with a new convention. Consistency is only one of the myriad quality attributes of an API (read [3] for a good overview).

```
import com.fasterxml.jackson.annotation.JsonCreator;
import com.fasterxml.jackson.annotation.JsonProperty;

@XmlRootElement(name = "AboutPage")
public final class AboutPage extends ResourceSupport {
    @JsonProperty @XmlAttribute
    private final String name = "About the Problem Reports service";

    @JsonProperty @XmlAttribute
    private final String about = "Stores problem reports registered in a system";

    @JsonProperty @XmlAttribute
    private final String text = "The example micro-service for chapter 7.";

    @JsonCreator
    public AboutPage() { }

    public final String getName() {
        return name;
    }

    public final String getAbout() {
        return about;
    }

    public final String getText() {
        return text;
    }
}
```

To serve resource representations (handle HTTP requests) you must define the corresponding resource controller classes. A resource controller will attach the necessary links to the base resource representation. This is a fine example of how internal data storage details are not necessarily mapped to resource representations. Again, everything happens via annotations. Here is the code for the about page resource controller (watch out for the sections shown in bold).

```
package rs.exproit.problem_reports.controller;

import static org.springframework.hateoas.mvc.ControllerLinkBuilder.*;

import org.springframework.http.HttpEntity;
import org.springframework.http.HttpStatus;
import org.springframework.http.ResponseEntity;
import org.springframework.web.bind.annotation.RestController;

import rs.exproit.problem_reports.resource.AboutPage;

import org.springframework.web.bind.annotation.RequestMapping;
import org.springframework.web.bind.annotation.RequestMethod;
```

```
@RestController
public class AboutPageController {
    @RequestMapping(path = "/About", method = RequestMethod.GET)
    public HttpEntity<AboutPage> aboutPage() {
        AboutPage aboutPage = new AboutPage();
        aboutPage.add(linkTo(methodOn(AboutPageController.class).aboutPage()).
        withSelfRel());
        aboutPage.add(linkTo(HomePageController.class)
                .withRel("http://xmlns.com/foaf/spec/#term_homepage"));

        return new ResponseEntity<AboutPage>(aboutPage, HttpStatus.OK);
    }
}
```

The benefit of reusing the link handling from Spring HATEOAS is that many background tasks are carried out for you automatically. For example, a usual practice is to hide services behind a proxy. If you configure the proxy to pass the X-FORWARDED-HOST header, then the serialized links will pick up the host provided by the proxy instead of reflecting the current location of the running service. Nevertheless, the main benefit is the existence of the ControllerLinkBuilder class, which allows you to point back to controller classes (either to a full class, or to one of its HTTP request handler methods). Imagine how hard would it be to manually construct those absolute URLs for links. Because a controller class already specifies relative paths, all the rest (protocol, host, port number, and base path) is dynamically attached by the Spring HATEOAS link handling facility. The self-link is so important that it is even predefined.

Finally, to create a working HTTP service we need to package everything up. There are two possibilities: create the WAR file to be used inside an external web server, or make a fat jar file with an embedded HTTP server. We use the latter choice by using Spring's Tomcat servlet container. The Spring Boot Maven plug-in does most of the packaging work for us, so we just need to create the main application class. Here is the listing (notice the part shown in bold).

```
package rs.exproit.problem_reports;

import org.springframework.boot.SpringApplication;
import org.springframework.boot.autoconfigure.SpringBootApplication;

@SpringBootApplication
public class ProblemReportsService {
    public static void main(String[] args) {
        SpringApplication.run(ProblemReportsService.class, args);
    }
}
```

The single @SpringBootApplication annotation performs all the work. It triggers the scan for resource controller classes and brings them in. Also, Spring will read the configuration file application.properties (located inside the src/main/resources folder) and set the base path and port number of the service accordingly. The last line deactivates automatic HAL responses (a client needs to explicitly ask for HAL via content negotiation). Here is the content of the configuration file.

```
server.contextPath=/api/ProblemReports
server.port=8080

spring.hateoas.use-hal-as-default-json-media-type=false
```

The Remaining Representations and Controllers

The problem reports are going to be stored in an ad-hoc, prepopulated, in-memory database. It will contain for now some basic methods to manipulate the data set. Nonetheless, we first need to define the problem report resource representation. Its listing is provided here (the getters are omitted for brevity).

```java
package rs.exproit.problem_reports.resource;

import javax.xml.bind.annotation.XmlAttribute;
import javax.xml.bind.annotation.XmlRootElement;

import org.springframework.hateoas.ResourceSupport;
import org.springframework.hateoas.core.Relation;

import com.fasterxml.jackson.annotation.JsonCreator;
import com.fasterxml.jackson.annotation.JsonInclude;
import com.fasterxml.jackson.annotation.JsonProperty;

@XmlRootElement(name = "problem")
@Relation(collectionRelation = "items")
@JsonInclude(JsonInclude.Include.NON_EMPTY)
public final class ProblemReport extends ResourceSupport {
    @JsonProperty @XmlAttribute
    private final String reportNumber;

    @JsonProperty @XmlAttribute
    private final String type;

    @JsonProperty @XmlAttribute
    private final String title;

    @JsonProperty @XmlAttribute
    private final Integer status;

    @JsonProperty @XmlAttribute
    private final String correlationId;

    public ProblemReport(String id, String type, String title, Integer status,
                         String correlationId) {
        this.reportNumber = id;
        this.type = type;
        this.title = title;
        this.status = status;
        this.correlationId = correlationId;
    }

    @JsonCreator
    public ProblemReport() { }
```

The @Relation annotation is useful for HAL serialization to control the name of the collection JSON property. @JsonInclude is required to avoid empty links sections in the output. It is very important to define a default no-arg constructor, otherwise XML serialization wouldn't work. The following code is the implementation of our simple database[3] (you can browse the associated unit test class in the accompanying source code for this book).

```java
package rs.exproit.problem_reports.db;

import java.util.ArrayList;
import java.util.Iterator;
import java.util.List;

import rs.exproit.problem_reports.resource.ProblemReport;

public final class ProblemReportDB {
    private static List<ProblemReport> database = new ArrayList<>();

    static {
        database.add(new ProblemReport("1",
                "http://example.org/errors/out-of-memory", "Out of memory error", 500,
                "T1"));
        database.add(new ProblemReport("2",
                "http://example.org/errors/authorization-error", "Invalid token", 401,
                "T2"));
        database.add(new ProblemReport("3",
                "http://example.org/errors/resource-not-found", "Resource not found", 404,
                "T2"));
        database.add(new ProblemReport("4",
                "http://example.org/errors/out-of-credit", "Out of credit", 403, "T3"));
        database.add(new ProblemReport("5",
                "http://example.org/errors/invalid-request", "Invalid request", 400, "T4"));
    }

    public static ProblemReport findProblemReport(String reportNumber) {
        for (ProblemReport report : database) {
            if (report.getReportNumber().equals(reportNumber)) {
                return report;
            }
        }
        return null;
    }

    public static List<ProblemReport> getAllProblemReports() {
        return database;
    }
}
```

---

[3]This is throwaway code, and is using static methods, which aren't proper for an API. See the exercises at the end of this chapter for more directions on how to refactor it.

```java
    public static List<ProblemReport> findAllProblemReports(String correlationId) {
        List<ProblemReport> result = new ArrayList<>();

        for (ProblemReport report : database) {
            if (report.getCorrelationId().equals(correlationId)) {
                result.add(report);
            }
        }
        return result;
    }

    public static void deleteProblemReport(String reportNumber) {
        Iterator<ProblemReport> it = database.iterator();
        while (it.hasNext()) {
            ProblemReport report = it.next();
            if (report.getReportNumber().equals(reportNumber)) {
                it.remove();
                return;
            }
        }
    }
}
```

In production, you would not store the resource representations directly, but use separate domain model entities. The problem report resource controller[4] is depicted here (the imports are omitted).

```java
package rs.exproit.problem_reports.controller;

@RestController
@RequestMapping("/Reports/{reportNumber}")
public class ProblemReportController {
    @RequestMapping(method = RequestMethod.GET)
    public HttpEntity<ProblemReport> getReport(@PathVariable String reportNumber) {
        ProblemReport report = ProblemReportDB.findProblemReport(reportNumber);
        if (report == null) {
            return new ResponseEntity<ProblemReport>(HttpStatus.NOT_FOUND);
        } else {
            report.add(linkTo(methodOn(ProblemReportController.class)
                    .getReport(reportNumber)).withSelfRel());
            report.add(linkTo(methodOn(ProblemReportsController.class)
                    .getReports(report.getCorrelationId())).withRel("related"));
            report.add(linkTo(methodOn(ProblemReportController.class)
                    .getReport(reportNumber)).withRel("edit"));
            report.add(linkTo(ProblemReportsController.class).withRel("collection"));

            return new ResponseEntity<ProblemReport>(report, HttpStatus.OK);
        }
    }
```

---

[4]Read more about the PathVariable annotation in the Spring documentation.

```
@RequestMapping(method = RequestMethod.DELETE)
public HttpEntity<ProblemReport> deleteReport(@PathVariable String reportNumber) {
    ProblemReportDB.deleteProblemReport(reportNumber);
    return new ResponseEntity<ProblemReport>(HttpStatus.NO_CONTENT);
    }
}
```

It already supports the deletion of problem reports (the update is left as an exercise). Finally, we present the problem reports controller, which creates a collection of problem reports (the imports are omitted).

```
package rs.exproit.problem_reports.controller;

@RestController
@RequestMapping(value = "/Reports")
public class ProblemReportsController {
    @RequestMapping(method = RequestMethod.GET)
    public Resources<ProblemReport> getReports(
            @RequestParam(value = "correlationId", required = false) String correlationId) {
        List<Link> links = new ArrayList<Link>();
        links.add(linkTo(methodOn(ProblemReportsController.class)
                .getReports(correlationId)).withSelfRel());
        links.add(linkTo(HomePageController.class)
                .withRel("http://xmlns.com/foaf/spec/#term_homepage"));
        links.add(createSearchLink());

        List<ProblemReport> reports =
                correlationId != null ? ProblemReportDB.findAllProblemReports(correlationId) :
                                ProblemReportDB.getAllProblemReports();

        return new Resources<>(toResources(reports), links);
    }

    private Link createSearchLink() {
        UriComponents uriComponents = UriComponentsBuilder.fromUri(
                linkTo(ProblemReportsController.class).toUri()).build();
        UriTemplate template = new UriTemplate(uriComponents.toUriString())
            .with("correlationId", TemplateVariable.VariableType.REQUEST_PARAM);

        return new Link(template, "search");
    }

    private List<ProblemReport> toResources(List<ProblemReport> reports) {
        for (ProblemReport report : reports) {
            if (!report.hasLink("self")) {
                report.add(linkTo(methodOn(ProblemReportController.class)
                        .getReport(report.getReportNumber())).withSelfRel());
            }
        }

        return reports;
    }
}
```

There is no separate collection resource representation; this is created on the fly by the controller. The createSearchLink method is an example of how to create links with URI templates. The toResources method illustrates how to produce a collection of resource representations. In our case, it just adds a self-link to each report, if it doesn't already have one.

Smoke Testing the Service

We are now ready to start our service by invoking the next Maven command from the project's home folder: mvn clean test spring-boot:run. To hit the entry point of our service you should issue the following command (the -v flag triggers a more verbose output):

```
curl -v -H "Accept: application/json" http://localhost:8080/api/ProblemReports/
```

We will get the same response as we expected at the beginning of this section. The same is true if we follow the about link. If we would like to alter the embedded hostname in the links, then we should issue this:

```
curl -v -H "Accept: application/json" -H "X-FORWARDED-HOST: example.org" http://
localhost:8080/api/ProblemReports/
```

The response would reflect the new host definition, and localhost:8080 will be replaced with example. org. We can request an XML message with this:

```
curl -v -H "Accept: application/xml" http://localhost:8080/api/ProblemReports/
```

We will receive the following response (cleaned up a bit):

```
> GET /api/ProblemReports/ HTTP/1.1
> Host: localhost:8080
> Accept: application/xml
>
< HTTP/1.1 200
< Content-Type: application/xml

<?xml version="1.0" encoding="UTF-8" standalone="yes"?>
<HomePage xmlns:atom="http://www.w3.org/2005/Atom"
          name="Problem Reports service's home page">
  <atom:link rel="self" href="http://localhost:8080/api/ProblemReports/"/>
  <atom:link rel="about" href="http://localhost:8080/api/ProblemReports/About"/>
  <atom:link rel="contents" href="http://localhost:8080/api/ProblemReports/Reports"/>
</HomePage>
```

This is an Atom protocol message, but signaled as pure XML. We can specifically ask for an Atom format by demanding the application/atom+xml media type.

There is also an interesting feature of Spring HATEOAS (you can read an excellent blog about URLs with and without an ending slash at https://webmasters.googleblog.com/2010/04/to-slash-or-not-to-slash.html). If you issue the following command:

```
curl -v -H "Accept: application/json" http://localhost:8080/api/ProblemReports
```

you will get back a 302 redirect with the Location header set to http://localhost:8080/api/ProblemReports/. You can instruct curl to automatically follow such redirects by specifying the -L option. Let us now get back all the registered problem reports:

```
curl -v -H "Accept: application/json" http://localhost:8080/api/ProblemReports/Reports
```

The response is as follows (notice the search link relation):

```
> GET /api/ProblemReports/Reports HTTP/1.1
> Host: localhost:8080
> Accept: application/json
>
< HTTP/1.1 200
< Content-Type: application/json;charset=UTF-8

{
  "links":[
    {
      "rel":"self",
      "href":"http://localhost:8080/api/ProblemReports/Reports"
    },
    {
      "rel":"http://xmlns.com/foaf/spec/#term_homepage",
      "href":"http://localhost:8080/api/ProblemReports"
    },
    {
      "rel":"search",
      "href":"http://localhost:8080/api/ProblemReports/Reports{?correlationId}"
    }
  ],
  "content":[
    {
      "reportNumber":"1",
      "type":"http://example.org/errors/out-of-memory",
      "title":"Out of memory error",
      "status":500,
      "correlationId":"T1",
      "links":[
        {
          "rel":"self",
          "href":"http://localhost:8080/api/ProblemReports/Reports/1"
        }
      ]
    },...
  ]
}
```

The search link gives a clear instruction for a client on how to filter this collection. The embedded problem reports are denoted with self-links. Without such links, this couldn't be treated as a true hypermedia-driven representation. Let's retrieve the first problem report:

```
curl -v -H "Accept: application/json" http://localhost:8080/api/ProblemReports/Reports/1
```

We will receive the following response (notice the parts shown in bold).

```
> GET /api/ProblemReports/Reports/1 HTTP/1.1
> Accept: application/json
>
< HTTP/1.1 200
< Content-Type: application/json;charset=UTF-8

{
  "reportNumber":"1",
  "type":"http://example.org/errors/out-of-memory",
  "title":"Out of memory error",
  "status":500,
  "correlationId":"T1",
  "links":[
    {
      "rel":"self",
      "href":"http://localhost:8080/api/ProblemReports/Reports/1"
    },
    {
      "rel":"related",
      "href":"http://localhost:8080/api/ProblemReports/Reports?correlationId=T1"
    },
    {
      "rel":"edit",
      "href":"http://localhost:8080/api/ProblemReports/Reports/1"
    },
    {
      "rel":"collection",
      "href":"http://localhost:8080/api/ProblemReports/Reports"
    }
  ]
}
```

The related link tells how to get all the other interlinked reports having the same correlation Id (groups together reports sharing a common context). The edit link assumes that the client will maintain its own application state (this is different than a resource state taken care of by the server), and will know that it should use POST only for edit links associated with a problem reports collection (see the exercises at the end of this chapter). For an individual problem report, the client can use PUT or DELETE. More advanced hypermedia formats even allow you to transfer the exact template for edits (e.g., HTML has the notion of a form to specify how the request's body should look). We now use the edit link, and issue an HTTP DELETE action:

```
curl -v -X DELETE http://localhost:8080/api/ProblemReports/Reports/1
```

We will receive the following response.

```
> DELETE /api/ProblemReports/Reports/1 HTTP/1.1
>
< HTTP/1.1 204
```

If we now try to get the same report back, the server will generate the HTTP 404 Not Found error.

131

Adding an Ontology

We are left with the task of adding an ontology to the returned representations. The ontology adds machine-processable statements about the terms used in the representations. Moreover, it clearly specifies the types of those terms. The ontology can be attached as the `profile` link relation. Here is the minimal JSON-LD document for our service.

```
{
  "@context": {
    "@vocab": "http://example.org/terms#",
    "as": "http://www.w3.org/ns/activitystreams#",
    "schema": "http://shema.org/",
    "xsd": "http://www.w3.org/2001/XMLSchema#",
    "content": {
      "@id": "as:items"
    },
    "reportNumber": {
      "_comment": "The unique report number.",
      "@type": "xsd:string"
    },
    "type": {
      "_comment": "The URI for the type of the problem.",
      "@type": "@id"
    },
    "title": {
      "_comment": "The short description of this problem.",
      "@type": "xsd:string"
    },
    "status": {
      "_comment": "The HTTP reponse code.",
      "@type": "xsd:positiveInteger"
    },
    "correlationId": {
      "_comment": "The ID to group together related reports.",
      "@type": "xsd:string"
    }
  }
}
```

The `content` is an alias for the `items` (part of the *Activity Streams* vocabulary). We could produce similar aliases for the other terms. For example, instead of saying `"schema:WebPage"` we might just say `"WebPage"` when designating a type. This JSON document can be served from a stable URL with a content type of `application/ld+json`. Another option is to embed this context definition inside each representation, but this should be avoided.

Summary

You have now experienced the power of hypermedia controls in crafting maintainable APIs. Instead of hard-coding all the details in code, the server is able to actively shape the communication and inform the client what options are available. This is how the Web works using HTML. There is no reason why the programmable Web cannot function in a similar fashion.

In addition to hypermedia controls, you have also witnessed the effectiveness of content negotiation. The client dictates the response format, and if the server cannot support that media type, it will return an error. New formats can be added without jeopardizing the compatibility of an API.

Providing an ontology helps in boosting the expressiveness of our API. Reusing common terms is far better than reinventing the wheel with each new service. Linking documents is a solved problem; now we need to seek opportunities to link data at a web scale (read [4] for an extensive treatment of this topic).

FINALIZE THE IMPLEMENTATION

Practice Spring HATEOAS

You should implement the following features:

- **Creating new problem reports.** You must add a POST request handler to the problem reports controller. You should decide how to specify the input template. Don't forget to add the matching edit link to the representation. This will send a green light for a client that it is now allowed to create new reports, too.

- **Updating an existing problem report.** You have to add a PUT request handler to the problem report controller. You may reuse the same template as for creating a new report.

- **Attaching the ontology to the returned representations as described earlier.** You may reuse the ALPS profile for XML serialization format, which you created in Chapter 5.

You might want to replace the rudimentary in-memory database with a real one. The static methods there go against sound testing principles; that is, the tests running this code would influence each other. I would advocate proper engineering, and allow multiple instances of ProblemReportDB class. As a final note, should the static nature be kept in some other context, then the ProblemReportDB class misses private constructor(s) to prevent instances of this class to be created (a common API design mistake in Java).

References

1. Sletten, Brian. *Resource-Oriented Architectures: Hypermedia*. Sebastopol, CA: O'Reilly Media, 2015.

2. Sletten, Brian. *Resource-Oriented Architectures: Linking Data*. Sebastopol, CA: O'Reilly Media, 2015.

3. Myers, Brad A., and Jeffrey Stylos. "Improving API Usability," *Communications of the ACM,* June 2016, Vol. 59, No. 6. doi:10.1145/2896587

4. Sikos, Leslie F. *Mastering Structured Data on the Semantic Web: From HTML5 Microdata to Linked Open Data*. New York: Apress, 2015.

■ ■ ■

CHAPTER 8

Implementing Synchronous and Asynchronous REST APIs

There are two broad categories of API quality attributes: *usability* (simplicity, consistency, learnability, risk mitigation, productivity, etc.) and *power* (expressiveness, maintainability, evolution, etc.). These are not always in sync. For example, research studies have shown some empirical evidence that the factory pattern might lower an API's usability. On the other hand, we definitely know that using factory methods instead of constructors gives us more control over performance, security, and evolution. Therefore, there are always some trade-offs pertaining to API design (good IDEs can offer you a list of factory methods for a class or its subclasses, so they might remedy the usability issue a bit). A similar story holds with the synchronous and asynchronous programming models. The former is surely easier to understand, but the latter could be critical to achieving the desired performance level. The HTTP 1.x protocol is inherently synchronous and sequential (this has radically changed in 2.0), but also has abilities to support the asynchronous reactive paradigm (consult the *Reactive Manifesto* for a good summary of the benefits of this style at `http://www.reactivemanifesto.org`). In this chapter, we analyze the available options and see how we can use them in REST APIs.

In the synchronous communication model the client waits for the server to generate the response. This could be a waste of time for a client, as it might perform some other background tasks. Moreover, end users don't like to see an hourglass spinning in front of them. The asynchronous approach is nonblocking. The client is allowed to do other tasks while the server is processing the request. The communication pattern can be elected by both a client and a server. Traditionally, servers only supported the synchronous model, so clients needed a way to enable an asynchronous style even though servers were still running in a purely synchronous fashion. However, this emulated regime, which brings in a separate client-side API, doesn't have any impact on the server-side REST API. The story about asynchronous processing might also emanate from the server, as it solves many performance issues there. We investigate both sides.

We do not delve into HTML 2.0 (you can read about it at `https://tools.ietf.org/html/rfc7540`) and how it speeds up both sides in an unobtrusive way. It reinforces the so-called *Half-Sync Half-Async* architectural pattern (see [1] or `http://www.cs.wustl.edu/~schmidt/PDF/PLoP-95.pdf`), hiding many optimization complexities at the HTTP protocol level (header compression, binary format instead of textual, efficient pipelining of requests, etc.). The good news is that transitioning to HTML 2.0 shouldn't be disruptive. Our browsers already support it, as do many web sites.

Client-Controlled Asynchrony

The most popular client-side web architectural style is *Asynchronous JavaScript and XML* (AJAX), which relies on a multitude of technologies to deliver an asynchronous programming model (there is a good tutorial at `http://www.w3schools.com/ajax/`). All this happens in a totally opaque manner from the server's viewpoint. In other words, any existing synchronous REST API can be transformed into an asynchronous one by introducing this extra AJAX layer. AJAX is responsible for handling all communication with a server

© Ervin Varga 2016
E. Varga, *Creating Maintainable APIs*, DOI 10.1007/978-1-4842-2196-9_8

and emulating asynchrony. Figure 8-1 shows the AJAX model. The client might exchange a bit of simplicity for considerable performance and user experience gains. I'm saying this because AJAX does complicate the client-side API. It isn't that transparent, and it might get convoluted when clients want to synchronize multiple requests in parallel (when the ordering of those requests matter). Here is an example to show how this works in practice (it is simple enough that even the exposed asynchrony doesn't make the code difficult to understand). You can alter the target web site to try retrieving different content. The core of AJAX revolves around the XMLHttpRequest class[1] (the main API) responsible for driving all data exchanges with a server. The following code can be run directly from a browser (notice the parts shown in bold).

```
<!DOCTYPE html>
<html>
  <body onLoad = "loadDocument()">
    <h1>AJAX Demo</h1>
    <div id="placeholder" /div>
  </body>

  <script type="text/javascript">
    function loadDocument() {
      var xhttp = new XMLHttpRequest();
      xhttp.onreadystatechange = function() {
        if (this.readyState == 4) {
          if (this.status == 200) {
            document.getElementById("placeholder").innerHTML = this.responseText;
          } else {
            document.getElementById("placeholder").innerHTML = this.statusText
          }
        };
      }
      xhttp.open("GET", "http://exproit.rs?t=" + Math.random());
      xhttp.send();
      document.getElementById("placeholder").innerHTML = "Waiting for the response...";
    }
  </script>
</html>
```

---

[1]The XMLHttpRequest class has nothing to do with XML, and it can work on any protocol. Furthermore, it isn't only a request, but also a response handler as well. This is an example of a naming problem in an API.

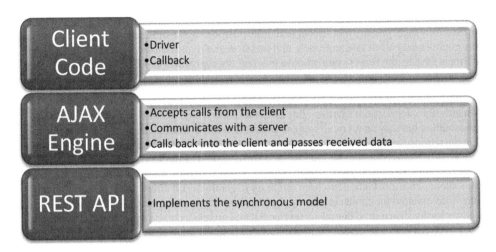

Figure 8-1. *The AJAX engine sits at the front of the client's code and emulates an asynchronous programming model*

The loadDocument function is started by a browser when the page is loaded. The inner anonymous function is the callback, which is registered with the AJAX engine by assigning it to the onreadystatechange field. The AJAX engine calls this function multiple times during the request processing (we are interested in reacting after the last stage, denoted 4). The rest of the code is the driver. The HTTP request is set up in the open method (the extra URL parameter is used to circumvent caching to better illustrate the asynchronous pattern), and activated via the send method. By default, the open method assumes an asynchronous regime (you can set the third parameter to false to switch into a synchronous mode[2]). Nevertheless, the last statement will execute before the page is retrieved from the remote server. This is an example of how things happen in "parallel" on the client side.

With asynchronous processing, you might want to control the time you are ready to wait for an answer. Properly setting a timeout value is even more critical in synchronous calls (remember that here you're blocked while waiting for a response). This is supported by AJAX by setting the timeout value in the property named timeout. After the expiration of this wait time, the engine generates an error.

You might think that using AJAX solves all the problems regarding asynchronous communication. Well, it isn't that simple. Although the client software can increase its throughput and UX (user experience), it cannot solve the problem on the server side (there is an apt term DevX, which stands for developer experience). It might be the case that the server is overloaded and simply cannot accept more requests. It would be much better if the server could store the request and handle it when appropriate. This is the reason merely client-side intervention isn't enough.

Server-Controlled Asynchrony

The server might expose endpoints, which aren't going to be handled in real time. There are three types of endpoints from the viewpoint of asynchrony (looked at from outside).

- An endpoint is always served in a synchronous manner.

- An endpoint is always served in an asynchronous manner.

---

[2]You are highly discouraged from using a synchronous mode, and Firefox even prints a warning into its console that it isn't recommended.

- An endpoint is served in a mixed mode. For example, the server might choose to process only high-priority requests in real time, postponing the others; or the server might choose a fail-fast approach, and just store the request until the peak load drops. Finally, the server could choose to let off the client after estimating the processing time.

There is no hypermedia support for a server to suggest whether the endpoint is synchronous or asynchronous. Similarly, the client cannot negotiate this aspect with the server, as is the case with media types. There are some possibilities, but they aren't quite sophisticated. The main mechanism by which a server signals back to a client that the request isn't going to be served immediately is the 202 Accepted response code. A client receiving this code can rest assured that the request was valid and accepted by the server. The only problem is when and how to receive the actual result. Of course, in some use cases waiting is the most reasonable approach.

Suppose that a client gets a 202 code. The client might try to get the result after a long period of time. If the server just indefinitely waited for clients to pick up their results, this would open up a security hole (the server would be easy prey for distributed denial-of-service [DDoS] attacks). On the other hand, if the clients started polling the server at a high pace, taking into account a potentially huge number of such clients, those polling activities combined would be a kind of a DDoS assault.

A client could tell the server how long it is willing to wait for a response before being "rejected" with 202. The HTTP Prefer request header serves this purpose (for more information visit https://tools.ietf.org/html/rfc7240). This header could contain many more preferences, but we focus our attention here only on the wait time. For example, the client might issue this request:

```
curl -v -X POST
        -H "Prefer: respond-async, wait=5"
        -H "Content-Type: application/json"
        -H "Accept: application/json"
        -d '{"data":"Sample data"}' http://example.org/some-collection
```

The server could choose either to process the request or respond with 202 if it judges that the command will take more than five seconds to complete. In case of 202, the server should set the Location header toward the URL to be used to pick up the final result, or to monitor the progress of an operation. Another possibility for the server is to simply describe the estimate and the location of the status check endpoint inside a document returned in the response body. This document would be part of an API, and specified using an XML or JSON schema.

If the server has provided a status check URL inside the Location header, then the client should receive a 303 See Other response code when the result is ready (after hitting this URL via GET). Again, the location from which to pick up the final result should be given inside the Location header.

For the server to control the polling frequency, it might choose to provide its guess when clients should expect the result. The server can set this expectation inside the Retry-After HTTP response header (for more information, visit http://www.w3.org/Protocols/rfc2616/rfc2616-sec14.html#sec14.37). This header is also used with 5xx and 3xx codes, but can be handy with 202, too. The unit of time is seconds, as in the case of the Prefer header's wait attribute.

All the previous possibilities can be combined with an alternate method to polling by leveraging the Callback pattern.[3] The idea is for a client to register with the server a callback URL. The server would use this URL to call the client and inform it about the result (or provide error information if something went wrong). Despite the fact that this method does avoid polling, it has its own drawbacks. With a callback the client must run a web server to receive HTTP requests. Therefore, most clients would not be able to use this method. Moreover, there are many situations in which the server simply cannot reach the client; that is, establish a new connection and perform the call (these reasons are primarily related to security and firewall setups).

---

[3]A variant of this pattern is known as Webhooks. It is a very popular way to connect a source code repository with the build server. For example, GitHub uses this approach a lot, and you can read about this topic at https://help.github.com/articles/about-webhooks/.

The biggest issue inherent in asynchronous REST APIs is dealing with persistence. The server must reliably store the requests as well as the responses to be picked up at a later time by clients. There must be some associated time-to-live (TTL) period after which the server should simply return 404 Not Found. Due to all these issues, messaging systems are a much better fit for achieving event-driven asynchronous solutions. This is the topic of Part III of this book.

Case Study: Favorite Problem Report

Suppose that we would like to extend our sample service from Chapter 7, and introduce a special subcollection type called *Favorite Problem Reports*. Furthermore, we presume that computing this collection is a very time-consuming process, so it would be very expensive to stall server threads while waiting for the result (those threads could fulfill other requests in the meantime). A new endpoint would be an extension of the main collection's URL, so it will be Reports/favorite. The idea is to mimic a synchronous GET request in an economic manner. Clients should be oblivious to the fact that the server is just simulating a synchronous model (the Jetty web server was among the first one supporting this with its Continuations API). Again, we are seeing the Half-Sync Half-Async pattern at work. Of course, a client could also apply a nonblocking behavior using AJAX. Both sides would be doing useful work while the request is being processed.

▉ **Note**   If you can provide a synchronous API for clients while using fully asynchronous processing in the background, then you would achieve a true win–win situation (operating systems have been using this approach for decades in managing devices). You will increase both the usability and power aspects of your API at the same time!

We first extend our simple database with a method to retrieve these favorite problem reports (the actual implementation isn't at all important, and you can go fancy with Futures). The method will simulate a long-running process by sleeping for five seconds. Here is the listing.

```
public static List<ProblemReport> getFavoriteProblemReports() {
    // Simulate a long running process.
    try {
        Thread.sleep(5000);
    } catch (InterruptedException e) {
        e.printStackTrace();
    }
    return database.subList(0, database.size() / 2);
}
```

Next we must implement an endpoint for this subcollection of problem reports. We just add a new method to our ProblemReportsController class. Here is the implementation (notice the parts shown in bold).

```
@RequestMapping(path = "/favorite", method = RequestMethod.GET)
DeferredResult<Resources<ProblemReport>> getFavoriteReports() {
    final DeferredResult<Resources<ProblemReport>> result = new DeferredResult<>();
    final RequestAttributes requestAttributes = RequestContextHolder.
currentRequestAttributes();

    // Simulate that we wait for the result using a separate thread.
    new Thread(new Runnable() {
        @Override
        public void run () {
```

```
            RequestContextHolder.setRequestAttributes(requestAttributes);

            List<Link> links = new ArrayList<Link>();
            links.add(linkTo(methodOn(ProblemReportsController.class)
                    .getFavoriteReports()).withSelfRel());
            links.add(linkTo(HomePageController.class)
                    .withRel("http://xmlns.com/foaf/spec/#term_homepage"));

            List<ProblemReport> favoriteReports =
                    toResources(ProblemReportDB.getFavoriteProblemReports());
            result.setResult(new Resources<>(favoriteReports, links));
        }
    }).start();

    return result;
}
```

The core of the solution revolves around the DeferredResult class (similar to the Java Future). If you return an instance of this class, then Spring will not tie up its request processing thread. The result will be delivered back to the client when it is ready (signaled by calling the setResult method). The other lines shown in bold are needed to preserve the proper context and reestablish it inside a new thread. At any rate, it is mandatory to set up the context before making any link-related calls.

If we now issue the following curl command, then it will wait for the result, but the server will not waste any resources.

```
curl -v -H "Accept: application/json" http://localhost:8080/api/ProblemReports/Reports/
favorite
```

We will get the following response (the output is cleaned up a bit).

```
> GET /api/ProblemReports/Reports/favorite HTTP/1.1
> Accept: application/json
>
< HTTP/1.1 200
< Content-Type: application/json;charset=UTF-8

{
  "links":[
    {
      "rel":"self",
      "href":"http://localhost:8080/api/ProblemReports/Reports/favorite"
    },
    {
      "rel":"http://xmlns.com/foaf/spec/#term_homepage",
      "href":"http://localhost:8080/api/ProblemReports"
    }
  ],
  "content":[
    {
      "reportNumber":"1",
      "type":"http://example.org/errors/out-of-memory",
      "title":"Out of memory error",
```

```
      "status":500,
      "correlationId":"T1",
      "links":[
        {
          "rel":"self",
          "href":"http://localhost:8080/api/ProblemReports/Reports/1"
        }
      ]
    },...
  ]
}
```

Notice that we don't support searching inside the favorite collection, so there is no search link. This is the beauty of a hypermedia-driven design. Clients would immediately get the message.

Summary

In this chapter we enrolled various options to boost concurrency of REST services, and analyzed the impact of an asynchronous model on APIs. We have seen that there are many available choices, but the best solution is to leverage the Half-Sync Half-Async pattern as much as possible.

COMPLETE THE HYPERMEDIA STORY

Continue to Practice Hypermedia Controls with Spring HATEOAS

The new endpoint isn't reachable from the Billboard URL (our entry point into the service). Your task is to augment the set of links available from the home page. You should also consider documenting the new *favorite* term inside our ontology.

Always refactor your code after making changes. For example, the newly added method repeats the line for creating the home page link. This redundancy should be eliminated from the code (create a common private method). Your task is to find all opportunities to tidy up the source code.

Reference

1.   Schmidt, Douglas C., Michael Stal, Hans Rohnert, and Frank Buschmann. *Pattern-Oriented Software Architecture: Patterns for Concurrent and Networked Objects.* New York: Wiley, 2000.

CHAPTER 9

■ ■ ■

Documenting REST APIs

We have seen in the previous chapters that one of the main goals of having a hypermedia-driven REST service is to get rid of human-targeted documentation as much as possible. Of course, due to sematic gaps, we cannot completely eliminate such documentation, but we can reduce its magnitude. The ideal situation would be to just describe the meaning of domain-specific terms, and let the rest be kept in a machine-processable form. For example, instead of explicitly writing "this field's type is a positive integer," we should express this fact inside the corresponding schema (both XML and JSON schema allows attaching human-readable descriptions to elements in the schema). A step further would be to produce an executable version of the documentation and allow users to interact with a system through its own documentation. In this sense, the documentation wouldn't be a passive dust collector artifact (if stored in a printed form), but a handy UI to communicate with software. From a maintenance viewpoint, this is a huge improvement. Any stale part of the documentation would be revealed immediately. There is really no difference between a bug in the documentation or the software; both can cause damage.

There are two opposite approaches to documenting HTTP REST APIs.

- *Adding documentation-related annotations to an existing code base, and producing API documentation based on them*: This is the style mimicking the Javadoc mechanism, where instead of annotations a developer uses special comments inside the code. The main idea is to let the documentation faithfully follow the actual implementation. Therefore, it is beneficial to keep it close with the source code to enhance its truthfulness. However, for a REST API documentation (it is a high-level description of a service) things aren't quite that straightforward. Before marking up your code with annotations, you need to ensure that REST-related entities are properly delineated from the rest of the system. It is very easy to reveal implementation details inside an API, thus restricting future opportunities to refactor the code (all changes must be done without affecting an API). Nevertheless, the main limitation of this approach is that your API's documentation can only embrace static things from the code. For example, if some parts of the resource representation are produced dynamically (like the links in our example service), then it is nearly impossible to include such details in the REST API documentation. It is definitely a suspicious strategy to alter the code base at the expense of clarity, maintainability, and comprehensibility just to fit into a concept of annotation-based API documentation. Another disadvantage is that your development environment must be equipped with tools to produce such documentation, although the major frameworks (e.g., Swagger, RAML, and Apiary) do have a broad spectrum of supported languages.

© Ervin Varga 2016
E. Varga, *Creating Maintainable APIs*, DOI 10.1007/978-1-4842-2196-9_9

- *Create API documentation independently,[1] and optionally generate client/server code based on it*: This is a more flexible way to create an API documentation, as you're not limited to code constructs to drive the process. You can even generate client/server code by the documentation tool (to speed up the implementation). The main benefit of this approach is that you can create API documentation well in advance (before commencing the implementation), and use it as a facility to help in distributed development. Teams dependent on your service wouldn't need to wait for you to finish the implementation. Moreover, by focusing solely on the API documentation, it can be distributed early on to other stakeholders for review (together with a mock implementation usually supplied automatically by the documentation tool). In this way, rapid change cycles can be carried out without throwing away any code. It is proven that people tend to have fewer issues with throwing away documentation or screen mockups than real source code.

■ **Caution**   As demonstrated in Chapter 5, it is very easy to abuse modern tools and eventually produce a Level 2 REST service, where all assumptions are fixed and hard-coded both by the clients and the server. This is especially true with an irresponsible code generation usage.

We continue with our sample service from previous chapters and add documentation to it. The documentation will be created as a stand-alone entity, retrievable by clients at the relative URL /swagger.json.[2] The API documentation would contain template definitions for creating and updating problem reports (something we still miss in our response documents). Again, you wouldn't want to make documentation in this fashion after finishing up the implementation, but the book must follow some linear sequence. Chapters 5 through 8 have established a common ground regarding hypermedia-based REST APIs, and this chapter builds on that foundation.

■ **Caution**   You should be cautious of various marketing fluffs, like the next one cited (at the time of this writing) from the web site of Apiary[3] (https://apiary.io/how-it-works): "Write an API in 30 minutes." You can never write a moderately complex hypermedia-driven API in that short amount of time! The crux of the Level 3 REST API revolves around careful design work. An API should reflect the decisions made during that period. If you can squeeze all that into 30 minutes, then you're a genius, at least. I have shown in Chapter 5 that you can write an API in an even shorter time, but that is far from being a maintainable API.

Currently, all tools are essentially oriented toward Level 2 REST services (Swagger, RAML, Apiary, Hydra, etc.). However, this chapter shows you some ideas for how to use them in supporting Level 3 REST APIs (this is the reincarnation of a well-known *programming into vs. programming in* a language philosophy). To cross the chasm between a Level 2 API documentation[4] for a Level 3 REST service, you should limit code generation as much as possible. Moreover, by introducing an endpoint to retrieve the current API documentation, you allow clients to get a Level 2 projection of a Level 3 API. Maintaining these snapshots is a repetition of the truth, but there is no efficient substitute until the appearance of API documentation tools for Level 3 services.

---

[1]There are even IDEs (for example, the Restlet Studio) to help you produce the REST API specification in a generic fashion (without a need to prematurely stick to the concrete documentation system, like, Swagger, RAML, etc.). However, such tools hit their limits quite early, as we will showcase in this chapter.

[2]As this is a static file, without a chance to negotiate content, then it is okay to have a file extension inside the URL.

[3]Apiary is an excellent API specification framework with good support for testing.

[4]Something that is nicely illustrated at http://xkcd.com/1481/.

Case Study: Attempting the Universal Method

We will start with the Restlet Studio (I assume that you have already created a username at restlet.com) to create REST API documentation in a format amenable for translation into Swagger 2.0 and RAML 0.8 (these are the targets supported by the version of Restlet Studio at the time of this writing). Who could object to the vision (dream) of having a single API source from which you can generate all other variants? Well, the reality itself, because all this is too good to be true in more advanced cases.

Our first step is to fill out some generic attributes of the API. We reference an Apache 2.0 License, and require an HTTP Basic authentication scheme for accessing our service (this is definitely something you should avoid in a production setup). Here is the output generated for Swagger 2.0 YAML (more human-readable than raw JSON), which does contain superfluous double quotes (a first sign that it was produced by a machine).

```
---
swagger: "2.0"
info:
  description: "This is the sample service for Part II of the book \"Creating Maintainable\
    \ APIs.\" The service exposes a level 3 HTTP REST API (hypermedia-driven) for\
    \ storing and searching problem reports (per RFC 7807)."
  version: "0.2.0"
  title: "Problem Reports Service"
  contact: {}
  license:
    name: "Apache 2.0"
    url: "http://www.apache.org/licenses/LICENSE-2.0"
host: "localhost:8080"
basePath: "/api/ProblemReports"
schemes:
- "http"
security:
- problem-reports-realm: []
paths: {}
securityDefinitions:
  problem-reports-realm:
    description: "The service should be protected by a minimal basic authentication\
      \ mechanism to prevent inadvertent usage (the assumption is that this service\
      \ will run behind a corporate firewall)."
    type: "basic"
```

The lines shown in bold should be removed, as they would indicate that you want to protect all paths. We will only secure those related to problem reports (see [1] for more details about the HTTP basic authentication mechanism). The associated RAML 0.8 file doesn't contain the licensing details, nor does it have a placeholder for a contact person (its value above is marked as an empty JSON object). Therefore, the Restlet Studio provides a bridge for different formats, but eventually you might need to tweak the outputs "manually" (e.g., by using the Swagger Editor for Swagger stuff). The internal format used by the Restlet Studio isn't observable.

The next task is to define sections of an API (Swagger calls them tags). These are handy to group related content together. We define three sections: Home Page, About Page and Reports. The corresponding Swagger definition is shown here (this time in pure JSON).

```
"tags": [
  {
    "name": "Home Page",
```

```
    "description": "This is the entry point of the service."
  },
  {
    "name": "About Page",
    "description": "Some generic information about the service."
  },
  {
    "name": "Reports",
    "description": "Stuff related to collection of reports as well as individual reports."
  }
]
```

So far, so good. Let us now fully specify the Home Page section. We first add the home page resource representation (called Representation in the Restlet Studio) and afterward an HTTP GET endpoint of the home page (called Resource in the Restlet Studio). Figure 9-1 shows the screen shot of Restlet Studio reflecting the work so far. Both will be put into the Home Page section. The corresponding Swagger 2.0 YAML sections (paths and definitions) look like this (notice the parts shown in bold).

```
paths:
  /:
    get:
      tags:
      - "Home Page"
      summary: "Gets available options."
      description: "Retrieves the initial list of options for a client as well as\
        \ some top level information (like the name of the service)."
      produces:
      - "application/json"
      - "text/xml"
      - "application/xml"
      - "application/atom+xml"
      parameters:
      - name: "Accept"
        in: "header"
        description: "The media type requested by a client: application/json, application/xml,\
          \ application/hal+json or application/atom+xml. The default is application/json."
        required: false
        type: "string"
        x-example: "Accept: application/xml"
      responses:
        200:
          description: "The list of affordances for a client accessing this service.\
            \ The response contains links to further content offered by this service."
          schema:
            $ref: "#/definitions/HomePage"

definitions:
  HomePage:
    type: "object"
    required:
    - "links"
    - "name"
```

```
properties:
  links:
    type: "array"
    description: "The hypermedia links to drive behavior of a client."
    items:
      type: "object"
      properties:
        href:
          type: "string"
          description: "The URL to the resource representation."
        rel:
          type: "string"
          description: "The relation's name; for example, self, about, contents, etc."
        required:
        - "href"
        - "rel"
  name:
    type: "string"
    description: "The name of this page."
  description: "The resource representation of this page. It contains\
    \ dynamic links to drive the behavior via hypermedia controls."
```

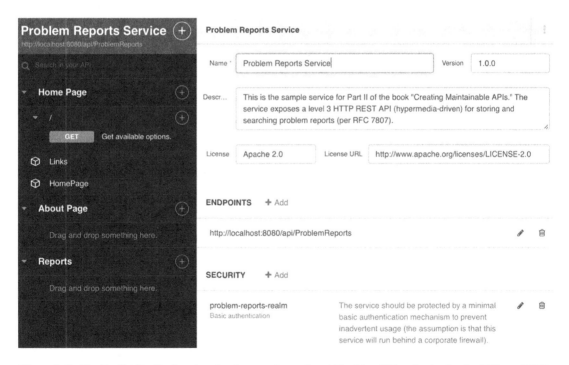

Figure 9-1. *The Restlet Studio showing the three sections of an API with a GET endpoint for the Billboard URL.*

The Restlet Studio has included the x-example vendor extension into Swagger (extensions are prefixed with x-). This attaches an example snippet of how someone might use the request header. Swagger allows examples to be associated with definitions.

The next couple of arguments regarding the Restlet Studio are applicable at the time of this writing. Once they become implemented, then you might be able to achieve lot more from the tool itself. However, a general remark applies: You might need to go back and forth between a GUI tool and a text editor to alter the underlying file. The first problem that we cannot currently solve inside the Restlet Studio is to add application/hal+json to the list of available response formats. Another issue is that we cannot specify generic parameters. For the Accept request header, which is applicable to all endpoints, it is cumbersome to repeat (redefine) it multiple times. We also want to refactor the HomePage representation by pulling out the links as a separate representation (we will need it later on). Finally, the links array definition is too lenient (e.g., it allows duplicates). Hence, we have to add some constraints, again something not yet supported by the Restlet Studio. Consequently, we will have to import the current Swagger definition into the Swagger Editor (available at http://editor.swagger.io), perform all the changes there, and import the new Swagger file back into Restlet Studio; at least, that is the plan. Here is the refactored, condensed Swagger 2.0 YAML file (observe the parts shown in bold).

```
swagger: "2.0"

info:
    ...
  contact:
      name: Ervin Varga
      email: e.varga@ieee.org
    ...
consumes:
- "application/json"
- "text/xml"
- "application/xml"
produces:
- "application/json"
- "text/xml"
- "application/xml"
- "application/atom+xml"
- "application/hal+json"
externalDocs:
    description: "Click here for more details about the RFC 7807."
    url: "https://tools.ietf.org/html/rfc7807"

paths:
  /:
    parameters:
    - $ref: "#/parameters/Accept"
    get:
      ...

parameters:
  Accept:
    name: "Accept"
    in: "header"
    description: "The media type requested by a client: application/json,\
      \ application/xml, application/hal+json or application/atom+xml."
    required: false
    default: "application/json"
    type: "string"
    x-example: "Accept: application/atom+xml"
```

```
definitions:
  Links:
    description: "Contains links related to all resource representations."
    type: "array"
    minItems: 1
    uniqueItems: true
    items:
      type: "object"
      title: "LinkItem"
      properties:
        href:
          type: "string"
          description: "The URL to the resource representation."
        rel:
          type: "string"
          description: "The relation's name; for example, self, about, contents, etc."
      required:
      - "href"
      - "rel"

  HomePage:
    type: "object"
    required:
    - "links"
    - "name"
    properties:
      links:
        $ref: "#/definitions/Links"
      name:
        type: "string"
        description: "The name of this page. "
    description: "The resource representation of this page. It contains\
      \ dynamic links to drive the behavior via hypermedia controls."
```

I've kept the extra double quotes. The following major changes have been incorporated:

- The contact field is now properly defined.

- The consumes and produces sections are global, as all endpoints are "working" with these media types. The produces list contains the application/hal+json format.

- The externalDocs points to the web site of RFC 7807 as a convenience for users.

- The Accept request header is a global parameter, so it can be easily referenced. The references are JSON Pointers, and # denotes the current document (see RFC 6901 at https://tools.ietf.org/html/rfc6901). Some reusable definitions (like Links in our case) could even be placed in external files. Furthermore, the default value is explicitly stated in machine-processable way instead of being kept as part of a human-readable description.

- The Links representation is a separate entity with additional constraints. The internal object of an item has a title property. This is not required, but if you want to avoid having ModelXY autogenerated names inside a generated code, then I recommend you override the naming of any such internal entity with this property.

If you try to import this new Swagger file into the Restlet Studio the tool will accept the command, but the content will not be accessible. Therefore, this *Restlet Studio → Swagger Editor → Restlet Studio* trick, to still be able to create an equivalent RAML file for free, will need to wait until the tool becomes more feature rich.

■ **Note**   GUI tools are good to jump-start you with development, but sooner or later you will hit their limits. Working directly with a Swagger YAML file inside the Swagger Editor does require more learning (you must comprehend Swagger's specification) than clicking around and filling in some forms, but it gives you full control. Moreover, text editing is still superior to GUI manipulations for refactoring the code.

Case Study: Producing a Swagger API Specification

We continue only with Swagger, and create the full REST API documentation for our example service. Here are the incremental additions for the about page resource representation (notice the line shown in bold).

```
/About:
  parameters:
  - $ref: "#/parameters/Accept"
  get:
    tags:
    - "About Page"
    summary: "Gets general information about this service."
    responses:
      200:
        description: "The general information about this service, and a links to\
          \ navigate through this service."
        schema:
          $ref: "#/definitions/AboutPage"

AboutPage:
  allOf:
  - $ref: "#/definitions/HomePage"
  - type: "object"
    title: "AboutExtraData"
    required:
    - "about"
    - "text"
    properties:
      about:
        type: "string"
        description: "A short summary about this service."
      text:
        type: "string"
        description: "A detailed description of this service."
```

At first glance, the /About endpoint isn't anything different than the Billboard URL / (except that it doesn't contain a separate description element). Nonetheless, this isn't true. Whereas the / route is intuitive and pretty stable, the /About path is something the server can dynamically provide. A client should not hard-code the fact that the about page is accessible via /About. This is the major difference between a

Level 2 and Level 3 REST service. On the other hand, we have no other way to describe the about page inside Swagger (or with any other tool for that matter). Moreover, what can be done with an about page resource is again something a server might tell via hypermedia controls. All in all, this is the reason we can only talk about a Level 2 snapshot of our service.

The AboutPage definition contains the allOf construct. This is a way to combine elements in Swagger. The AboutPage is everything that is contained inside the HomePage plus those additional properties (denoted here as AboutExtraData).

What follows is the extra materials related to the individual problem report entity (observe the parts shown in bold).

```
/Reports/{reportNumber}:
  parameters:
  - $ref: "#/parameters/Accept"
  - name: "reportNumber"
    description: "The unique report number."
    in: "path"
    type: "string"
    required: true
  get:
    security:
    - problem-reports-realm: []
    tags:
    - "Reports"
    summary: "Gets data about an individual problem report."
    responses:
      200:
        description: "The data associated with this problem report, and a links to\
          \ available options regarding this entity."
        schema:
          $ref: "#/definitions/ProblemReport"
      default:
        $ref: "#/responses/UnexpectedServiceError"
  delete:
    security:
    - problem-reports-realm: []
    tags:
    - "Reports"
    summary: "Deletes the given problem report."
    responses:
      204:
        description: "This problem report has been removed from the system."
      default:
        $ref: "#/responses/UnexpectedServiceError"

responses:
  UnexpectedServiceError:
    description: Unexpected service error (4x or 5x type of error).
    schema:
      $ref: "#/definitions/ProblemReport"

ProblemReport:
  type: "object"
```

```
required:
- "type"
- "title"
- "status"
- "correlationId"
properties:
  links:
    $ref: "#/definitions/Links"
  reportNumber:
    type: "string"
    description: "The globally unique report identifier."
  type:
    type: "string"
    description: "The type of this report (used to categorize problems)."
  title:
    type: "string"
    description: "The name of this problem report."
  status:
    type: "integer"
    description: "The status code associated with this problem."
  correlationId:
    type: "string"
    description: "The identifier to group related reports together."
description: "The resource representation of an individual problem report.\
  \ It contains dynamic links to drive the behavior via hypermedia controls."
```

The endpoint of the problem report entity contains a path parameter reportNumber. This is signaled by saying in: path. Both the GET and DELETE methods are marked with a default response (the other endpoints have been refactored in the same way; you can look up the complete Swagger file in the source code repository). This is a convenient way to define generic error conditions. We are returning an instance of a problem report for our own error, too. The global responses are defined inside the responses section.

The problem report resource representation doesn't require the links and reportNumber properties. Recall that this template will be used to create a new report with POST (we don't know in advance the report number), and also for returning our own error message (the links field has no meaning in this context).

The security clause designates the corresponding endpoint as protected. We demand all requests regarding problem reports to be authenticated.

Finally, we add details for the collection of problem reports as shown here (see the lines shown in bold).

```
/Reports:
  parameters:
  - $ref: "#/parameters/Accept"
  - name: "correlationId"
    description: "The identifier for grouping reports."
    in: "query"
    type: "string"
  get:
    security:
    - problem-reports-realm: []
    tags:
    - "Reports"
    summary: "Gets all registered problem reports, or just its subset filtered by the\
      \ correlation identifier."
```

```
    responses:
      200:
        description: "The collection of problem reports, and links to\
          \ available options regarding this entity."
        schema:
          $ref: "#/definitions/ProblemReports"
      default:
        $ref: "#/responses/UnexpectedServiceError"
/Reports/favorite:
  parameters:
  - $ref: "#/parameters/Accept"
  get:
    security:
    - problem-reports-realm: []
    tags:
    - "Reports"
    summary: "Gets the favorite problem reports."
    responses:
      200:
        description: "The collection of favorite problem reports, and links to\
          \ available options regarding this entity."
        schema:
          $ref: "#/definitions/ProblemReports"
      default:
        $ref: "#/responses/UnexpectedServiceError"


ProblemReports:
  type: "array"
  uniqueItems: true
  items:
    $ref: "#/definitions/ProblemReport"
  description: "The collection of problem reports.\
    \ It contains dynamic links to drive the behavior via hypermedia controls."
```

We see here an example of an optional query parameter definition. The problem reports resource representation just references an individual problem report as its items. We are left with just adding the endpoint for retrieving this Swagger file by clients. Here is the necessary section (notice the parts shown in bold).

```
/swagger.json:
  get:
    produces:
    - "application/json"
    summary: "Gets API specification of this service."
    responses:
      200:
        description: "The API specification of this service in Swagger format."
        schema:
          type: "object"
      default:
        $ref: "#/responses/UnexpectedServiceError"
```

We override here the generic produces directive, and restrict it only to application/json. The response is any valid JSON document, so we just denote that the type is object.

Extending the Service to Implement This New Specification

We must add some extensions to our service to fully obey this new API. We should return a Swagger JSON file via the /swagger.json route as well as incorporate the HTTP basic authentication mechanism. Also, we should replace the default Spring Boot's *whitelabel* error page with our custom problem report instance (see more at http://docs.spring.io/spring-boot/docs/current/reference/html/howto-actuator.html).

The first part is rather trivial. Inside the Swagger Editor you should select File → Download JSON. It will show inside the browser the content of the JSON file. We will save this file into the src/main/resources/static folder under the name swagger.json. That is all that is required (the rest is handled by the Spring framework).

To replace the default error handler, we should introduce a new controller for the /error route, and create an instance of a problem report class as the response (we will base our approach on the example published at https://gist.github.com/jonikarppinen/662c38fb57a23de61c8b). Here is the shortened listing of this controller (notice the parts shown in bold).

```
package rs.exproit.problem_reports.controller;

@RestController
public class DefaultErrorController implements ErrorController {
    private static final String ERROR_PATH = "/error";
    private static final String NOT_APPLICABLE = "N/A";

    @Autowired
    private ErrorAttributes errorAttributes;

    @RequestMapping(value = ERROR_PATH, produces = "application/json")
    public ProblemReport errorHandler(HttpServletRequest request,
                                      HttpServletResponse response) {
        return createReport(request, response);
    }

    @Override
    public String getErrorPath() {
        return ERROR_PATH;
    }

    private ProblemReport createReport(HttpServletRequest request,
                                       HttpServletResponse response) {
        assert errorAttributes != null : "Error attributes should have been set by Spring";

        RequestAttributes requestAttributes = new ServletRequestAttributes(request);
        Map<String,Object> errorFields =
                errorAttributes.getErrorAttributes(requestAttributes, false);

        return new ProblemReport(
                errorFields.getOrDefault("path", NOT_APPLICABLE).toString(),
                errorFields.getOrDefault("error", NOT_APPLICABLE).toString(),
                errorFields.getOrDefault("message", NOT_APPLICABLE).toString(),
                response.getStatus(),
                errorFields.getOrDefault("exception", NOT_APPLICABLE).toString());
    }
}
```

The `ErrorController` interface is essentially a marker interface to denote that the controller implementing it is used to render error responses. The controller needs to implement the `getErrorPath` method. In our case it just returns the `/error` route.

The `ErrorAttributes` attribute is autowired, which means that Spring will provide a concrete instance. This is used inside the `createReport` method to read out information about the error. The `reportNumber` will contain the path on which the error has occurred (as a way to identify this report).[5] The correlation identifier will contain the root exception's class name. All these assignments are protected via the `getOrDefault` method.

Finally, let us implement the HTTP Basic authentication scheme. The idea is to force clients to provide the username and password on each request accessing problem reports (the home and about pages can be accessed freely). For our service we will use the venerable Oracle's combination scott/tiger (you might read stories about from where all this came on the Web).

We need to add the following dependency into the `pom.xml` file.

```xml
<dependency>
    <groupId>org.springframework.boot</groupId>
    <artifactId>spring-boot-starter-security</artifactId>
</dependency>
```

Here is the listing of the security configurator class (the imports are omitted).

```java
package rs.exproit.problem_reports.security;

@Configuration
@EnableWebSecurity
public class SecurityConfiguration extends WebSecurityConfigurerAdapter {
    @Override
    protected void configure(AuthenticationManagerBuilder auth) throws Exception {
        auth.inMemoryAuthentication()
            .withUser("scott").password("tiger").roles("USER");
    }

    @Override
    protected void configure(HttpSecurity http) throws Exception {
        http.authorizeRequests()
            .antMatchers("/", "/swagger.json", "/About").permitAll()
            .anyRequest().fullyAuthenticated();
        http.httpBasic();
        http.csrf().disable();
    }
}
```

We see that the paths `/`, `/swagger.json`, and `/About` are unprotected. All the other paths require full authentication. Cross-Site Request Forgery (CSRF) support is usually not needed for a non-browser-driven system, so it is disabled (for more details, see `https://www.owasp.org/index.php/Cross-Site_Request_Forgery_(CSRF)_Prevention_Cheat_Sheet`).

---

[5]You might want to refactor the problem report entity and rename `reportNumber` to `reportId`. You might also want to add a timestamp when the error has ensued. Don't forget to update the API documentation after these changes.

Smoke Testing the Service

We will smoke test the service using the Swagger UI rendered by the Swagger Editor. To overcome the CORS issues (see `https://github.com/swagger-api/swagger-editor/blob/master/docs/cors.md`), I recommend you use Google Chrome, and activate the *Allow-Control-Allow-Origin:** browser extension (it is freely available). Start up the service in the same way as previously, but this time from the `chapter9` folder. Go to the `http://editor.swagger.io/` web site, and choose the File → Import URL... command. Make sure that the Use CORS proxy check box is cleared. Now enter the following address into the URL field, and click Import: `http://localhost:8080/api/ProblemReports/swagger.json`. The API specification should be loaded without problems, and the Swagger UI rendered properly on the right side (you can maximize it by clicking on the left arrow on the divider line).

Select the Authenticate button in the Security section, and provide the user credentials scott/tiger. Doing this means all protected requests will have the `Authorization` header set to `Basic c2NvdHQ6dGlnZXI=`. Try out various requests by clicking Try this Operation. You will be offered the possibility to set values to input parameters. When you are ready, then click Send Request (make sure that the problem-reports-realm check box is selected for protected calls). You will also get a hint on how to construct the matching `curl` request. This is useful in case you get strange errors in your browser related to CORS handling.

Generating the Dynamic HTML Client

It is interesting to investigate the dynamic HTML autogenerated client. You should select Generate Client → Dynamic HTML in the Swagger Editor. It will produce an archive, which you can unpack into some folder on disk. Now, open a command shell, and `cd` into this folder. From there execute the following commands:

```
npm install
node main.js
```

If all goes well, you should be able to open a web site at `http://localhost:8002`. It presents the API of your service in an interesting way.

Summary

We have experienced the comfort of having our REST API properly documented in Swagger. Suddenly we were able to use our service through the Swagger UI facility. However, all this documentation, as mentioned earlier, is just a snapshot of the hypermedia-driven service. You should not use it as the basis for generating client and server code. All the assumptions would become fixed, and evolving the API would be nearly impossible without breaking existing clients. This is usually what happens in the industry today.

AUGMENT THE API SPECIFICATION

Practice Swagger

If you haven't already done so, solve the exercise from Chapter 7. Augment the API specification from this chapter to include the extensions of the service as described in the previously mentioned exercise. You basically have all the major pieces at your disposal.

As additional training, try to break out the current monolithic Swagger specification into multiple parts.

Reference

1.   Gourley, David, Brian Totty, Marjorie Sayer, Anshu Aggarwal, and Sailu Reddy. *HTTP: The Definitive Guide.* Sebastopol, CA: O'Reilly, 2002.

■ ■ ■

CHAPTER 10

Testing REST APIs

Classical testing approaches are exercising REST APIs in a piecewise manner (for a good overview of different sorts of tests and related processes see [1]). Each path is treated in isolation, with fixed assumptions about affordances pertaining to the particular resource behind that path. They teleport themselves from one path to the other without bothering about their interconnectedness (those details are hard-coded on both sides). This is radically different in a Level 3 REST API. The connections are first-class citizens, and matter as much as anything else in the API. Islands of interrelated paths shouldn't exist inside a system API (I'm not talking here about interoperability concerns of disparate systems). Everything must be accessible by starting from the home page. Tests should reflect these characteristics.

The tests should follow the use cases (both main and exceptional routes) by always starting from the home page, and reacting to content presented by the server. The tests should be equipped with just enough knowledge to understand the ontology. If a link is missing in the response, then the functionality related to that link should be skipped accordingly; that is, teleportation and presupposed affordances are strictly forbidden. Consequently, if a particular use case demands a nonexistent link, then the test would simply fail.

The major problem is that current testing tools favor Level 2 REST APIs. Level 3 REST APIs can be exercised via their Level 2 projections (see Chapter 9 for an explanation regarding Level 2 views), and in that sense they can be tested with current testing methods. These tests cannot cover aspects like linkage completeness, context-dependent affordances, and so on. However, with some cleverness we could leverage current tools to carry out Level 3 REST API tests. We also demonstrate some distinct Level 3 testing facilities. Again, in the spirit of TDD, you would want to write these tests before commencing the construction phase.

Case Study: Testing with a Level 2 Tool

There are many tools targeted for Level 2 REST APIs, like, Apache JMeter[1], Postman for Chrome, SoapUI, and so on. We use the SoapUI 5.2.1 community (open source) edition. It has a nice integrated environment for performing functional and load tests as well as support for testing JMS-based systems (something we will need in the next part of the book). Before proceeding further, you should download SoapUI (http://soapui.org) for your OS.

The main advantage of SoapUI is that you can structure your tests in the same familiar way as with JUnit. The `TestSuite` contains multiple `TestCases`, which are made up of `TestSteps`. The steps are actionable items. Moreover, you can turn your functional tests into semiload tests very easily (complex load tests require more work than a simple button click).

---

[1]The Swagger Editor could even generate a JMeter client based on your API specification. It will contain an initial test script for each section of your API. Nonetheless, the generated tests will exercise the Level 2 projection of your Level 3 REST API.

© Ervin Varga 2016
E. Varga, *Creating Maintainable APIs*, DOI 10.1007/978-1-4842-2196-9_10

■ **Tip** I suggest you familiarize yourself with SoapUI by following its "Getting Started" guide (available at `https://www.soapui.org/getting-started/introduction.html`). It contains a simple REST sample project, too.

Examine the Service Use Case

Let's start by testing an easy use case, examine the service. Figure 10-1 shows the general test structure inside SoapUI (the tests for the other use cases will follow a similar structure). There is only one GET request to reach the home page. All the rest should happen via hypermedia controls. You can find the whole test setup inside the accompanying source code for this chapter (it is best to import the `Problem-Reports-Service-soapui-project.xml` file into SoapUI, and browse it from the tool).

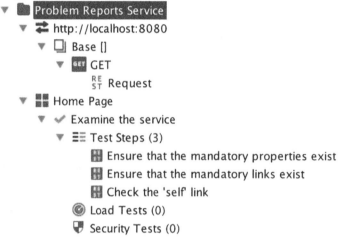

Figure 10-1. *The use case is mapped onto a test case, and the test suite represents a group of related use cases (in our case it has a 1:1 mapping with tags in the Swagger API documentation from Chapter 9).*

The simplest test step is to check that the name property exists. It uses as an assertion the JSONPath expression `$.name`, and ensures that it is evaluated to true (this kind of assertion is termed a JSONPath existence match). `$` marks the current document, and `.name` is the field inside the top-level JSON object. The test doesn't care about the actual content of this field, though.

■ **Tip** You can learn more about JSONPath at `http://jsonpath.com`. There you will find a useful online JSONPath evaluator, too.

The next test interrogates that all pertinent links exist. It has three assertions, one for each link. For example, the `self` link is checked by ensuring that the value of the `$.links[*].rel[?(@==self)]` JSONPath expression equals `[self]`. The `links[*]` matches all items from the `links` collection. We want to search for an item with a `rel` field that has a value of `self`. The `@` symbol denotes the current context. In our case, it is the value of the `rel` field. The `?` designates the "find" action; that is, defines a filter (its form is `?(<expression>)`).

Finally, the last test checks that the self link indeed points to itself (i.e., to the Billboard URL). It assures that the expression $.links[*][?(@.rel==self)].href[0] evaluates to ${Check 'self' link#Endpoint}. The .href[0] suffix selects the href field of the self-link (the zero index is there purely to convert the expression into an ordinary value). The expected value uses an expression instead of a literal, which is a neat way to avoid hard-coding the Billboard URL (including the host and port number). It references the Endpoint property of our test step (given here with its name). There are many other built-in SoapUI properties that you can reference in your tests. Another possibility is to define custom properties. Besides JSONPath statements, you may even use a Groovy script. This provides you with the greatest flexibility in specifying a test step.

The generic GET request is having its endpoint "empty." The other test steps define their endpoints explicitly, and use it as a single source of record. This will become handy for dynamic updates of the endpoints through property-transfer test steps. Another possibility is to leverage custom properties (you can create a dedicated *properties* test step), and keep the Base Path property (a built-in SoapUI property) set to the root of the API (in our case /api/ProblemReports). This is a better option, as it gives more flexibility in managing the paths. I have chosen the former solution for simplicity reasons.

If we run our test suite inside the SoapUI's TestRunner (assuming that the Problem Reports service is running in the background), we will get the following abbreviated output in the console (only the most salient parts are presented):

```
23:07:22,500 INFO  [SoapUITestCaseRunner] Running SoapUI testcase [Examine the service]
23:07:22,504 INFO  [SoapUITestCaseRunner] running step [Ensure that the mandatory properties
                                          exist]
23:07:23,086 INFO  [SoapUITestCaseRunner] Assertion [Find 'name' property] has status VALID
23:07:23,086 INFO  [SoapUITestCaseRunner] running step [Ensure that the mandatory links exist]
23:07:23,114 INFO  [SoapUITestCaseRunner] Assertion [Find 'self' link] has status VALID
23:07:23,114 INFO  [SoapUITestCaseRunner] Assertion [Find 'about' link] has status VALID
23:07:23,114 INFO  [SoapUITestCaseRunner] Assertion [Find 'contents' link] has status VALID
23:07:23,115 INFO  [SoapUITestCaseRunner] running step [Check the 'self' link]
23:07:23,197 INFO  [SoapUITestCaseRunner] Assertion [Validate self-link] has status VALID
23:07:23,198 INFO  [SoapUITestCaseRunner] TestCase [Examine the service] finished with
                                          status [FINISHED] in 222ms
```

The test steps are actions comprising distinct scenarios. I recommend you be vigilant when naming tests and their segments. Don't be satisfied with default names assigned by the tool. You should even properly name individual assertions. All is green, and the tests were finished in about quarter of a second. Notice the output, and the importance of suitably naming the elements of the test (test suites, test cases, test steps, and assertions). You get a nice report, and everybody can understand what is going on here.

Find General Information Use Case

In this test case we need to actually follow the about link from the home page. When we arrive at the about page, then we need to examine its content (properties and links). In a classical REST API test, you would simply hard-code the URL toward the about page. This is strictly forbidden here, though. Figure 10-2 shows the structure of the matching test suite (it is named About Page).

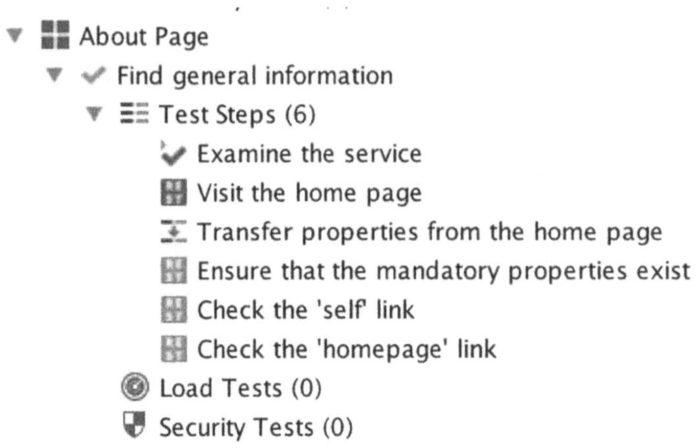

▼ ▦ About Page
   ▼ ✔ Find general information
      ▼ ☰ Test Steps (6)
         ✔ Examine the service
         ▦ Visit the home page
         ⤨ Transfer properties from the home page
         ▦ Ensure that the mandatory properties exist
         ▦ Check the 'self' link
         ▦ Check the 'homepage' link
      ◉ Load Tests (0)
      🛡 Security Tests (0)

Figure 10-2. *This test case has two new elements: the test case runner test step, and the property-transfer test step. These are crucial to implement the Level 3 REST API testing method.*

The about page contains a link back to the home page. To test this link, we need to know what our Billboard URL is. This data comes from the self-link of the home page. Therefore, before using any data from the home page, we would like to have guarantees that it is valid. This is the reason for calling the previous test case (examine the service) as our first step. All subsequent test cases will follow this approach.

The next test step's purpose is to retrieve the content of the home page. This redundancy is intentional to make the test case self-contained. If the home page changes its content in a noncompatible way (e.g., altering the ontology or restructuring the representation), then all affected test cases must fail. The induced extra pain is desirable as a price that anyone has to pay when introducing an incompatible change. It develops empathy with the clients of a service.

■ **Note** Always remember that your REST API tests should care more about the clients of your service than saving the comfort for you and your development team. Developers can always come up with ingenious solutions for incompatibility-tolerant tests, but these will not keep clients happy.

Once we have the content of the home page, then we can extract the relevant details (like the `self` and about links). This time we will get the home page in XML format by specifying the HTTP `Accept` header to be `application/xml`.[2] We need XML to be able to use the `responseAsXml` property of the `Source` section of the property-transfer step. This will be a fine opportunity to introduce you XPath (you can find an XPath tester at `http://www.freeformatter.com`).

The property-transfer test step is the central piece of this test case. The idea is to read out the about link's URL, and pass it down to all consequent test steps. The next three test steps will have their `Endpoint` set to the content of the about link. In this way, they will hit the about page, and be able to perform necessary assertions on it. Besides the about link we also need to transfer the self-link from the home page to the test step validating the back link.[3] The last test step will receive the self-link in its `Domain` property (as it is the

---

[2]Changing output formats might potentially leave some code paths untested. In our case, the representation formats are handled by the Spring HATEOAS framework, whereas our code only contains the core logic of the service. This is a fine example of the *separation of concerns* principle, and the importance of using a powerful underlying framework.

[3]At first glance, you might think that a back link could be transferred inside the HTTTP `Referer` request header. However, this would entail the need for extra contextual information for interpreting the response message. In Level 3 REST APIs, a message must be self-describing. The information inside the previously mentioned header would vanish after the matching request/response cycle is done.

domain referenced by the home page link). Notice that this test step will have its endpoint set (as mentioned earlier) to the about page.

The property-transfer test step might contain multiple transfer definitions. In our case, it has three transfers of the about link to all subsequent steps, and one transfer of the self-link. SoapUI allows you to easily clone all sorts of entities (including transfer definitions), so you don't need to retype them (not a true reuse, but a time saver nevertheless). Figure 10-3 shows the content of the window for this test step.

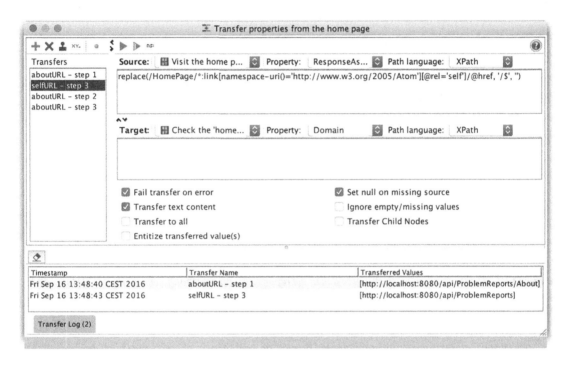

Figure 10-3. *For each transfer you need to fill out the Source and Target sections. The selected content from the source is moved into the target, hence we transfer properties from one place to another.*

All our transfers have their source as the test step to visit the home page. The three transfers of the about link use the following XPath expression:

```
string(/HomePage/*:link[namespace-uri()='http://www.w3.org/2005/Atom'][@rel='about']/@href)
```

It selects the about link's (notice the filtering part [@rel='about']) href property. The namespace definition is mandatory, as the response XML format is based on Atom (although returned here as a bare application/xml). Another possibility is to use the declare namespace statement before the expression to select the content. The self-link transfer is similar, but instead of the string function it uses replace with the regular expression /$ to get rid of the trailing / in the path.

The Transfer Log (lower part of the window) shows the outcomes of these XPath expressions. SoapUI allows you to execute test steps individually. For this step to work you first need to execute the step to get the home page's content. Running steps separately is a good way to debug.

It is also worth mentioning that the next three test steps use a JSON response document, as they ask for application/json. This is a fine example that you can freely mix content formats inside the same test case if you are supported by a great framework such as Spring HATEOAS. Also, notice that the self-link check step is a pure clone (SoapUI allows you to easily create such a clone) of the same test step from the previous test case.

Delete a Problem Report Use Case

This is the final use case that we present in this chapter (the rest will be left as an exercise). It contains some novelties completing the picture about SoapUI (it is still just the tip of the iceberg compared to the possibilities offered by the tool). We will start from the home page, get the contents link, retrieve the list of reports (verifying that we have at least one), select the self-link of the first report from the list, and delete it. Finally, we will make an additional check that the report is really gone. Figure 10-4 shows the structure of this test case.

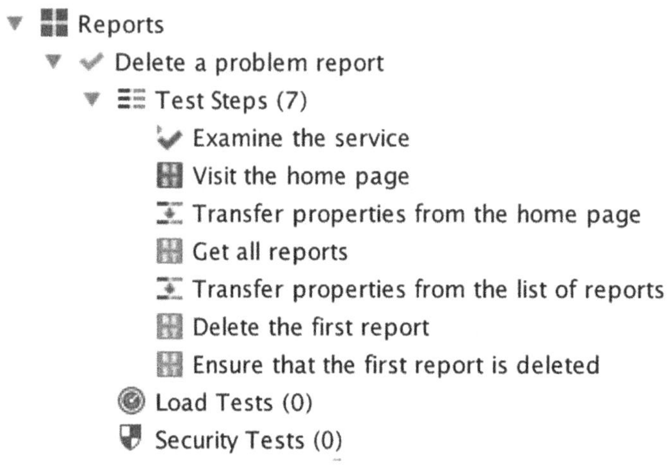

▼ ▪▪ Reports
   ▼ ✔ Delete a problem report
      ▼ ☰☰ Test Steps (7)
            ✔ Examine the service
            ▦ Visit the home page
            ⮂ Transfer properties from the home page
            ▦ Get all reports
            ⮂ Transfer properties from the list of reports
            ▦ Delete the first report
            ▦ Ensure that the first report is deleted
         ⊚ Load Tests (0)
         🛡 Security Tests (0)

Figure 10-4. *This test case uses a test step to delete the report with an assertion to check the HTTP status code. Observe that we don't know anything about URLs except the Billboard URL. Also, we don't care what the first report is. Nothing is hard-coded.*

This test case, as it is currently implemented, leaves the system in an altered state (not a great practice). A better sequence would be as follows (this will be possible after you've implemented the exercise to create new problem reports):

1. Insert a new dummy report.

2. Confirm that this report exists.

3. Delete this report.

4. Confirm that this report doesn't exist anymore.

The get all reports uses a simple assertion to verify that we can reach the first element in the collection of reports. The JSONPath existence expression is $.content[0]. Of course, because accessing reports is a privileged action, the Authorization header is properly set.

The property-transfer step uses the next JSONPath expression for both transfers to select the self-link of the first report from the Response property of the previous step:

```
$.content[0].links[*][?(@.rel==self)].href[0]
```

The step to delete the report is executing an HTTP DELETE method with its Endpoint set by the previous transfer step (you will need to first create a generic DELETE request besides GET; see Figure 10-1). It uses an assertion to check that the returned status value is 204 No Content. The next step is trying to get this report (after being deleted), and an assertion to verify that the status code is 404 Not Found.

Load Testing the Examine the Service Use Case

Load testing this use case is a matter of selecting Case → New Load Test. SoapUI will open a window in which you can set various load test parameters. Figure 10-5 shows the outcome of load testing our use case with a maximum of 10 virtual users using the Thread strategy. We have also set an assertion that the transactions per second (TPS) metric cannot go below 100. Any discrepancy with this threshold is treated as an error. In the middle you can see the statistics graph.

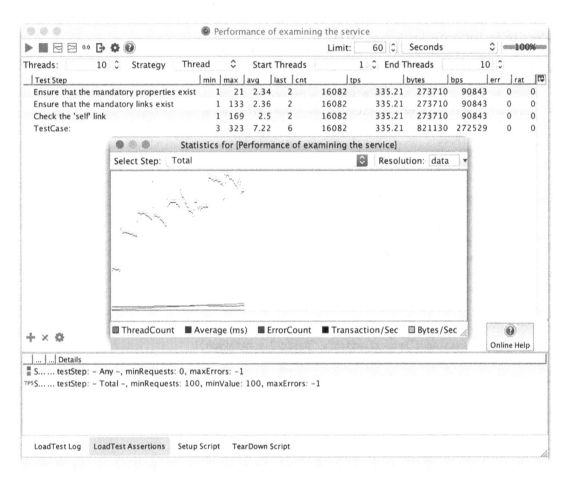

Figure 10-5. *The end result of load testing our use case. All this is available with a single selection of a menu item to create a new load test.*

Case Study: Testing with a Level 3 Tool

We demonstrate here Spring HATEOAS's Traverson API, which is a client-side service traversal facility (see the Spring HATEOAS reference guide's client API theme). This time our task is to test the use case for searching problem reports. We start from the home page, follow the contents link, then use the search link to hit a specific problem report. The correlationId query parameter will be set to T1. Finally, we should ensure that we really got the proper problem report.

We request our resources in HAL hypermedia format, as this will give us more flexibility in handling links. Otherwise, we would always need to use an explicit JSONPath expression to find the URL of a link. With HAL it is just enough to reference the link via its name. This is again a testimony to the power of content negotiation. You can choose the format that best fits the job in a given context.

Here is the source code of the integration test related to searching problem reports (the Java imports are omitted, and the essential details are shown in bold).

```java
package rs.exproit.problem_reports.integration;

@RunWith(SpringJUnit4ClassRunner.class)
@SpringBootTest(webEnvironment = WebEnvironment.RANDOM_PORT)
public final class SearchProblemReports {
    private static final String USERNAME = "scott";
    private static final String PASSWORD = "tiger";
    private static HttpHeaders httpHeaders = new HttpHeaders();

    @LocalServerPort
    private int port;

    @Autowired
    private ServletContext servletContext;

    private Traverson traverson;
    ParameterizedTypeReference<Resources<ProblemReport>> collectionReference =
            new ParameterizedTypeReference<Resources<ProblemReport>>() {};

    @BeforeClass
    public static void setupHTTPHeaders() throws UnsupportedEncodingException {
        String authHash =
                Base64.getEncoder().encodeToString((USERNAME + ":" + PASSWORD).getBytes());
        httpHeaders.add("Authorization", "Basic " + authHash);
    }

    @Before
    public void setupTraversonClient() throws URISyntaxException {
        traverson = new Traverson(
                new URI("http://localhost:" + port + servletContext.getContextPath()),
                MediaTypes.HAL_JSON);
    }

    private Resources<ProblemReport> followTheSearchLink(String correlationId) {
        Map<String, Object> params = new HashMap<>();
        params.put("correlationId", correlationId);

        return traverson.follow("contents")
                        .withHeaders(httpHeaders)
                        .follow("search")
                        .withTemplateParameters(params)
                        .toObject(collectionReference);
    }
}
```

```
@Test
public void searchForTheReportWithTheGivenCorrelationIdAndVerifyIt() throws Exception {
    Resources<ProblemReport> resources = followTheSearchLink("T1");
    assertThat(resources).isNotNull();

    Collection<ProblemReport> reports = resources.getContent();
    assertThat(reports).isNotNull();
    assertThat(reports).hasSize(1);

    ProblemReport report = reports.iterator().next();
    assertThat(report).isNotNull();
    assertThat(report.getReportNumber()).isEqualTo("1");
    assertThat(report.getType()).isEqualTo("http://example.org/errors/out-of-memory");
    assertThat(report.getStatus()).isEqualTo(500);
    assertThat(report.getTitle()).isEqualTo("Out of memory error");

    Link selfLink = report.getId();
    assertThat(selfLink).isNotNull();
    assertThat(selfLink.getHref()).endsWith("/" + report.getReportNumber());
    }
}
```

This test case is marked to be run by Spring's JUnit4 test runner. Our integration test demands a running instance in the background. Test instances should be run frequently, avoiding port collisions. Manually handling port assignments is quite tedious. This is the reason Spring Boot provides you with the ability to use a random port number. Spring also takes care to automatically start up and shut down your service. The system runs using the test application properties (these are situated in the src/test/resources folder). The servlet context is injected by Spring, and we will need it to read out the context (base) path.

Performance tests are ordinarily postponed for later phases of the project, because they aren't intuitive to set up and run. However, that doesn't mean that this is a sacred rule. With SoapUI there is no reason to wait to see whether your service will meet the required Service Level Agreement (SLA). Performing measurements early and often isn't the same as optimizing prematurely and blindly. The latter is bad, whereas the former is wise.

The collectionReference uses the Resources template parameter, as it contains a collection of resources. For a single resource you would use Resource instead of Resources, though.

As our service will use privileged endpoints we need to set up the Authorization HTTP request header. The hash value is calculated by Base64 encoding the username:password string. The implementation uses the Base64 class of Java 8. At any rate, hard-coding login credentials in test cases isn't recommended, but here it is done to keep the example code as simple as possible.

Inside the setupTraversionClient method we clearly demarcate that we would like to get responses in the HAL hypermedia format. Spring HATEOAS has a very nice support for this format, and makes our life much easier (at least when links are in question).

The gist of the test is encompassed inside the followTheSearchLink method. This method accepts the correlation identifier as a parameter (criteria for filtering). This is put inside the template parameters map. The Traverson object is then used to follow the links. Finally, the result is converted into a collectionReference. Notice the technique by which we handle links. This is an example of declarative programming.

In the actual test method, we retrieve the content from our collectionReference, which is a collection of problem reports. We only have a single report satisfying the search condition. As a final step we make sure that the self-link ends with the report number in its path.

Summary

At this point it is instructive to compare the two approaches (SoapUI and Traverson Client API). Both achieve the same goal, although in a different manner. We miht expect more hypermedia support in the current web frameworks and tools. It would be critical to have a test step type in SoapUI that follows links and recognizes hypermedia formats to make SoapUI a Level 3 tool.

COMPLETE THE FUNCTIONAL TESTS

Practice SoapUI

First, complete the functional tests for the current code base. Once you implement the additional features as described in the exercise of Chapter 7, then add the corresponding test cases. Watch out for any potential interplays between tests, which might occur if state-changing test cases are run in an arbitrary order. After completing your functional tests, create the matching load tests, too.

As an additional assignment, refactor the test structure to avoid setting the `Authorization` header explicitly with a fixed Base64-encoded value. In the case of an HTTP Basic scheme, you can provide the username/password combination by using the following host definition (we use the `scot/tiger` pair): `http://scot:tiger@localhost`. See the Traverson-based test case for an example of how to perform Base64 encoding.

PRODUCE SECURITY TESTS

Learn About Web Security

SoapUI enables you to create very sophisticated security tests. These tests are critical, especially if your service is going to be publicly exposed on the Web. Your service will surely be scrutinized by malicious users for potential security issues. Suitably securing your service is a very complex endeavor.

The Basic authentication mechanism, which we have implemented without TLS, is good only for educational purposes. However, when used in combination with a secure channel, it can be a viable choice. Nevertheless, take a look at OAuth 2.0 for a more advanced solution.

YET ANOTHER UNUSUAL TESTING PRACTICE

Get Acquainted with mountebank

Mocking out dependencies is the cornerstone of many test scenarios. The goal is to be able to control the external dependencies while running the tests. There are many well-known frameworks to create stubs and mocks (Spring also has its own support). However, most of these efforts are related to creating mocks inside a local environment. Setting up test doubles over the wire (remote imposters) is a rather atypical case. Imagine that your application has to talk to a remote service, and you need to take control over things at the protocol level (e.g., HTTP, TCP, etc.). This is where mountebank (`http://www.mbtest.org`) comes to your rescue.

The idea is to let your test setup routine talk to mountebank (using its HTTP REST API) to define the remote service's behavior. This would include the protocol, port number, and all the endpoints together with mock data. Mountebank would set up a remote imposter (test double), and you could point your application to talk to that test instance. This approach can be very handy during development, too (when the dependent service isn't even available).

Set up a test double for our example service before running the SoapUI functional tests (SoapUI allows you to define test setup and teardown scripts). The test double would return the same data as our service.

Reference

1. Watkins, John, and Simon Mills. *Testing IT: An Off-the-Shelf Software Testing Process, Second Edition.* New York: Cambridge University Press, 2011.

CHAPTER 11

■ ■ ■

Implementing Messaging APIs

XML and JSON are language-independent and generic message formats, but they lag behind binary formats in efficiency. When you need to craft a system capable of processing high volumes of data, switching to a binary representation is a viable approach. This remark also applies for communication requirements of distributed internal services (many of them are RPC based).[1] The decision regarding the concrete format is very important, as it is usually difficult to switch later to a different one (especially when huge amounts of data are already stored in the old format). The message format is an important part of the system's API.

In a similar fashion as for REST services (they should satisfy a set of architectural constraints of networked systems), there are some desirable features that a binary message format should have. These are listed here (see [1] about the history of Apache Avro,[2] and how it incrementally gained these properties):

- *Generic*: This means that you can easily express arbitrarily complex data structures including nested constructs. For example, comma-separated values (CSV) files leverage a predefined table structure. You cannot intuitively arrange everything into this form.

- *Self-contained*: The format should be accompanied by a schema, and together with the serialized data comprise a unity. It should contain all details for any reader to be capable of understanding the overall structure of a message. Of course, we are neglecting here the semantic gap problem (see Part II of this book).

- *User friendly*: The schema should be specified in an effortless fashion. We definitely don't want to learn yet another cryptic format or to be forced to use some GUI tool to manipulate it. XML uses XML Schema, and JSON leverages JSON Schema. At any rate, each uses a generic, human-readable format for its own purposes. Relying on an already known format reduces the learning curve. Avro's schemas are written in JSON.

- *Efficient*: This immediately entails a binary format, as it is always more performant than its textual counterpart. There are various efficiency criteria. For us they will boil down to size and speed. Therefore, a serialized message should be compact with fast read/write operations. Consequently, the data should be kept separate from its schema to reduce its size.[3]

---

[1]The RPC style tends to introduce more coupling between clients and servers than the REST approach. This is why RPC services might efficiently flourish only inside corporate boundaries. Once again, I'm not stating that they cannot be successful in general, just that they are better suited for internal use. On the other hand, there is no justifiable reason to stick to REST, when RPC could deliver better performance for such inner systems.

[2]You can visit Avro's web site for extensive documentation at `http://avro.apache.org`. Avro does support JSON serialization (besides a binary one), but this is more useful for debugging purposes than in a production setup. REST services can also use this possibility, but using the bare `application/json` as a media type isn't advisable in a Level 3 REST service. All in all, this is the reason Avro is concomitant to a binary encoding of data.

[3]When using a stateless transport in Avro, which boils down to HTTP, each request/response cycle is prefixed with a handshake. During this period a schema is exchanged, too. Therefore, you might want to use this kind of a transport in cases when the actual message payload is much larger than the schema alone. You might also want to reduce the number of such request/response cycles.

© Ervin Varga 2016
E. Varga, *Creating Maintainable APIs*, DOI 10.1007/978-1-4842-2196-9_11

- *Evolvable*: The message format should permit dynamic transformations of a message in most cases without the hurdle of recompiling consumers and producers.[4] We talk more about rules governing schema evolution later in this chapter. This requires an unbound data representation, where data isn't confined inside strict temporal and spatial boundaries. The data should be usable with another schema (follow an open schema definition), and be able to live outside of the producer. Apparently, maintainability is tightly joined with the self-containment property.

- *Big Data friendly*: Handling large amounts of data is the most compelling reason for a binary message format (we have already stated that these are more performant than textual forms). However, solely possessing large data sets without an accompanying Big Data technology isn't a winning situation. Hadoop is currently one of the most popular open source batch processing technologies following the MapReduce paradigm. A binary format should be Hadoop friendly. Accordingly, it should be splittable even in a compressed form. These are quite contradictory requirements, as it is easy to compress a textual file, but nearly impossible to create independent chunks from such a compressed image.

This chapter presents Apache Avro (it is a full-fledged data serialization system), which satisfies all of these constraints. In Chapter 12, we will see how to use Avro in combination with an efficient messaging hub.

Case Study: Load Profile Generator

In this case study, we implement a small simulator of a smart meter, acting as our load profile (LP) generator inside a smart house (for more information about the overall structure of a smart grid, see `http://energy.gov/oe/services/technology-development/smart-grid`). LPs are patterns of electricity usage for a customer or a group of customers over some period of time. Each LP is associated with a context (denoted as a load condition) characterizing the corresponding time period. LPs are generated using historical power usage data. In smart grids, LPs are calculated and collected not only at a transmission and distribution parts of the network, but also at service delivery points via smart meters (see [2] for a neural-network based software framework to handle LPs in real time for classification purposes).

Figure 11-1 shows the components of our sample system. It is made up of the external controller triggering LP generation based on historical daily data (we assume a daily schedule). The controller is presumably connected with meteorological devices to collect load condition data (often designated LP metadata). For now, we assume that the generated LP is saved inside a shared file (accessible by other data processors). Moreover, we will design our load generator to be an RPC service accepting Avro messages. Smart meters are embedded devices with much less CPU power than ordinary computers. Therefore, choosing a lightweight protocol and message format is of utmost importance.

---

[4]Something we can do with XSL on XML documents (for more details visit `http://www.w3schools.com/xsl/`).

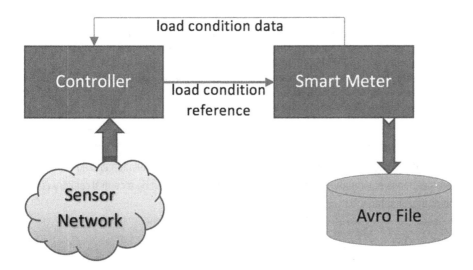

Figure 11-1. *After collecting daily sensor data, the controller triggers the LP creation. It passes only a reference to the daily load condition. An LP processor can use these references in a lazy fashion.*

There are three general data passing scenarios, listed here, where the last one is compliant with a spirit of building maintainable messaging APIs.

- *Send all data expanded at the schema level*: This results in bloated data as well as schema representations. Such shared extensions unnecessarily tie up otherwise disparate services.

- *Send all data, but put extra stuff into a generic field*: Here, the schema is kept lean while the data grows (we refer here to the number of new data elements put inside that generic field, not simply the amount of data).

- *Leverage references to data, and send only the pointer*: This approach builds up a directed acyclic graph (DAG) of referenced data elements. The references must be unique, stable identifiers, which could be used to retrieve the relevant data (in REST services this would always be URLs).

It is extremely tempting and dangerous to introduce so-called black holes into an API (the second case in the preceding list). For example, your service might create a generic extraData field, which presumably should behave as a black box from the perspective of the called service. However, if other services start to "communicate" via your service, and make assumptions about what they are going to put there, then you will open up a Pandora's box. Services will covertly become tightly coupled via this side channel, without anybody being aware of it. Therefore, generic sinks should be carefully monitored.

The third option is especially sensible in our case. Most LP classifiers (a special kind of LP processors) cannot mix metadata with primary LP data. Present LP handling methods have been mostly used for so-called *transversal grouping*, aimed at grouping customers belonging to the same macrocategory in a given period of time. For each customer, the load data monitored over some period of time is averaged and a representative load pattern is produced, which is then used as input for classification purposes. Unfortunately, during this averaging, crucial contextual information is lost. All in all, for these LP classifiers, passing metadata all the time would be a pure waste of bandwidth and storage capacity. The controller is thus better off providing a URL for the collected data. We assume that such data will be retained until the LP classification is done.

This brings us to the notion of *immutability* and *versioning* of data. Each serialized message should carry a version number (denoting the schema that was used for creating it), and a unique identifier.[5] Such a message becomes immutable, as the contained data is the same anytime and anywhere (we are assuming that the message will not be altered without changing its identifier). Avro ensures that data is always accompanied with the matching schema (Avro files are created with a schema as input). You will see in the exercises at the end of Chapter 12 how using schema identifiers instead of full schemas can tremendously boost messaging performance and facilitate maintenance.

■ **Note**   In our example, we compile the message schema using the Avro Maven plug-in. It better simulates the situation with embedded devices and demonstrates this particular technique. Compilation should be avoided for dynamic heterogeneous environments, and schemas should be managed by a central registry (see the exercises at the end of this chapter).

Message Design

Our first task is to design our message API for the smart meter service. This is important because external consumers of the produced data will have to comply with this structure. Avro schemas are specified in the JSON format (see the exercises at the end of this chapter for an Interface Definition Language [IDL] variant). We will demand that the caller provide a reference to the load condition data as URL (don't forget that a URL might designate a different protocol than HTTP). Here is the Avro schema in the JSON Object form for the message representing a daily LP (notice the parts shown in bold).

```
{
  "namespace": "rs.exproit.load_profile_generator.domain",
  "name": "LoadProfileModel",
  "type": "record",
  "doc": "Load profile (LP) data with a reference to the corresponding load condition.",
  "fields": [
    {
      "name": "organizationId",
      "type": ["null", "string"],
      "default": null,
      "order": "ignore",
      "doc": "The unique identifier of the power distribution company."
    },
    {
      "name": "consumerId",
      "type": ["null", "string"],
      "default": null,
      "order": "ignore",
      "doc": "The unique identifier of the consumer inside the power distribution company."
    },
```

---

[5]Often developers choose a simple timestamp (e.g., the creation time in UTC) as an identifier. In an asynchronous distributed system, there is no global clock. Any timestamp could be drifted away from the "current" time. It could happen that the same service would regenerate timestamps, if its clock was moved backward by an NTP daemon (it will try to slow down the fast node, but might even set the time backward in an extreme case). The major problem arises when such timestamps are also used for reasoning about ordering of events.

```
{
  "name": "createdAt",
  "type": "int",
  "logicalType": "date",
  "order": "descending",
  "doc": "The calendar date when this LP was created."
},
{
  "name": "deviceId",
  "type": "string",
  "doc": "The unique device identifier, which generated this LP."
},
{
  "name": "frequency",
  "type": "int",
  "default": 15,
  "order": "ignore",
  "doc": "The sampling frequency in minutes."
},
{
  "name": "consumerCategory",
  "type": {
    "name": "Category",
    "type": "enum",
    "symbols": ["INDUSTRIAL", "RESIDENTIAL"]
  },
  "default": "RESIDENTIAL",
  "doc": "The category of this consumer (industrial or residential)."
},
{
  "name": "loadCondition",
  "type": ["null", "string"],
  "default": null,
  "order": "ignore",
  "doc": "The identifier for the referenced data (may be null if the controller doesn't
  collect meta-data)."
},
{
  "name": "data",
  "type": {
    "type": "array",
    "items": "double"
  },
  "order": "ignore",
  "doc": "The array of samples (Double.NAN if the datum is missing)."
},
{
  "name": "messageHash",
  "type": [
    "null",
    {
```

```
              "type": "fixed",
              "name": "MD5",
              "size": 16
            }
          ],
          "default": null,
          "order": "ignore",
          "doc": "An MD5 hash value of this message (ensures data integrity)."
        },
        {
          "name": "meta",
          "type": [
            "null",
            {
              "type": "map",
              "values": "bytes"
            }
          ],
          "default": null,
          "order": "ignore",
          "doc": "Arbitrary meta data attached by the smart meter."
        }
      ]
    }
```

The schema elements can be placed into a namespace (either defined globally, for the whole message as in our case, or individually). The namespace is used to place the generated code into the designated package to avoid name collisions. You could also use an expanded name; that is, with a namespace part embedded in it (e.g., example.org.LoadProfile). It is mandatory for the message to be named and have a top-level type of record. Fields are defined inside the fields array. Every piece of the schema can be documented via the doc item (I do recommend you attach such documentation, as it is an important detail of your API).

The organizationId is an optional string field with a default value of null. The type of this item is a union, which is denoted by a JSON array (it could contain multiple type references). The serialized messages are ordered inside the object container (like an Avro file), and the order field controls the role of the current item in that process. The default is an ascending ordering, but for fields unimportant from the ordering perspective, it should be ignore.

The createdAt and deviceId fields comprise a composite identifier of this message. The former is a logical type of date with a descending ordering (we would like to have the most recent LPs listed first). A logical type is a semantic extension of the base type, in our case int. Avro defines a couple of logical types, which could become handy in making stricter statements about fields.

The consumerCategory is an enumeration, denoted by the type designator of enum. Enums behave in a similar way as in C++ (they are not full-blown classes as in Java). We need this enumeration to differentiate between industrial and residential consumers (they are treated differently in an electrical grid).

The LP data is stored inside the data field of type array. We see that elements of this array are all double precision floating point numbers (they are marked as double). They represent samples expressed in kW. The messageHash is an optional MD5 hash value of type fixed. This is a complex type with a predefined size (in our case 16 bytes = 128 bits). Finally, the meta is an optional field to store additional metadata produced by the smart meter. It is a map with keys that are strings (Avro strings are not the same as Java strings, so conversions are necessary), and values that are sequences of bytes. The Avro file could also contain metadata, but that applies to a whole file. The meta field in our schema is linked to an individual message.

> ■ **Caution** Can you spot a dangerous detail in the schema? A seemingly innocuous meta section might turn into a *black hole*, as discussed earlier. This could happen if it is abused by components in the system. I have put it here just to better illustrate the point. You should be very careful what you declare as meta in your API. This remark also applies in any context where messages are passed around; that is, it is universal.

Project Setup

We will set up a Maven project for our smart meter simulator. The pom.xml file should contain the following elements pertaining to Avro (the avro.version property is set to be 1.8.1).

```
<dependency>
    <groupId>org.apache.avro</groupId>
    <artifactId>avro</artifactId>
    <version>${avro.version}</version>
</dependency>
<dependency>
    <groupId>org.apache.avro</groupId>
    <artifactId>avro-ipc</artifactId>
    <version>${avro.version}</version>
</dependency>

<plugin>
    <groupId>org.apache.avro</groupId>
    <artifactId>avro-maven-plugin</artifactId>
    <version>1.8.1</version>
    <executions>
        <execution>
            <phase>generate-sources</phase>
            <goals>
                <goal>schema</goal>
                <goal>protocol</goal>
            </goals>
            <configuration>
                <sourceDirectory>${project.basedir}/src/main/avro/</sourceDirectory>
                <outputDirectory>${project.basedir}/src/main/java/</outputDirectory>
            </configuration>
        </execution>
    </executions>
</plugin>
```

We will also save our message Avro schema inside the src/main/avro folder in a file named load-profile.avsc. After invoking Maven to generate sources (summon mvn compile) we will get three new source files inside the rs.exproit.load_profile_generator.domain package: Category.java, LoadProfile.java, and MD5.java.

Before proceeding, it would be beneficial to read the Avro specification, and take a look at some RPC examples (like https://github.com/phunt/avro-rpc-quickstart). If you haven't worked with Netty before, you should take a look at that, as well.

RPC Protocol Design

Avro also supports RPC, and allows you to define the RPC API using JSON. For now, we only add a single method for a controller to trigger the LP creation process. The controller will only pass the URL for load condition data or null. Here is the Avro protocol schema in JSON, situated inside the same folder as the message schema, with the name load-profile.avpr (observe the parts shown in bold).

```
{
  "namespace": "rs.exproit.load_profile_generator.protocol",
  "protocol": "LoadProfileRPC",
  "doc": "The RPC API of our smart meter.",
  "types": [
    {
      "name": "LPCreationRequest",
      "type": "record",
      "fields": [
        {
          "name": "loadCondition",
          "type": ["null", "string"],
          "default": null,
          "doc": "The identifier for the referenced data (may be null if the controller
          doesn't collect meta-data)."
        }
      ]
    },
    {
      "name": "ServiceError",
      "type": "error",
      "fields": [
        {
          "name": "code",
          "type": "int",
          "doc": "The application error code."
        },
        {
          "name": "message",
          "type": "string",
          "doc": "The application error message."
        }
      ]
    }
  ],

  "messages": {
    "lpCreate": {
      "request": [{"name": "request", "type": "LPCreationRequest"}],
      "response": "string",
      "errors": ["ServiceError"]
    }
  }
}
```

RPC is about passing messages containing data about remote method invocations over the network. Our smart meter implements the LoadProfileRPC protocol with a single method lpCreate. We define two types here: the LPCreationRequest for describing what to provide as input, and the ServiceError for explaining the service-specific error response. The messages section contains all the endpoints of our RPC API (currently only one). These message definitions reference the types we defined earlier in the protocol schema. As a response we pass back the string representation of the produced load profile. Finally, the error is effectively a union type of ["string", "ServiceError"], which is constructed for us by Avro. The ordinary string type is used for internal server errors (those that don't even reach our service).

Service Implementation

The implementation is rather trivial, as we simulate most complex load profile data acquisition tasks with some dummy stuff. The RPC subsystem uses the Netty client server framework (see http://netty.io). We have a service wrapper (to start and stop the internal Netty server) as well as the remote method handler. Here are the listings for these (Java imports are omitted, and salient details are shown in bold), respectively.

```
package rs.exproit.load_profile_generator;

public final class App {
    private static final String DATA_FILE = "load_profiles.avro";
    private volatile Server server;
    private volatile LoadProfileRPCImpl loadProfileRPC;

    public App() throws IOException {
        loadProfileRPC = new LoadProfileRPCImpl(DATA_FILE);
    }

    public App(LoadProfileRPCImpl loadProfileRPC) throws IOException {
        this.loadProfileRPC = loadProfileRPC;
    }

    /**
     * Starts the service if not already started. Trying to start a previously started
       service
     * does nothing.
     * @throws IOException if any error occurs during the startup.
     */
    public void start(int port) throws IOException {
        if (server == null) {
            server = new NettyServer(
                    new SpecificResponder(LoadProfileRPC.class, loadProfileRPC),
                    new InetSocketAddress(port));
        }
    }

    /**
     * Stops the service if it is running. Once stopped it cannot be restarted anymore.
     */
    public void stop() {
        if (server != null) {
            try {
```

```java
                loadProfileRPC.shutdown();
            } finally {
                server.close();
            }
        }
    }

    /**
     * Get the port number on what the service is running.
     * @throws IllegalStateException if the service isn't running.
     */
    public int port() {
        if (server != null) {
            return server.getPort();
        } else {
            throw new IllegalStateException();
        }
    }

    /**
     * The main entry point of this service.
     *
     * @param args the only command line argument is the port number.
     * @throws IOException if any error occurs during the startup.
     */
    public static void main(String[] args) throws IOException {
        if (args.length != 1) {
            System.err.println("You need to specify the port number!");
            System.exit(1);
        }

        final App app = new App();
        int port = Integer.parseInt(args[0]);
        app.start(port);

        Runtime.getRuntime().addShutdownHook(new Thread() {
            @Override
            public void run() {
                app.stop();
            }
        });

        try {
            // We should wait until the Netty server starts up.
            Thread.sleep(5000);
        } catch (InterruptedException e) {
            e.printStackTrace();
        }
    }
}

package rs.exproit.load_profile_generator;
```

```
final class LoadProfileRPCImpl implements LoadProfileRPC {
    static final String DEVICE_ID_PREFIX = "SM_";
    private static final DatumWriter<LoadProfileModel> lpDatumWriter =
            new SpecificDatumWriter<>(LoadProfileModel.class);
    private final File dataFile;

    LoadProfileRPCImpl(String dataFile) {
        this.dataFile = new File(dataFile);
    }

    private List<Double> doubleArrayToList(double[] array) {
        return DoubleStream
                .of(array)
                .mapToObj(Double::valueOf)
                .collect(Collectors.toList());
    }

    private final Random rnd = new Random(1L);
    private final Category[] consumerTypes = Category.values();

    private LoadProfileModel acquireLP() {
        double[] lpData = new double[4 * 24];
        for (int i = 0; i < lpData.length; i++) {
            lpData[i] = rnd.nextDouble() * 1000;
        }

        return LoadProfileModel
                .newBuilder()
                // Simulate LP creation for various days.
                .setCreatedAt(rnd.nextInt(Integer.MAX_VALUE))
                .setDeviceId(DEVICE_ID_PREFIX + rnd.nextInt(100))
                .setData(doubleArrayToList(lpData))
                // Simulate different category of consumers.
                .setConsumerCategory(consumerTypes[rnd.nextInt(consumerTypes.length)])
                .build();
    }

    public CharSequence lpCreate(LPCreationRequest request)
            throws AvroRemoteException, ServiceError {
        LoadProfileModel lpModel = acquireLP();
        lpModel.setLoadCondition(request.getLoadCondition());

        try (
            DataFileWriter<LoadProfileModel> dataFileWriter =
                    new DataFileWriter<>(lpDatumWriter);
        ){
            if (dataFile.exists() && !dataFile.isDirectory()) {
                dataFileWriter.appendTo(dataFile);
            } else {
                dataFileWriter.setMeta("about", "Sample generated data file for chapter 11.");
                dataFileWriter.setCodec(CodecFactory.snappyCodec());
                dataFileWriter.create(lpModel.getSchema(), dataFile);
```

```
            }
            dataFileWriter.append(lpModel);
            return lpModel.toString();
        } catch (Exception e) {
            throw ServiceError
                    .newBuilder()
                    .setCode(1)
                    .setMessage$(e.getMessage())
                    .build();
        }
    }

    public void shutdown() {
    }
}
```

In the main App class, we start up the Netty server, passing it an instance of our remote method handler LoadProfileRPCImpl. The LoadProfileRPC class is autogenerated by Avro's Maven plug-in. We just need to ensure that the server gets closed on exit. The service can be started up in stand-alone mode using the following commands from the project's home folder (the first step is only needed the first time):

```
mvn clean test
mvn -q exec:java -Dexec.mainClass=rs.exproit.load_profile_generator.App -Dexec.args=<port>
```

The method handler uses Avro's DatumWriter to serialize load profile messages (instances of the LoadProfileModel class). The method acquireLP creates a new dummy load profile instance via the provided builder facility (it automatically sets all default values). It uses the auxiliary method doubleArrayToList for converting an array of doubles (double[]) into a list of doubles (List<Double>). The trick is to leverage Java 8 Streams API.

The lpCreate method uses the *try-with-resources* statement to guarantee that the file writer is properly closed at the exit of the method. If a data file already exists, then the next write is prepared via the appendTo call. Otherwise, a new data file is produced. The about meta field[6] tells what this file contains, and the codec is set to Google's Snappy (it protects data blocks with CRC checks, something we definitely want with sensitive data as load profiles). Finally, the new load profile is appended to a data file via the append method. In the case of an error, we throw our custom ServiceError instance.

It should be noted that the concurrency model of the LoadProfileWriter class implements the *one writer per file* rule. If you want multiple parallel writers per file, then additional synchronization would be needed (you should really question why would you want this here). The lpDatumWriter field is static, as it is assumed that all data files will follow the same schema per smart meter directive.

Notice the setMessage$ method of the ServiceError class, which extends the SpecificExceptionBase checked exception class (it is an indirect child of Exception). ServiceError inherits the getMessage method from its parent class (for a tool, a "getter" is enough to figure out the property's name). However, we have specified that our custom exception should have code and message properties. Naively, we will hope that the latter will be mapped onto the message property of an Exception. Avro automatically attaches the $ symbol to avoid name collisions, and doesn't try to interpret what you mean by message. Nonetheless, this can create a problem, as anybody expecting to find a custom exception message by calling the usual getMessage method would be surprised (the compiler will not issue an error). You must be careful with such name collisions. Any time you find $ in a generated method name, simply change your specification. In our case, instead of message we should have used reason. Hours of debugging time can be spent on these silly mistakes, so being acquainted with the nuances of the target framework is always beneficial.

---

[6]You can use the isReservedMeta method of the DatumFileWriter class as a sanity check, whether or not your meta field is already reserved by Avro.

Integration Test

It is quite straightforward to implement an integration test with our service running in the background (it is automatically started and stopped by the test). The test code triggers two load profile creations, and checks the responses. Here is the listing (Java imports are omitted, and important sections are shown in bold).

```java
package rs.exproit.load_profile_generator;

public class ClientServerTest {
    private static final String TEST_DATA_FILE ="load_profiles_test.avro";
    private static final int PORT = 65111;

    private App app;
    private NettyTransceiver client;

    @Before
    public void createClient() throws IOException {
        app = new App(new LoadProfileRPCImpl(TEST_DATA_FILE));
        app.start(PORT);
        client = new NettyTransceiver(new InetSocketAddress(PORT));
    }

    @After
    public void closeClient() {
        client.close();
        app.stop();
        new File(TEST_DATA_FILE).delete();
    }

    private LPCreationRequest createRequest(String loadCondition) {
        LPCreationRequest request = LPCreationRequest.newBuilder().build();
        if (loadCondition != null) {
            request.setLoadCondition(loadCondition);
        }
        return request;
    }

    @Test
    public void triggerLPCreationsAndValidateThatDataIsSaved() throws IOException {
        LoadProfileRPC proxy = SpecificRequestor.getClient(LoadProfileRPC.class, client);

        String response;
        for (int i = 0; i < 100; i++) {
            response = proxy
              .lpCreate(createRequest("http://example.org/api/Controller/LoadConditions/"
              + i))
              .toString();
            assertNotNull(response);
            assert(response).contains(
        "\"loadCondition\": \"http://example.org/api/Controller/LoadConditions/" + i
        + "\"");
```

```
    }
    response = proxy.lpCreate(createRequest(null)).toString();
    assertNotNull(response);
    assert(response).contains("\"loadCondition\": null");
  }
}
```

The createClient and closeClient methods are setting up as well as tearing down the stage, respectively. Of course, a client cannot be created before the smart meter service is up and running. The Avro RPC provides a client with a proxy for remote methods (a classical technique in the RPC world). A client's programming model follows the local one. If the remote call is successful, then the response contains the string representation of the created LP. This is validated inside the test case. This test case can serve as an elementary tutorial on how to use the service and implement a client.

Summary

We have seen a new type of service API based on the RPC model together with binary formatted messages. Apache Avro delivers a universal model to build efficient internal services with Hadoop-friendly data representations. All schemas are specified in JSON (there are even tools to convert an Avro schema into a JSON Schema). Avro is designed for evolution, and the rules about extending the schemas (both message and protocol) in compatible fashion are encoded in the official specification itself (see http://avro. apache.org/docs/current/spec.html#Schema+Resolution). Avro schemas can even contain aliases to map terms from one schema into another.

SCHEMA REGISTRY

A Truly Dynamic Solution

An Avro container file is always preserved with the schema, so any service can figure out the structure of the contained messages by reading it out. In RPC the schemas are exchanged during the handshaking phase. Nevertheless, there are situations when schemas should be transmitted before message transfer can begin (e.g., when messages are encoded or decoded directly). A proper solution would be to introduce a central place where schemas can be stored, searched, and retrieved.

One really sophisticated Avro schema registry (a perfect choice with Kafka) is available at https:// github.com/confluentinc/schema-registry. It stores a versioned history of schemas, and even understands compatibility directives. Try to set up this registry, and put your message and protocol schemas there.

IDL

Practice the IDL Format for Protocol Schemas

Avro also supports an alternative protocol schema format called Interface Definition Language (IDL). Visit the documentation at http://avro.apache.org/docs/current/idl.html, and convert our JSON protocol schema into IDL. Don't forget to add the idl-protocol goal into the pom.xml file.

ANALYZING THE DATA

Embarking into the Big Data World

The Avro file is Hadoop friendly, as it is already stored as a compressed chain of blocks with end-of-block markers (it is very hard to achieve a perfect alignment between logical and physical blocks, so some tolerance is required). To process your data in Avro format you can either develop a Hadoop code, or use high-level frameworks like Pig or Hive. The latter provides you with a convenient SQL view over your data. For an excellent introduction how to use Hive with Avro, visit `https://cwiki.apache.org/confluence/display/Hive/AvroSerDe`. I recommend that you use the latest version of Hive and Avro. For more information about Hive (it is part of the Hadoop ecosystem), you can visit `https://hive.apache.org`.

You should first generate some test data by reusing the `ClientServerTest` class (you might want to avoid the deletion of a test data file, so create a new version of this class), or directly using an instance of the `LoadProfileWriter` class in your code. You should then connect Hive with your data file, and map the contained load profile data as a Hive table.

Create a SQL `SELECT` statement to find the global minimum and maximum consumption values separately for residential and industrial customers. To be able to judge the correctness of your SQL statement, don't produce random load profile consumption values in your bootstrap code (the code you used to generate the Avro file).

References

1. Cutting, Doug . *Avro Data*. Sebastopol, CA: O'Reilly Media, 2011.

2. Varga, Ervin D., Sándor F. Beretka, Christian Noce, and Gianluca Sapienza, "Robust Real-Time Load Profile Encoding and Classification Framework for Efficient Power Systems Operation." *IEEE Transactions on Power Systems*, Volume 30, Issue 4, July 2015.

3. Helland, P. "Data on the Outside versus Data on the Inside." Paper presented at the 2005 CIDR Conference.

CHAPTER 12

■ ■ ■

Apache Kafka as a Messaging Hub

A message-oriented middleware (MOM) with an associated system built on top of it is targeting scenarios where the action–reaction cycle is desirable to be separated both in space and time. This allows clients and servers[1] to be detached from each other, and follow their intrinsic life cycle. The Java Message Service (JMS) includes a generic API for interfacing with MOMs fulfilling its specification (a typical example is ActiveMQ available at http://activemq.apache.org). Many MOMs don't follow the JMS standard to offer lightweight or specialized messaging hubs (e.g., ZeroMQ is an ultralight distributed messaging solution, available at http://zeromq.org). Apache Kafka (see https://kafka.apache.org) trades JMS support for superb performance and scalability. It is worth noting that ActiveMQ, ZeroMQ, and Kafka have drastically different designs, and are intended for different purposes. Therefore, by using Kafka in this chapter I'm not favoring it over the others. In many use cases, Kafka would be overkill (if you don't expect a huge load of about 100,000+ messages per second, then you should consider an alternative, lighter MOM). We cover the major features of Kafka throughout the following case study.

Case Study: Distributed LP Classification System

Chapter 11 introduced an example system made up of a central controller and a smart meter. The latter generates a daily load profile when triggered by the controller. However, it stores the data locally. Usually, low-capacity devices send data to a place where it can be analyzed. A device might keep short-term historical data, but definitely cannot perform any serious exploration of that data. Moreover, in an electrical grid you are interested in collecting data from many devices to observe trends. Therefore, fast data movement becomes an enabler for the efficient operation of a smart grid.

Each produced load profile is essentially an event[2] in the smart grid (it is a large-scale distributed system), and a sequence of such events make up the event log. Devices should only know about the destination log, where to announce events. We talk here about events instead of ordinary messages, as we do care about their structure and semantics (the foremost goal is to produce machine-processable data). Using Avro to serialize load profiles has equipped us with events (schema + data) together with an RPC API for the smart meter. Apache Kafka is here to solve our problem of efficiently delivering those events to their destinations (there can be many interested parties to watch for those events). The crucial point is that devices shouldn't know anything about the consumers of published data. In other words, producers

---

[1] A client/server model is an abstraction in distributed systems, where at a given moment in time, we can identify a pair of collaborating components; one as a service provider (server), and the other as its user (client). In MOMs, it is better to speak of peers, as the roles of clients and servers can change quite rapidly.

[2] By an *event* we assume a compact, well-structured, and machine-processable message.

© Ervin Varga 2016
E. Varga, *Creating Maintainable APIs*, DOI 10.1007/978-1-4842-2196-9_12

and consumers should be shielded from both referential and temporal couplings.[3] This is the essence of the *publish-subscribe* messaging style. Kafka is its principal representative as a fault-tolerant, durable, and distributed event log (Kafka uses the term *message* for a unit of data, but we stick to event).

■ **Note**   To create a rich data ecosystem, where producers and consumers can evolve independently, you need to establish a sound system to provide maintainable message schemas. This is the reason Avro and Kafka make a superb combination. Working directly with XML/JSON documents isn't a performant solution, especially in the context of Big Data.

Figure 12-1 shows the architecture of our extended example, with Kafka sitting between a smart meter and the LP classifier. Once we standardize on an event format, then we can easily attach new consumers or chain them together (consumers of input data might become producers of the transformed data).

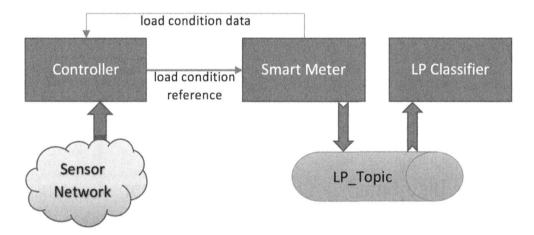

Figure 12-1. *The controller triggers the LP creation by passing the load condition reference. The smart meter generates the LP event, and publishes it inside the Kafka topic for LP. Finally, the LP classifier consumes the event, and processes it (either stores it, or handles it immediately).*

Our task here is to set up a stand-alone Kafka broker, change the `LoadProfileRPCImpl` class of the smart meter, and implement the LP classifier (it will read events from Kafka, and just dump them on the console).

Setting Up Kafka

The easiest way to set up Kafka (at the time of this writing its version is 0.10.0.1) is to use Docker Compose (see `https://docs.docker.com/compose/overview/`) with the following `docker-compose.yaml` file (it is located inside the `docker` folder of this chapter's source code).

---

[3]Establishing direct connections with all types of data processors wouldn't scale. The only allowable direct connection is between a smart meter and a broker (a component that facilitates event publication). By using a MOM any temporal coupling is eliminated by letting the producer emit a message even if nobody is listening on the other side of a channel. Referential decoupling means that a producer doesn't know or care who will consume the message. Of course, you might have higher level temporal dependencies and ordering constraints in a distributed system, but we are talking here about a single request/response cycle.

```
version: '2'
services:
  zookeeper:
    image: wurstmeister/zookeeper
    restart: always
    ports:
      - "2181:2181"
  kafka:
    image: wurstmeister/kafka
    restart: always
    ports:
      - "9092:9092"
    environment:
      KAFKA_ADVERTISED_HOST_NAME: ${DOCKER_HOST_IP}
      KAFKA_AUTO_CREATE_TOPICS_ENABLE: "false"
      KAFKA_DELETE_TOPIC_ENABLE: "true"
      KAFKA_CREATE_TOPICS: "load_profile:3:1"
      KAFKA_ZOOKEEPER_CONNECT: zookeeper:2181
    volumes:
      - /var/run/docker.sock:/var/run/docker.sock
```

This Docker Compose file requires the DOCKER_HOST_IP environment variable to be set to the IP address of the host machine. On Mac OS X and Linux this can be easily retrieved using the ifconfig command (on Windows it is ipconfig). To start up the Kafka broker, simply issue: docker-compose up -d. The output from docker-compose ps should be as follows:

```
Name                  Command                    State  Ports
----------------------------------------------------------------------------------------
-----
docker_kafka_1        start-kafka.sh             Up     0.0.0.0:9092->9092/tcp
docker_zookeeper_1    /bin/sh -c /usr/sbin/sshd  ... Up 0.0.0.0:2181->2181/tcp, 22/tcp,
                                                        2888/tcp, 3888/tcp
```

This startup file will create the topic load_profile for our sample system (with three partitions[4] and a replication factor of 1). To test that the broker is properly running you might want to create a test topic, put messages into it, read them out, and finally remove the topic (notice that we have enabled topic deletion in the startup file). Here is the dump of the command-line session, where each command is separated with a horizontal line (the first line happens on the host, and the rest occur inside the running container).

```
docker exec -it docker_kafka_1 /bin/bash
----------------------------------------------------------------------------------------
-----
bash-4.3# cd /opt/kafka_2.11-0.10.0.1/bin/
----------------------------------------------------------------------------------------
-----
bash-4.3# ./kafka-topics.sh --create --zookeeper $KAFKA_ZOOKEEPER_CONNECT --replication-
factor 1 --partitions 1 --topic test
```

---

[4]A configuration with three partitions per topic with a single broker is only good for educational purposes (we use this setup to showcase our custom partitioner).

```
Created topic "test".
---------------------------------------------------------------------------------
-----
bash-4.3# ./kafka-topics.sh --zookeeper $KAFKA_ZOOKEEPER_CONNECT --describe --topic test
Topic:test     PartitionCount:1    ReplicationFactor:1        Configs:
Topic: test    Partition: 0        Leader: 1001    Replicas: 1001    Isr: 1001
---------------------------------------------------------------------------------
-----
bash-4.3# ./kafka-console-producer.sh --broker-list localhost:9092 --topic test
Event 1
Event 2
^D
---------------------------------------------------------------------------------
-----
bash-4.3# ./kafka-console-consumer.sh --zookeeper $KAFKA_ZOOKEEPER_CONNECT --topic test
--from-beginning
Event 1
Event 2
^CProcessed a total of 2 messages
---------------------------------------------------------------------------------
-----
bash-4.3# ./kafka-topics.sh --zookeeper $KAFKA_ZOOKEEPER_CONNECT --delete --topic test
Topic test is marked for deletion.
Note: This will have no impact if delete.topic.enable is not set to true.
---------------------------------------------------------------------------------
-----
bash-4.3# exit
exit
```

Overall, we see that our Kafka broker is properly functioning (we have created a new topic, sent a couple of messages into it, read them out, and deleted the topic). To fully remove the Kafka broker issue docker-compose kill and docker-compose rm. To stop just the "cluster," summon docker-compose stop. At any rate, the setup here isn't viable for large systems (for small ones it will work[5]). You would want to create a full cluster of machines, and fine-tune the settings (see [1] for details). After all, Kafka is designed for an enormous load, and is rarely justifiable for tiny systems.

Refactoring the Smart Meter to Use Kafka

Kafka comes with its own Client API for implementing custom producers and consumers. Kafka also has its own binary wire protocol, and it is also possible to hook into this low-level network layer (there are many clients available; see https://cwiki.apache.org/confluence/display/KAFKA/Clients). We use the materials provided by Kafka itself for simplicity reasons (otherwise, Kafka's Client API has a satisfactory performance for most use cases).

---

[5]Our docker-compose.yaml file is set up for a single broker (the port number on the host is fixed; notice the bold part in the listing). To create multiple brokers on a single machine (to boost performance on a multicore machine) you should delete that bolded 9092: part (we are assuming that at this moment the cluster isn't yet created). You would then be able to scale the running cluster (after starting it up) with a simple command of docker-compose scale kafka=3 (for three brokers). Don't forget that the port numbers on the host for those brokers will be dynamically allocated (they are visible after executing docker-compose ps). Therefore, you will need to alter the bootstrap.servers property inside the configuration file for both a producer and a consumer.

As there are potentially lots of smart meters in a smart grid, we envisage a high aggregate load (the throughput should be high for the Kafka cluster as well as for the consumers). The latency for producers of daily load profiles will not be that important. As LP classification is often used to decide on prices, it is imperative that we don't lose messages or duplicate them. All these decisions affect how we are going to craft our custom producer, and what configuration options will we use. Of course, the primary setup revolves around the Kafka cluster itself, and for production use it could be very complicated (refer to the Kafka documentation for all possible broker, producer, and consumer parameters that you can set).

As a first step, we need to add the following dependency to the pom.xml file, where the kafka.version is set to 0.10.0.1:

```
<dependency>
    <groupId>org.apache.kafka</groupId>
    <artifactId>kafka-clients</artifactId>
    <version>${kafka.version}</version>
</dependency>
```

This brings in the Kafka Client API artifacts. We configure our producer using the following settings (the others are kept with their defaults) stored inside the config/kafka-producer.properties file:

```
bootstrap.servers=localhost:9092
acks=all
retries=3
batch.size=2048
compression.type=snappy
key.serializer=org.apache.kafka.common.serialization.StringSerializer
value.serializer=org.apache.kafka.common.serialization.ByteArraySerializer
```

In production, the list of candidate brokers would be greater than one (this increases the fault tolerance of the system). The acks is set to all, which means that the producer will wait for all brokers to acknowledge the reception of the event (see also the broker configuration parameter min.insync.replicas in the Kafka documentation). This option increases reliability, but is acceptable only in situations when latency isn't a concern. The retries is set to 3, which also boosts reliability by letting Kafka automatically retry the delivery of an event in the case of errors.[6] The batch size is reduced to 2K, as a smart meter will only send a full LP once per day. The compression algorithm is Snappy, as it has good performance, and low CPU requirements (perfect for embedded devices). We use the deviceId as our event key, and serialize our load profile data into a sequence of bytes.

■ **Caution**   Even if we perfectly tune everything pertaining to our Kafka producer, we might still end up with duplicate events. If the controller doesn't receive a response from a smart meter, then it cannot reliably conclude that the previous RPC request has failed. Therefore, it might retry the RPC call. We are assuming that the idempotency will be assured by the LP classifier (events are uniquely identified by a composite key made up from the LP creation date and device identifier). This means that it must keep track of events that it has received, and ignore duplicates.

---

[6]In our case we don't bother about an ordering issue. However, if you want to keep proper ordering of records with multiple retries, then you should also set the max.in.flight.requests.per.connection producer configuration parameter to 1.

The custom partitioner puts industrial customers into a separate partition (always the last one in the cluster), while using distributed hashing over the remaining partitions for the residential customers. This simulates the situation of having much less industrial customers than residential ones. Here is the listing of the LoadProfilePartitioner class (the Java imports are omitted, and important parts are shown in bold).

```
package rs.exproit.load_profile_generator;

final class LoadProfilePartitioner {
    public int partition(String topic, String key, LoadProfileModel value, int
numPartitions) {
        int lastPartitionIdx = numPartitions - 1;
        try {
            if (value.getConsumerCategory() == Category.INDUSTRIAL) {
                return lastPartitionIdx;
            } else {
                if (lastPartitionIdx > 0) {
                    return (Math.abs(Utils.murmur2(key.getBytes()))) % lastPartitionIdx;
                } else {
                    return lastPartitionIdx;
                }
            }
        } catch (NullPointerException | ClassCastException e) {
            throw new InvalidRecordException("Key or value is missing or isn't valid.");
        }
    }
}
```

The partition method is called for each event. The interesting part is the Utils.murmur2 method, which does the hash computation (the output from the murmur2 method is a noncryptographic hash used for lookups). The index of the output partition is then a modulus of this uniform hash function in regard to the number of partitions (in our case one less than the total number of partitions, as industrial customers are put into the last one). Kafka also has a property called partitioner.class, which should point to a class implementing the Partitioner interface. However, in that case the class has to be public, and implement other methods not relevant in our case. In the spirit of TDD, the design of this class was driven by the following unit test:

```
package rs.exproit.load_profile_generator;
// Imports are omitted...

public class LoadProfilePartitionerTest {
    private static final String TEST_TOPIC = "test";
    private final LoadProfilePartitioner partitioner = new LoadProfilePartitioner();
    private final LoadProfileModel lp;

    public LoadProfilePartitionerTest() {
        List<Double> data = Arrays.asList(0.1, 200.2);
        lp = LoadProfileModel
                .newBuilder()
                .setCreatedAt(0)
                .setDeviceId("SM_05")
                .setConsumerCategory(Category.RESIDENTIAL)
                .setData(data)
                .build();
    }
```

```
@Test
public final void getPartitionIndexForTheTopicWithASinglePartition() {
    assertEquals(0, partitioner.partition(TEST_TOPIC, lp.getDeviceId().toString(), lp,
    1));
    lp.setDeviceId("SM_12");
    assertEquals(0, partitioner.partition(TEST_TOPIC, lp.getDeviceId().toString(), lp,
    1));
    lp.setConsumerCategory(Category.INDUSTRIAL);
    assertEquals(0, partitioner.partition(TEST_TOPIC, lp.getDeviceId().toString(), lp,
    1));
}

@Test
public final void getPartitionIndexForTheTopicWithMultiplePartitions() {
    assertEquals(0, partitioner.partition(TEST_TOPIC, lp.getDeviceId().toString(), lp,
    3));
    lp.setDeviceId("SM_12");
    assertEquals(1, partitioner.partition(TEST_TOPIC, lp.getDeviceId().toString(), lp,
    3));
    lp.setConsumerCategory(Category.INDUSTRIAL);
    assertEquals(2, partitioner.partition(TEST_TOPIC, lp.getDeviceId().toString(), lp,
    3));
}
}
```

Figure 12-2 shows the situation with a single broker, three partitions per topic, and a single consumer. With three brokers each partition would be assigned to one broker. With a replication factor of three, each partition would also be replicated on each broker. Every partition will have its primary broker, and the others will be part of the replica set. Increasing the number of partitions of a topic is the principal scaling mechanism in Kafka. The same logic applies for consumers. If you increase the number of consumers (assuming they all belong to the same group), then they will start consuming events only from partitions assigned to them. Kafka will guarantee that the set of partitions, assigned to consumers belonging to the same group, are disjunctive. In this way, you could speed up the processing of events from a topic without a danger of picking up the same event by multiple consumers (there are edge cases when duplication might occur, but refer to [1] for more details).

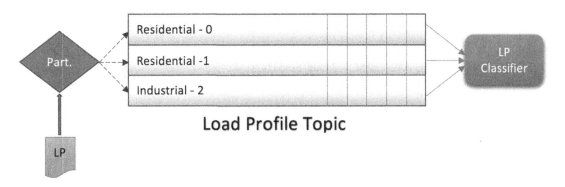

Figure 12-2. *The event is passed to a partitioner, which decides into what partition it will go. The consumer is reading out events from a topic (in our case all partitions are assigned to a single consumer). Events are only guaranteed to be ordered inside the same partition.*

The refactored part inside the LoadProfileRPCImpl class looks like the following (notice the lines shown in bold).

```
private final LoadProfileWriter lpWriter;

LoadProfileRPCImpl() throws IOException {
    lpWriter = new LoadProfileWriter();
}

LoadProfileRPCImpl(LoadProfileWriter lpWriter){
    this.lpWriter = lpWriter;
}

public CharSequence lpCreate(LPCreationRequest request)
        throws AvroRemoteException, ServiceError {
    LoadProfileModel lpModel = acquireLP();
    lpModel.setLoadCondition(request.getLoadCondition());

    try {
        lpWriter.sendLP(lpModel);
        return lpModel.toString();
    } catch (Exception e) {
        throw ServiceError
                .newBuilder()
                .setCode(1)
                .setMessage$(e.getMessage())
                .build();
    }
}

void shutdown() {
    lpWriter.shutdown();
}
```

The bulk of the work is happening inside the LoadProfileWriter class. It implements all the necessary logic to send events over Kafka. Here is the listing (observe the sections in bold).

```
package rs.exproit.load_profile_generator;

final class LoadProfileWriter {
    static final String TOPIC_NAME = "load_profile";
    private static final String CONFIGURATION_FILE = "config/kafka-producer.properties";

    private final Producer<String, byte[]> producer;

    LoadProfileWriter() throws IOException {
        Properties config = new Properties();
        config.load(new FileReader(CONFIGURATION_FILE));
        producer = new KafkaProducer<>(config);
    }
```

```
LoadProfileWriter(Producer<String, byte[]> producer) {
    this.producer = producer;
}

private final DatumWriter<LoadProfileModel> eventWriter =
        new SpecificDatumWriter<>(LoadProfileModel.class);

private byte[] serializeLP(LoadProfileModel lp) throws IOException {
    assert lp != null : "The load profile reference cannot be null";

    ByteArrayOutputStream out = new ByteArrayOutputStream();
    BinaryEncoder encoder = EncoderFactory.get().binaryEncoder(out, null);

    eventWriter.write(lp, encoder);
    encoder.flush();
    out.close();

    return out.toByteArray();
}

private final LoadProfilePartitioner partitioner = new LoadProfilePartitioner(). ;

void sendLP(LoadProfileModel lp)
        throws IOException, ExecutionException, InterruptedException {
    String deviceId = lp.getDeviceId().toString();
    int numPartitions = producer.partitionsFor(TOPIC_NAME).size();
    ProducerRecord<String, byte[]> record = new ProducerRecord<>(
            TOPIC_NAME,
            partitioner.partition(TOPIC_NAME, deviceId, lp, numPartitions),
            deviceId,
            serializeLP(lp));

    producer.send(record).get();
    }
}

void shutdown() {
    producer.close();
}
```

The LoadProfileWriter creates a KafkaProducer object inside its default constructor (the other accepts a Producer instance). The producer is configured with settings specified in the previously mentioned properties file. The serializeLP method shows the technique of directly serializing an Avro object. This binary representation has no reference to the associated schema (see the exercises at the end of this chapter for a solution). The method sendLP sends the event wrapped inside the ProducerRecord object. Notice the immediate get() method call on the returned Future instance. This is a way to implement a fully synchronous communication model in Kafka (it is the most reliable approach, but also the slowest). Kafka will throw an exception only if it cannot resolve a problem after a specified number of retry attempts. We can use our old ClientServerTest test case to fill in the load_profile topic with records (we devote Chapter 13 to performing integration tests with Kafka.).

Implementing the LP Classifier

We configure our consumer using the following settings (the others are kept with their defaults) stored inside the `config/kafka-consumer.properties` file.

```
bootstrap.servers=localhost:9092
group.id=LPClassifier
auto.commit.offset=false
key.deserializer=org.apache.kafka.common.serialization.StringDeserializer
value.deserializer=org.apache.kafka.common.serialization.ByteArrayDeserializer
partition.assignment.strategy=org.apache.kafka.clients.consumer.RoundRobinAssignor
```

We have chosen a manual offset handling by turning off the autocommit feature, which gives better control over offsets. Essentially, we realize the *at least once* semantics. It is hard to achieve only at this level the *exactly once* delivery mechanism (one idea is presented in [1]). The controller can always trigger a duplicate call, and idempotency has to be handled at the data store level. This nicely aligns with one of the most fundamental principles of distributed systems called the *End-to-End Principle* (see [5]). You might reduce the chance of problems in the middleware, but guarantees can only be achieved at the ends of the system. The partition assignment strategy is chosen to be Round Robin, which spreads out partitions to consumers much more smoothly than the Range Assignor (this is the default). All consumers belong to a single group, whose identifier is `LPClassifier`. To achieve better throughout you can add more consumers to the group, but never more than there are available partitions. That would be a waste of resources. Of course, you could always increase the number of available partitions, although you must be careful when deleting partitions to avoid data loss.

The LP classifier is made up of two main parts: the event reader and the bootstrapper. The event reader is responsible for tracking the matching Kafka topic, and is intended to be run from a single thread (Kafka follows the *one consumer per thread* rule). Multithreaded setup is easily achieved by spinning up many instances of readers in different threads. This is the task of the main application. Here is the listing of the reader (imports are omitted, and notice the parts shown in bold).

```
package rs.exproit.load_profile_classifier;

final class LoadProfileReader extends Observable implements Runnable {
    static final String TOPIC_NAME = "load_profile";
    private static final String CONFIGURATION_FILE = "config/kafka-consumer.properties";

    private final Consumer<String, byte[]> consumer;

    LoadProfileReader() throws IOException {
        Properties config = new Properties();
        config.load(new FileReader(CONFIGURATION_FILE));
        consumer = new KafkaConsumer<>(config);
        consumer.subscribe(Collections.singletonList(TOPIC_NAME), new RebalanceHandler());
    }

    LoadProfileReader(Consumer<String, byte[]> consumer) {
        this.consumer = consumer;
    }

    private final DatumReader<LoadProfileModel> eventReader =
            new SpecificDatumReader<>(LoadProfileModel.class);

    private LoadProfileModel deserializeLP(byte[] lpData) throws IOException {
```

```
        final Decoder decoder = DecoderFactory.get().binaryDecoder(lpData, null);
        return eventReader.read(null, decoder);
}

private class RebalanceHandler implements ConsumerRebalanceListener {
    @Override
    public void onPartitionsRevoked(Collection<TopicPartition> partitions) {
        // Before being revoked from partitions make sure that offsets are saved.
        // This is the reason that we use a synchronous call here.
        consumer.commitSync();
    }

    @Override
    public void onPartitionsAssigned(Collection<TopicPartition> partitions) {
        // This method is useful to seek into the matching offset, when offsets are
            saved
        // outside of Kafka (for example, inside a database).
    }
}

@Override
public void run() {
    try {
        while (true) {
            ConsumerRecords<String, byte[]> records = consumer.poll(Long.MAX_VALUE);
            for (ConsumerRecord<String, byte[]> record : records) {
                setChanged();
                notifyObservers(deserializeLP(record.value()));
            }

            consumer.commitAsync();
        }
    } catch (WakeupException e) {
        // This should be ignored, as it is a normal way to signal exit.
    } catch (IOException e) {
        // In production you should properly log the error.
        e.printStackTrace();
    } finally {
        try {
            // Before exiting we want to make sure that offsets are saved.
            // This is the reason that we use a synchronous call here.
            consumer.commitSync();
        } finally {
            consumer.close();
        }
    }
}

public void shutdown() {
    consumer.wakeup();
}
}
```

The LoadProfileReader is an Observable, and expects observers to register for events. The main application class has a simplistic event processor, which just dumps events on the console.

The Kafka consumer is set up in a very similar manner as the producer except that it needs to subscribe to a topic. During subscription we also pass an instance of the ConsumerRebalanceListener. This is a mechanism by which Kafka notifies a consumer that some partitions are revoked from it. This is the moment when offsets have to be reliably saved. The same remark applies when a consumer is exiting from its main loop. Otherwise, the consumer could use an asynchronous offset committing method, which is much faster. It is also mandatory to close the consumer at exit. The way to signal an exit is shown in the shutdown method (the thread executing the event loop will receive a WakeupException).

■ **Caution**   The poll method is also used to piggyback heartbeats from a consumer to a group coordinator broker. You shouldn't spend too much time in an event processing method. You might want to store events in a concurrent queue (like Java's ConcurrentLinkedQueue), and do further processing from other threads. Otherwise, Kafka might think that your consumer has died, and will start a rebalance procedure.

The polling time is set to a maximum value, as our consumer doesn't have to do anything more meaningful than wait for new events. The event processing is rather trivial. The byte sequence is decoded, and the load profile is dumped onto the console. The abridged wrapper code is shown next (observe the sections shown in bold).

```java
package rs.exproit.load_profile_classifier;

public final class App {
    private static class EventProcessor implements Observer {
        @Override
        public void update(Observable o, Object arg) {
            System.out.println(arg);
        }
    }

    /**
     * The main entry point of this service.
     *
     * @param args the number of readers to start up (if it is bigger then the number
     * of available partitions, then some of them will be idle).
     * @throws IOException if any error occurs during the startup.
     */
    public static void main(String[] args) throws IOException {
        if (args.length != 1) {
            System.err.println("You need to specify the number of consumers!");
            System.exit(1);
        }

        int numReaders = Integer.parseInt(args[0]);
        ExecutorService executor = Executors.newFixedThreadPool(numReaders);
        final List<LoadProfileReader> readers = new ArrayList<>();

        for (int i = 0; i < numReaders; i++) {
            LoadProfileReader reader = new LoadProfileReader();
```

```
        reader.addObserver(new EventProcessor());
        readers.add(reader);
        executor.submit(reader);
    }

    Runtime.getRuntime().addShutdownHook(new Thread() {
      @Override
      public void run() {
          readers.forEach(LoadProfileReader::shutdown);
          executor.shutdown();
          try {
              executor.awaitTermination(10, TimeUnit.SECONDS);
          } catch (InterruptedException e) {
              e.printStackTrace();
          }
      }
    });
  }
}
```

This is the recommended way to implement message consumers in Kafka. Always separate the core logic from the boilerplate code to add multithreading. It is effortless to smoke test our whole system. Start up the Kafka broker and open two command shell windows. In the first one, execute the following command to start the LP classifier with three concurrent readers (we are assuming that you have already executed a full Maven build):

```
mvn -q exec:java -Dexec.mainClass=rs.exproit.load_profile_classifier.App -Dexec.args=3
```

In the other window, execute mvn test. You should see 101 load profiles printed on the first screen. Notice that they are not dumped in the same order as they were sent. The reason is that they land in various partitions, and Kafka guarantees strict ordering only inside a single partition.

Summary

We have seen how Kafka allows you to easily implement messaging solutions, where messages are treated as events thanks to Avro. Combining Avro as a binary format, which inherently supports evolution of schemas in compatible manner, with Kafka gives you a powerful data ecosystem.

SCHEMA EXCHANGE IMPROVEMENT

Learn How to Pass Around Schema Identifiers

In the previous chapter you have been asked to set up the Avro schema registry. This exercise assumes that you have accomplished that task. Our current implementation doesn't solve the schema exchange problem. The smart meter and the LP classifier share the same Avro schema file by having their own copies of it. This isn't a scalable approach. Your task here is to leverage the registry.

The solution is to keep schemas inside the registry, and set the following properties for a producer:

```
key.serializer=<The serializer for keys>
value.serializer=io.confluent.kafka.serializers.KafkaAvroSerializer
schema.registry.url=<The URL where your registry is running>
```

For a consumer you would use the following properties:

```
key.deserializer=<The deserializer for keys>
value.deserializer=io.confluent.kafka.serializers.KafkaAvroDeserializer
schema.registry.url=<The URL where your registry is running>
```

You would then instantiate a producer with a custom Avro object (like `LoadProfileModel` in our case), and leave the rest to the Avro serializer. The serializer will generate a schema identifier, and only attach that to the message (instead of sending the full schema each time). The consumer would find the schema from the registry based on that identifier, and use the schema while deserializing the message. See [1] for more details.

WORKFLOW API AND MESSAGE GATEWAYS

Practice Creating Workflows with Apache Nifi

Suppose that the electrical power distribution company has merged with another regional distributor, whose customers have different smart meters. They are sending events into a JMS queue (e.g., ActiveMQ), using a different Avro event format, although the `data` section is the same (you might think about how this schema looks). The idea is to move all messages from the JMS queue into Kafka, so that the LP classifier can receive all data from a central place.

It is possible to write a custom solution by coding everything manually. However, this is a very fragile method. A better approach would be to use some kind of a workflow manager. This is where Apache Nifi (`https://nifi.apache.org`) might help.

Your task is to implement this scenario using Nifi. You might want to take a closer look at the following Nifi processors: ConsumeJMS, ConvertAvroSchema, and PublishKafka_0_10. Examine all the other processors (especially those related to Avro), too. This example illustrates an approach to create JMS ➤ Kafka or Kafka ➤ JMS gateways.

References

1. Narkhede, Neha, Gwen Shapira, and Todd Palino. *Kafka: The Definitive Guide - Early Release.* Sebastopol, CA: O'Reilly Media, 2016.

2. Shapira, Gwen. *Introduction to Apache Kafka.* Sebastopol, CA: O'Reilly Media, 2015.

3. Kreps, Jay. *I Heart Logs.* Sebastopol, CA: O'Reilly Media, 2014.

4. Gustafson, Jason. "Introducing the Kafka Consumer: Getting Started with the New Apache Kafka 0.9 Consumer Client." `http://www.confluent.io/blog/tutorial-getting-started-with-the-new-apache-kafka-0.9-consumer-client/`

5. Saltzer, J. H., D. P. Reed, and D. D. Clark. "End-to-End Arguments in System Design." *ACM Transactions in Computer Systems,* Vol. 2, No. 4, 1984, 277–288. `http://www.it.uu.se/edu/course/homepage/datakom2/vt10/papers/e2e_84.pdf`

CHAPTER 13

■ ■ ■

Testing Messaging APIs

Smoke tests are good to quickly assess whether the system functions or not (they are usually performed before deployment as a swift sanity check). This is a kind of test that we had executed at the end of Chapter 13. The main problem is that running tests manually isn't a scalable tactic (you cannot perform fast regression tests after each change by relying on manual labor). This is the reason we need to seek a better alternative. The main idea is to put the infrastructure under our control, and scrutinize all parts in an automated fashion. We will see how Kafka has a built-in support for this.

Testing messaging APIs is quite different than what you might experience with regular applications. The former is inherently asynchronous, and the broker is outside of application boundaries (it doesn't run embedded inside it, like an embedded web server in a REST service). Moreover, it isn't based on a simple response/request cycle. You need to coordinate multiple components to see what is happening. The main issue is controlling the clock. Many testing approaches are based on emulating a global clock, to be able to reason about the sequence of events. Even if you manage to come up with a proper solution, it is still more work than to clone a source repository (making it available locally), and summon mvn test from your project folder. However, this should be the goal for rapid automated integration tests. You should strive to a find a way to "squash" the whole setup into a single location (introduce a *single point of control*) and try out all sorts of scenarios (both happy and bad). If you don't have such a control, then you cannot successfully exercise edge cases. Finally, by running everything locally you immediately solve the test data problem. You should never worry whether your tests will spoil someone else's stuff, or suffer from side effects of others doing something on the shared asset.

At any rate, the level of achieved automation is directly proportional to the testability of your code. To boost your code's quality, you must follow the principles of TDD, and start thinking about testability from the very beginning. A poorly written code cannot benefit from the test support classes provided by Kafka, or for that matter any testing framework. You will notice that both the LoadProfileWriter and the LoadProfileReader classes are already prepared for automated integration tests. They don't have fixed external dependencies, and accept producer and consumer instances, respectively (see the exercises at the end of this chapter for a hint about how dependency injection might help further from the testability perspective). Moreover, the LoadProfileReader class is based on the Observer pattern, and it is straightforward to customize its event processing logic. They were designed by applying the TDD paradigm.

Case Study: Attaining Automated Integration Tests

The ClientServerTest test case, together with the manual supervision of the output produced by the LP classifier, required a running Kafka broker in the background. Although, we had managed to spin up a stand-alone instance using Docker Compose, we were still unable to automatically check whether the events have been properly sent and received. This study has the following goals:

- Fully automated independent testing of the smart meter and the LP classifier.

- No reliance on an external Kafka broker.

© Ervin Varga 2016
E. Varga, *Creating Maintainable APIs*, DOI 10.1007/978-1-4842-2196-9_13

- Tests should run fast. The word *fast* is an unquantifiable goal, so we need to be more precise. Any test suite that can be completed in less than a minute will be fast enough for us. You should decide yourself what fast means for you. The point is that you shouldn't leave adjectives underspecified.

Our revised test harness is depicted in Figure 13-1. We would like to inject a mock Kafka producer and consumer, so that we can isolate our tests from the underlying pipe.

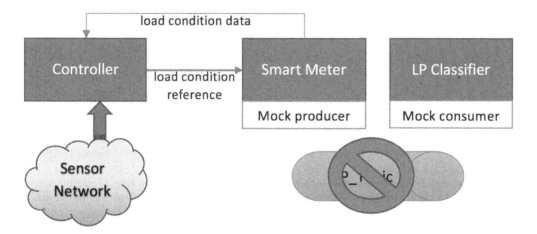

Figure 13-1. *The structure of the test harness allowing an independent testing of the smart meter and the LP classifier. Also, this setup doesn't need a running Kafka broker in the background.*

Both the LoadProfileWriter and the LoadProfileReader classes accept an instance of the Producer and the Consumer interfaces, respectively. This is the preparation for dependency injection to easily inject mock variants. Without any further support you can create mocks of these interfaces using any available mock framework. However, we don't even need to perform this step. Kafka already ships with the MockProducer and MockConsumer classes.

Refactoring the ClientServerTest Test Case

We will refactor the ClientServerTest test case to use the MockProducer class instead of sending events to an existing Kafka broker. By default, the MockProducer completes all calls synchronously. However, we can customize its behavior, and even instruct the producer to throw an exception (this is hard to achieve with a real Kafka cluster, especially when it is shared with other developers). Here is the listing of the refactored test case for a smart meter including its client API (imports are omitted, and crucial sections are shown in bold).

```
package rs.exproit.load_profile_generator;

public class ClientServerTest {
    private static final int PORT = 65111;

    private static App app;
    private static NettyTransceiver client;
    private static LoadProfileRPC proxy;
```

```
private static MockProducer<String, byte[]> mockProducer;
private static ExecutorService executor = Executors.newFixedThreadPool(1);

@BeforeClass
public static void setup() throws IOException {
    PartitionInfo partitionInfo =
            new PartitionInfo(LoadProfileWriter.TOPIC_NAME, 0, null, null, null);
    Cluster cluster = new Cluster(
            Collections.<Node>emptyList(),
            Arrays.asList(partitionInfo),
            Collections.<String>emptySet());
    mockProducer = new MockProducer<>(
            cluster,
            false,
            new DefaultPartitioner(),
            new StringSerializer(),
            new ByteArraySerializer());
    app = new App(new LoadProfileRPCImpl(new LoadProfileWriter(mockProducer)));
    app.start(PORT);
    client = new NettyTransceiver(new InetSocketAddress(PORT));
    proxy = SpecificRequestor.getClient(LoadProfileRPC.class, client);
}

@Before
public void clearMockProducer() {
    mockProducer.clear();
}

@AfterClass
public static void teardown() {
    client.close();
    app.stop();
    executor.shutdown();
}

private LPCreationRequest createRequest(String loadCondition) {
    LPCreationRequest request = LPCreationRequest.newBuilder().build();
    if (loadCondition != null) {
        request.setLoadCondition(loadCondition);
    }
    return request;
}

@Test
public void triggerSuccessfulLPCreationsAndValidateThatDataIsSent() throws IOException {
    // We need to set up the notifier thread to propel the main test.
    executor.execute(new Runnable() {
        private int requestCount = 101;

        @Override
        public void run() {
```

```
            while (requestCount > 0) {
                if (mockProducer.completeNext()) {
                    requestCount--;
                }
                Thread.yield();
            }
        }
    });

    // Sends requests and check responses.
    String response;
    for (int i = 0; i < 100; i++) {
        response = proxy
            .lpCreate(createRequest("http://example.org/api/Controller/LoadConditions/"
            + i))
            .toString();
        assertNotNull(response);
        assertTrue(response.contains(
        "\"loadCondition\": \"http://example.org/api/Controller/LoadConditions/" + i +
        "\""));
    }
    response = proxy.lpCreate(createRequest(null)).toString();
    assertNotNull(response);
    assertTrue(response.contains("\"loadCondition\": null"));

    // Check history of sent events.
    mockProducer.flush();
    List<ProducerRecord<String, byte[]>> records = mockProducer.history();
    assertEquals(101, records.size());

    for (ProducerRecord<String, byte[]> record : records) {
        assertTrue(record.key().startsWith(LoadProfileRPCImpl.DEVICE_ID_PREFIX));
        assertNotNull(record.value());
    }
}

@Test(expected = ServiceError.class)
public void triggerABadLPCreationAndValidateThatExceptionHasOccurred() throws
IOException {
    // We need to set up the notifier thread to announce an exception.
    executor.execute(new Runnable() {
        @Override
        public void run() {
            while (!mockProducer.errorNext(new RuntimeException())) {
                Thread.yield();
            }
        }
    });

    proxy.lpCreate(createRequest(null));
    }
}
```

The fields inside the ClientServerTest class are all static for performance reasons, as they represent a common heavy state for all test cases here. Generally, introducing shared state for tests is a bad practice, but in our case they aren't designed to be run in parallel anyhow. Therefore, no collisions would occur. Moreover, the MockProducer class has a method clear, which is intended to be called at the beginning of each test. Another issue with running our test cases in parallel would be the maintenance of all those simultaneously running embedded Netty servers. Concurrently running the test cases here would cause more trouble than benefits. The JUnit test runner by default runs all tests sequentially in some arbitrary order (unless you use the FixMethodOrder annotation to request a particular ordering).

The setup method prepares the necessary context (a dummy partition and a cluster), and creates the MockProducer object. The MockProducer instance can work in one the following two regimes: autocompletion mode and manual mode. The former always successfully returns from the send method (this is a natural choice if you only use an asynchronous send without a callback). To have greater control over your send method's behavior, you should choose manual modus operandi. This is the regime chosen here (observe that the second parameter of the constructor is false). Now, in manual mode things are a bit strange. Each call to send is registered, but isn't acknowledged. If you use a synchronous send in your code (like we did in our LoadProfileWriter class), then your test would simply block indefinitely (it waits indeterminately for an answer). This is why we need another thread to acknowledge pending requests in a way we would like. There are two methods to signal a completion: completeNext and errorNext. Both return a logical value depending on whether they had anything to acknowledge (true) or not (false). This is important to track, because we don't want our thread to exit prematurely. In the happy test case earlier we produced exactly 101 true acknowledgements before exiting. The other one produces just one erroneous proclamation. Of course, you could implement a variant that would instruct the MockProducer object to perform N successful sends before throwing an error.

The MockProducer object registers all sent records, and you can retrieve them by calling the history method. Your test case is then able to see what exactly was transferred to Kafka. Now imagine how tedious would it be to force the Kafka broker into various states as well as to trace the send method calls without using the MockProducer facility.

Testing the LP Classifier

We will use the same strategy as before, this time relying on the MockConsumer class. The listing of the LP classifier's test suite is presented here (imports are omitted, and important parts are shown in bold).

```
package rs.exproit.load_profile_classifier;

public class LPClassifierTest {
    private final DatumWriter<LoadProfileModel> eventWriter =
            new SpecificDatumWriter<>(LoadProfileModel.class);

    private byte[] serializeLP(LoadProfileModel lp) throws IOException {
        assertNotNull("The load profile reference cannot be null", lp);

        ByteArrayOutputStream out = new ByteArrayOutputStream();
        BinaryEncoder encoder = EncoderFactory.get().binaryEncoder(out, null);

        eventWriter.write(lp, encoder);
        encoder.flush();
        out.close();

        return out.toByteArray();
    }
```

```
private final TopicPartition partition =
        new TopicPartition(LoadProfileReader.TOPIC_NAME, 0);
private final MockConsumer<String, byte[]> mockConsumer =
        new MockConsumer<>(OffsetResetStrategy.EARLIEST);

@Before
public void setup() {
    Map<TopicPartition, Long> offsets = new HashMap<>();
    offsets.put(partition, 0L);
    mockConsumer.updateBeginningOffsets(offsets);
    mockConsumer.assign(Arrays.asList(partition));
}

private class EventProcessor implements Observer {
    private int startIdx;

    @Override
    public void update(Observable o, Object arg) {
        assertTrue(o instanceof LoadProfileReader);
        assertNotNull(arg);
        assertTrue(arg instanceof LoadProfileModel);

        LoadProfileModel lp = (LoadProfileModel) arg;
        assertEquals(Integer.valueOf(100 + startIdx), lp.getCreatedAt());
        assertEquals("TEST_" + startIdx, lp.getDeviceId().toString());
        assertEquals(Double.valueOf(1.0), lp.getData().iterator().next());
        startIdx++;
    }
}

@Test
public final void consumeEventsFromATopicAndProcessThem() {
    final LoadProfileReader reader = new LoadProfileReader(mockConsumer);
    reader.addObserver(new EventProcessor());

    final Runnable pollTask = new Runnable() {
        private final List<Double> testData = new ArrayList<>();
        {
            testData.add(1.0);
        }

        private int pollCount;

        @Override
        public void run() {
            try {
                // We need to "get out" the consumer form its infinite loop
                // once all data were consumed.
                if (pollCount == 10) {
                    reader.shutdown();
                } else {
```

```
                    mockConsumer.schedulePollTask(this);
                    pollCount++;
                }

                LoadProfileModel.Builder builder = LoadProfileModel.newBuilder();
                LoadProfileModel lp = builder
                        .setCreatedAt(100 + pollCount)
                        .setDeviceId("TEST_" + pollCount)
                        .setData(testData)
                        .build();

                mockConsumer.addRecord(new ConsumerRecord<String, byte[]>(
                        partition.topic(),
                        partition.partition(),
                        pollCount,
                        lp.getDeviceId().toString(),
                        serializeLP(lp)));
            } catch (IOException e) {
                fail("Unexpected exception occurred in the poll controller thread.");
            } finally {
                reader.shutdown();
            }
        }
    };

    mockConsumer.schedulePollTask(pollTask);
    reader.run();
    }
}
```

Inside the setup method we create the necessary map to hold offsets (in our case just one), and set the beginning offsets for our mock consumer (we would set the ending offsets in case the offset reset strategy was LATEST). Also, we assign our test topic to the consumer.

The EventProcessor class checks the events as they are added to the consumer inside the test case. The startIdx variable holds the current position as we progress through test events. The most interesting parts are inside the test case method. Everything revolves around the schedulePollTask method of the MockConsumer class. The MockConsumer isn't thread-safe, so the technique is very similar to scheduling a GUI update in Swing (for more details, see https://docs.oracle.com/javase/tutorial/uiswing/concurrency/dispatch.html). The main thread (the thread executing the test case) will enter an infinite loop after calling reader.run. Because we cannot start up a new thread (as we did in the previous situation) the solution is to schedule a new poll task. This task will be executed by the main thread when it calls poll (see the implementation of the LoadProfileReader class). Inside the poll task we add a new record to the consumer (simulating an arrival of an event). It is mandatory that we keep track of the number of records processed so far (this is kept inside the pollCount variable). If we haven't yet added all our records, then we just increase the pollCount, and reschedule the same poll task for the next iteration. Otherwise, we signal to the main thread that it should exit.

Full End-to-End Test

There is a fundamentally different approach to test our system. Instead of trying to exercise it piece by piece, we can use an in-process Zookeeper/Kafka ensemble (if you don't mind pulling in lots of jars during the build), and examine how our system functions end to end. This might boost our confidence that all components are properly working together. Nevertheless, there are many drawbacks to this approach as well. It is much harder to localize a problem compared to the case, when we just interrogate the smart meter or LP classifier separately. The mock variant of a producer and consumer provides us with a greater visibility of what happened at the boundary of our application, and an external messaging hub. When using an in-process Zookeeper/Kafka system, there is a chance that our system will run against a different messaging infrastructure compared to the production version of Kafka. Furthermore, it is sometimes impossible to induce errors in a controlled manner. Overall, having these automated end-to-end tests is useful, but I would suggest you to mock out dependencies right at the borders.

You must add the following dependencies (all having scope set to test) to your pom.xml file (notice the use of the classifier directive):

```xml
<dependency>
    <groupId>org.apache.kafka</groupId>
    <artifactId>kafka_2.11</artifactId>
    <version>${kafka.version}</version>
    <scope>test</scope>
</dependency>
<dependency>
    <groupId>org.apache.kafka</groupId>
    <artifactId>kafka_2.11</artifactId>
    <version>${kafka.version}</version>
    <classifier>test</classifier>
    <scope>test</scope>
</dependency>
<dependency>
    <groupId>org.apache.kafka</groupId>
    <artifactId>kafka-clients</artifactId>
    <version>${kafka.version}</version>
    <classifier>test</classifier>
    <scope>test</scope>
</dependency>
```

Here is the listing of this new test suite (imports are omitted, and salient details are shown in bold).

```java
package rs.exproit.load_profile_system;

public class LoadProfileSystemTest {
    private static EmbeddedZookeeper zkServer;
    private static ZkClient zkClient;
    private static KafkaServer kafkaServer;

    @BeforeClass
    public static void setupKafka() throws IOException {
        zkServer = new EmbeddedZookeeper();
        String zkConnect = "127.0.0.1:" + zkServer.port();
        zkClient = new ZkClient(zkConnect, 10000, 10000, ZKStringSerializer$.MODULE$);
        ZkUtils zkUtils = ZkUtils.apply(zkClient, false);

        Properties config = new Properties();
        config.setProperty("zookeeper.connect", zkConnect);
        config.setProperty("broker.id", "0");
```

```
        config.setProperty("listeners", "PLAINTEXT://0.0.0.0:9092");
        config.setProperty("auto.create.topics.enable", "false");
        MockTime mockTime = new MockTime();
        kafkaServer = TestUtils.createServer(new KafkaConfig(config), mockTime);

        String topicName = "load_profile";
        int numPartitions = 3;

        AdminUtils.createTopic(
                zkUtils, topicName, numPartitions, 1, new Properties(),
                RackAwareMode.Disabled$.MODULE$);
        final List<KafkaServer> servers = new ArrayList<>();
        servers.add(kafkaServer);
        TestUtils.waitUntilMetadataIsPropagated(
                scala.collection.JavaConversions.asScalaBuffer(servers), topicName, 0, 5000);
    }

@AfterClass
public static void stopKafka() {
    kafkaServer.shutdown();
    zkClient.close();
    zkServer.shutdown();
}

private NettyTransceiver controller;
private ByteArrayOutputStream stdOutputBuffer = new ByteArrayOutputStream();
private PrintStream standardOutput = System.out;

@Before
public void startLoadProfileSystem() throws IOException {
    int port = 65111;
    rs.exproit.load_profile_generator.App.main(new String[] { Integer.toString(port) });
    controller = new NettyTransceiver(new InetSocketAddress(port));

    System.setOut(new PrintStream(stdOutputBuffer));
    rs.exproit.load_profile_classifier.App.main(new String[] { "3" });
}

@After
public void stopLoadProfileSystem() {
    controller.close();
    System.setOut(standardOutput);
}

private LPCreationRequest createRequest(String loadCondition) {
    LPCreationRequest request = LPCreationRequest.newBuilder().build();
    if (loadCondition != null) {
        request.setLoadCondition(loadCondition);
    }
    return request;
}
```

```
private void waitUntilAllEventsAreProcessed(int numEvents) {
    while (stdOutputBuffer.toString().split("\r?\n").length < numEvents) {
        Thread.yield();
    }
}


@Test(timeout = 60000)
public final void tiggerLoadProfileCreationsAndCheckResult()
        throws InterruptedException, IOException {
    LoadProfileRPC proxy = SpecificRequestor.getClient(LoadProfileRPC.class, controller);

    for (int i = 0; i < 100; i++) {
        String response = proxy.lpCreate(createRequest("Data: " + i)).toString();
        assertNotNull(response);
        assertTrue(response.contains("\"loadCondition\": \"Data: " + i + "\""));
    }

    waitUntilAllEventsAreProcessed(100);

    String result = stdOutputBuffer.toString();
    for (int i = 0; i < 100; i++) {
        assertTrue(result.contains("\"loadCondition\": \"Data: " + i + "\""));
    }
}
}
```

The setupKafka method does all the work to start up the Zookeeper/Kafka stack as well as to create the necessary topic for load profiles. This code is customized to the 0.10.0.x version of Kafka. In the past, there have been lots of changes regarding this test setup, so it might change in the future, too. When this method completes, producers and consumers will have a fully functional Kafka broker available on a local machine on port 9092 (the default port number). The stopKafka method shows the steps to shut down the Zookeeper/Kafka ensemble.

The startLoadProfileSystem method starts up all components of our LP system: controller, smart meter and LP classifier. The LP classifier is started with three concurrent consumers (notice the command-line argument of 3). The whole system is now running as it would in a normal situation. The test case tiggerLoadProfileCreationsAndCheckResult uses the controller to initiate load profile creations. Each generated load profile is put into the Kafka topic "load profile," and is processed by the LP classifier. The test case ensures that the smart meter has sent all load profiles to Kafka, and that the LP classifier has processed them correctly. The first part is straightforward, but to validate the second part we must capture the standard output.

After all load profiles are delivered to Kafka, the test case calls the waitUntilAllEventsAreProcessed method to wait for all events to appear on the standard output. This is achieved by counting the number of new line characters. If the counter matches the expected number of events, then we know that all of them are captured in the output. The next task is just to check that they are really valid. There is a danger that this test case might never end (if something goes wrong). This is the reason for that timeout value in the Test annotation. If the test doesn't end in one minute, then we treat it as failed.

Summary

We have examined the peculiarities of testing messaging APIs (our tests are oriented toward Kafka, but the approach is generic), and how it differs from a casual situation with synchronous request/response cycles. Kafka already provided us with the test classes for executing integration tests in an isolated fashion. Again, all this is useful if your code is prepared for such a customization; that is, to accept mock objects instead of real ones (if you build your code so that external dependencies are clearly declared, then they can be easily mocked).

EXTENDING THE LP CLASSIFIER'S TEST SUITE

Practice the MockConsumer Class

Add a new test case to the LPClassifierTest class, which would trigger an error during event consumption. This is similar to what we have done in our first test suite.

The MockConsumer class has a method called setException. If this method is called from the poll task, then the driver thread will get an exception from the poll method. To test for this error, you will need to refactor a bit the LoadProfileReader class. One possibility is to introduce another callback, called the *error* callback. This would be called inside the exception handler, which currently just dumps out a stack trace.

REFACTOR THE CODE TO USE DEPENDENCY INJECTION

Practice a Dependency Injection Framework

The LoadProfileWriter and LoadProfileReader classes use a static variable to denote the topic name. Also, they cannot be configured externally via a configuration file (you must programmatically set them up with a custom Kafka producer and consumer instances).

A dependency injection framework (Spring, Guice, etc.) allows you to completely describe your components and their dependencies in a configuration file. This added flexibility increases your classes' testability, too. Refactor the code base (including the tests, as they also hard-code configuration values) to leverage dependency injection, and use external configuration files.

SCHEMA COMPATIBILITY TEST

Practice Avro Schema Handling

One of the biggest issues during API evolution is to preserve backward compatibility. Ensuring that we haven't missed some detail isn't an easy task (even if we reread the schema resolution rules in the documentation every time). Therefore, it would be great if we could automate schema comparisons and create automated schema compatibility tests. The test would compare two schemas (usually a reader and a writer schema) and report all compatibility errors.

One of the reasons that this book has chosen Avro as a good choice for implementing messaging APIs is that it already contains such a schema compatibility checker. Take a look at the SchemaCompatibility class. Devise an automated test to check for any compatibility problems between a smart meter and an LP classifier schema (assume that they evolve separately).

Reference

1. Maddox, Philip. "Testing a Distributed System." *ACM Queue*, 2015.
    https://queue.acm.org/detail.cfm?id=2800697

CHAPTER 14

∎ ∎ ∎

Schema-Based Messages

Distributed systems built around the service-oriented architectural style contain services, which continuously exchange messages[1] (data) with one another. It doesn't matter whether such transfers happen over HTTP communication channels, via some message queues, or both. What matters is the robustness and maintainability of the corresponding message structures, which are generally different for synchronous and asynchronous communication. If a message structure isn't aligned to support distributed development and deployment,[2] then we cannot qualify that system as supportable. Such a system cannot expand beyond some level. This chapter is about important techniques and principles for crafting evolvable message structures.

Before delving into further details, it is useful to establish a common taxonomy about different kinds of message structures.[3] The following list is sorted by maintenance level in ascending order.

1. *Unstructured (ad-hoc)*: A message structure is arbitrary, and is hidden inside an application. Applications must share a common knowledge about the whole structure if they want to exchange data. The structure doesn't exist outside of an application. This means that even if a message (document) does adhere to some sophisticated structure, that structure is not publicly revealed. A good example of this is the Microsoft Word document format. The format was never fully publicized, so only Word can adequately handle its own documents (unless they are very simple). Nevertheless, the Word document format itself is really amazing.

2. *Semi-structured*: There are some public rudimentary rules about the structure. For example, the casual text file format is one such example. Here, we expect that the content is arranged by lines, with proper end-of-line markers. There is also an end-of-file (EOF) marker. The content of each line is arbitrary. Nevertheless, it is a huge step forward compared to an unstructured case. Most Unix shell commands rely solely on the text format as their input/output. This allows you to combine them together to perform more complex actions. For example, the sort utility doesn't care what is inside a line as long as it is a sequence of characters.

---

[1]For our discussion, these messages can be textual or binary; the same reasoning applies in both cases.
[2]For a good summary see http://wiki.apidesign.org/wiki/Distributed_development.
[3]This fulfills a role similar to the *Richardson Maturity Model* for REST (martinfowler.com/articles/richardsonMaturityModel.html).

© Ervin Varga 2016
E. Varga, *Creating Maintainable APIs*, DOI 10.1007/978-1-4842-2196-9_14

3. *Fixed, structured*: A typical example is the comma-separated values (CSV) file format for storing tabular data in plain text. The format of the file is well structured, and the structure itself is rock solid. There are many variations on this topic. For example, if a delimiter is configurable then we might get the delimiter-separated values format. However, it is impossible to break out from this tabular view of the world unless you depart from the standard.[4] At any rate, all structured message formats have a metaformat clearly specifying the conditions for *well-formedness*.

4. *Extensible, structured*: A classic example is eXtensible Markup Language (XML). The structure itself is part of the message. The structure is not fixed, and a message is self-contained. This means that the application, which created a message, might cease to exist without impeding our ability to reason about the custom message structure. JavaScript Object Notation (JSON) is another good example, although not as flexible as XML. At any rate, each message is just an instance of a template (schema) known only to an application. Although we cannot validate a message without contacting its originator, we do have an ability grasp the overall structure. This is possible thanks to the inherent structure (e.g., a tree in XML) present in a message. Moreover, both XML and JSON allow naming elements, and these names are also preserved in a message.

5. *Schema based*: This type of a message structure is the topic of this chapter. Here, the template for creating messages is fully externalized. Any application can independently validate a message based on this template. A message conforming to the proper template is said to be *valid*. This is in correlation with the type safety of an API. An API should strive to be as formal as possible, and prevent mismatches during runtime. Of course, this isn't always possible to achieve; that is, some aspects of the contract will need to be validated from code. There are lots of schema languages to specify the rules of what constitutes a valid document, but the principles are the same. Therefore, in the rest of this chapter we focus our attention purely on the JSON Schema[5] draft 4, as this is the schema language used by JSON API.

6. *Conventional interface based*: This is not a pure message structure type, but a structure combined with a set of interaction rules about handling messages. Chapter 15 introduces JSON API as one of the best representatives of this category.

■ **Note** It is possible to augment the fifth and sixth categories with semantic technologies. We will see examples of this in Chapters 15 and 16, respectively.

In the rest of this chapter we gradually evolve a base JSON schema[6] to introduce techniques and principles for achieving a high level of maintainability regarding message structures. There is a lot of overlap with methods to make our object-oriented software maintainable (see Part I of this book). Therefore, we will

---

[4]It is easy to fall into this trap; that is, to tweak a standard. Any deviation from a standard will basically drop you back into a semistructured, or even unstructured category from the viewpoint of services expecting standard stuff. There is no such thing as "Our format is CSV with some customizations."

[5]To learn about the JSON Schema and see some nice examples, visit `json-schema.org`. This site contains a link to the official JSON Schema specification as well as references to many JSON frameworks for several programming languages.

[6]Throughout this endeavor it is useful for you to load into your browser the JSON Schema Net (`http://jsonschema.net`) or JSON Schema Lint (`http://jsonschemalint.com`) online schema validator. A validator can help you write and test JSON schemas that conform to the draft 4 specification. Both tools expect as inputs a JSON schema and an instance document.

now highlight only the specifics related to message structures. The maintainability of a message structure is associated with an ability to preserve the next properties:

- Full compatibility (forward and backward) between versions.

- High degree of reuse across versions.

- Ease of change.

Version 1.0.0: Simple Lottery Ticket

Let us incrementally develop a hypothetical online lottery service. Our focus is purely on a message format containing a player's betting data. As we progress through versions we resolve various maintenance issues. The following sample JSON document incorporates what we would like to capture in version 1.0.0.

```
{
  "version": "1.0.0",
  "name": "Wednesday Lotto",
  "selection": [1, 4, 10, 33, 45, 48],
  "price": 3,
  "number-of-draws": 1
}
```

The document has a version number (1.0.0), contains the name of the game, a player's selection (in this case 6 out of 49 numbers), the unit price of a ticket ($3), and how many times this ticket should participate in future drawings (in our case only in the next one). The corresponding JSON schema, capturing these business rules, can be specified as shown here.

```
{
  "id": "http://example.com/schemas/1.0.0/simple-lotto-schema#",
  "$schema": "http://json-schema.org/draft-04/schema#",
  "title": "Simple Lotto Ticket",
  "description": "A player's betting data for our on-line lottery service",
  "type": "object",
  "properties": {
    "version": {
      "description": "The unique semantic version number (X.Y.Z) of the document",
      "type": "string",
      "pattern": "^\\d{1,2}\\.\\d{1,2}\\.\\d{1,3}$"
    },
    "name": {
      "description": "The unique name of the game",
      "type": "string"
    },
    "selection": {
      "description": "A player's selection of numbers",
      "type": "array",
      "items": {
        "type": "integer"
      },
      "minItems": 5,
      "uniqueItems": true
```

```
    },
    "price": {
      "description": "A price of a single ticket in USD",
      "type": "integer",
      "minimum": 1
    },
    "number-of-draws": {
      "description": "The number of draws in which a ticket should participate",
      "type": "integer",
      "minimum": 1,
      "maximum": 10
    }
  },
  "required": [
    "version",
    "name",
    "selection",
    "price",
    "number-of-draws"
  ],
  "additionalProperties": false
}
```

This schema captures most of the rules that we have identified previously. It is important to try to specify as much as possible through the schema, so that the number of implicit assumptions is kept at a minimum. Of course, you should not be too aggressive with constraints. It is better to make a schema more flexible than to be overly constraining. This is exactly the strategy chosen in the JSON API's schema.

We see that the schema is itself a JSON document, so it obeys the same metarules as any other JSON document. The metaschema is referenced at the root via the $schema member.

▪ **Note**   It is always a good idea to reference the metaschema from your JSON schema. It clearly denotes its version (always be exact with a version number; don't use the `latest` shortcut), and declares that the given JSON document is indeed a schema. The same reasoning applies to the instance document. Notice that the version is explicitly stated in the `version` member.[7] Versioning is of the utmost importance to gain control over changes. Finally, I also suggest you assign a unique identifier for each schema using the `id` property. In our case, it points to a fictitious web site of our example lottery service from which anybody can download the schema. Again, a value of an `id` property is a URL with a distinct version number. It is then easy to search for the matching schema after receiving an instance document with a `version` field.

Another important task is to document your schema. Set the title for your schema, describe its main purpose, and describe each property (field). This makes your schema more comprehensible, and thus aids with maintenance.

---

[7]The recommended practice is to apply semantic versioning. For more information, visit http://semver.org. In our schema the regular expression for checking the validity of a version number is very simplified. The semantic version number check is more complicated, as it might contain various suffixes (e.g., RC-1, Alpha-2, etc.).

There is one important aspect that remained unspecified in the schema. The `selection` member has a lower cardinality bound of 5. This is a reasonable choice given that most lottery games require at least five numbers. The upper bound is not that clear, though. It depends on the type of lottery game (e.g., 5 out of 35, 6 out of 49, etc.). This is very hard to describe purely in schema, as it is a more complex business rule. The JSON schema is just a JSON document (data) with only a declarative power. More sophisticated semantic checks need to be done from code.

■ **Caution**   Any tool can automatically validate only the structure of an instance document. Certain relationships between data elements of a document must be performed by a validation logic implemented using some general-purpose programming language.

Finally, our schema has two additional members that we need to explain: `require` and `additionalProperties`. The former specifies what the mandatory elements are in an instance document. In our schema all of them are required. If you leave out some field from the list of required ones, then it becomes optional. However, its structure is still governed by the schema. The `additionalProperties` member (when set to `true` or to some JSON object[8]) permits arbitrary content to be attached to the document. These are not going to be checked in any way. In some way, they are like having a wildcard * at the end of a schema (anything that follows is allowed). Of course, the document still has to be a well-formed JSON document. Allowing such additional unchecked properties is okay if you expect new fields to be part of a document without breaking validation rules.

■ **Caution**   Don't abuse the `additionalProperties` feature! It can easily lead to uncontrolled changes, as new fields might appear and disappear from version to version without any formal trace. I recommend you to set it to `false` unless you are absolutely sure that it must be different.[9] After all, the most flexible JSON schema is {}, but by itself it is not very useful, as it validates everything.[10]

Version 1.0.1: Bug Fix

Schemas should follow the same stringent quality assurance and control procedures as any other software. Proper testing is one of them. It is easy to fool yourself that the schema truthfully expresses all constraints. This usually happens when testing is done by producing instance documents[11] and validating them against the schema. Most often the test specimens don't cover strange edge cases. There is an effective trick, though. Why not try in an opposite direction, as well? Let us see what potential documents we can produce with our schema as input.

---

[8]It is possible to restrict what can be attached freely to a document. For example, if the value of this property is set to { "type": "string" }, then it will allow only string properties.

[9]As always, it is a good idea to see how others are using this feature. For example, the JSON API (see Chapter 15) schema allows additional properties in two places only: inside a meta object and for links. This is an understandable decision, as meta is reserved for nonstandard extensions, and the links section may contain custom links defined by application developers. Additionally, the JSON API schema is a good source for learning advanced schema constructs (e.g., look at how the `relationships` member is specified using the `patternProperties` feature of the JSON Schema).

[10]Nevertheless, it might be handy while you develop your schema in a top-down fashion. For a good illustration of this, study the advanced example available at http://json-schema.org/example2.html.

[11]Even in our simple example the number of all possible instance documents is innumerable.

We will use a JSON Schema Faker tool (`http://json-schema-faker.js.org`) to generate fake data that conforms to our schema. After a couple of runs it produced the following output:

```
{
  "version": "72.8.16",
  "name": "minim exercitation proident in",
  "selection": [
    44916645,
    -67649279,
    44228531,
    12698882,
    -1677911
  ],
  "price": 99544208,
  "number-of-draws": 1
}
```

Apparently, something is fishy with the lottery numbers. It makes no sense to have a negative number there (this is a bug in the schema), and they should undeniably have an upper limit (a good choice is 100, as there is no lottery game I'm aware of with more than 100 choices). The price is also exorbitant, but we will not deal with that now. We need to apply the following patch (change the definition of the selection member):

```
"items": {
  "type": "integer",
  "minimum": 1,
  "maximum": 100
}
```

Is this a compatible change? In theory, it breaks compatibility, because the old schema could produce invalid input for the new version. On the other hand, the new version always produces compatible instances with the previous one. This is a fine point to introduce the following important definitions.

- *Backward compatibility*: A change to a schema definition is backward compatible if all documents that validated against previous schema still validate against the new one. In our case, the bug fix doesn't satisfy this provision. An old message producer may generate a bad document from the perspective of the new version of the online lottery service. Therefore, message producers must also switch to the new schema.

- *Forward compatibility*: A change in a message producer is forward compatible if it generates documents that continue to be valid against the (previous) schema. In our case, the bug fix does satisfy this provision. The new message producer cannot generate a bad document from the perspective of the old version of the online lottery service.

What about the *practice*, is it different than the *theory*? The answer is a resounding yes! The bug fix can be treated as a fully compatible change. The wrong selection numbers would have been rejected by the old system anyhow. This same reasoning applies to the usability improvement to reduce the upper limit for selections. Even before, nobody was able to provide insane choices.

We need to make another critical amendment to our schema. Each change must be followed by a new version number. Because this was a bug fix, the new version should be 1.0.1. Overwriting old versions with new material is the most dangerous thing to do.

> ■ **Note** Making an implicit assumption explicit in your schema doesn't count as an incompatible change! After all, you are just exposing your business rules instead of burying them in code. Of course, it can only happen when all known producers are under our control.

Version 1.1.0: Going International

After great success with the first version of the system, the company has decided to go international. The lottery game per se remained the same, but it was no longer satisfactory to have only a bare price field. The price member required the following additional data:

- *Currency*: A predefined list of supported currency symbols.

- *Amount*: Given in 1/1,000 of units.

- *Exchange rate*: Fixed at the time of purchase to convert the amount from the source currency into US dollars.

The company knows that there is a huge customer base using the old format and associated client software. Therefore, the change must be backward compatible. Here is the patch (changes relative to a previous state) of the price member.

```
"price": {
  "oneOf": [{
    "description": "A price of a single ticket in USD",
    "type": "integer",
    "minimum": 1
  },
  {
    "description": "A price of a single ticket in the chosen currency",
    "type": "object",
    "properties": {
      "currency": { "enum": ["USD", "EUR", "CAD", "RSD", "HUF"] },
      "amount": {
        "description": "An amount in 1/1000 units",
        "type": "integer",
        "minimum": 1000
      },
      "exchange-rate": {
        "description": "A fixed exchange rate > 0.0 to convert the amount into USD",
        "type": "number",
        "minimum": 0.0,
        "exclusiveMinimum": true,
        "default": 1.0
      }
    },
    "required": ["currency", "amount"],
    "additionalProperties": false
  }]
}
```

The corresponding instance document using a new price model is as follows.

```
{
  "version": "1.1.0",
  "name": "Wednesday Lotto",
  "selection": [1, 4, 10, 33, 45, 48],
  "price": {
    "currency": "CAD",
    "amount": 3247,
    "exchange-rate": 0.77
  },
  "number-of-draws": 2
}
```

Of course, version 1.0.0 of an instance document is still valid. By using the oneOf feature of the JSON Schema draft 4, we basically say, "A price may be an amount in US dollars, or a triple (currency, amount, exchange rate)." The exchange rate is optional with a default value of 1.0. In our sample, we essentially specified the price to be $2.5.

As always, we need to increase the version number. As this was a new feature implemented in a backward-compatible manner, the new version number is 1.1.0.

Version 1.2.0: Automaton-Pick Feature

Players have started to complain that the system is not very user friendly. For multiweek coupons, which were targeted for multiple draws, they didn't want to have the same numbers repeated. On the other hand, filling in multiple coupons was too cumbersome for them. They have demanded a feature by which the system would automatically fill in the selection with random choices.[12]

You've probably already guessed that the change must be done in a backward-compatible manner. Here are the patches to the schema (an addition of the new optional property called automaton-pick, and a change in the selection member's lower cardinality bound):

```
"automaton-pick": {
  "type": "boolean",
  "default": false
}
-------------------
"minItems": 0
```

The next instance document demonstrates the new feature:

```
{
  "version": "1.2.0",
  "name": "Wednesday Lotto",
  "price": 3,
  "selection": [],
  "number-of-draws": 4,
  "automaton-pick": true
}
```

---

[12]This feature is very popular among lottery organizations, and is known under various names (e.g., Quick Pick, Fast Pick, Smart Pick, and Lucky Dip, just to name a few). I just hope that nobody has copyrighted it under the name Automaton-Pick (this is the reason for such a funny label).

Here, we have specified that all numbers should be chosen by a machine. We may also fix some numbers, and let the system choose the remaining ones.

```
{
  "version": "1.2.0",
  "name": "Wednesday Lotto",
  "selection": [4, 12, 22],
  "price": 3,
  "number-of-draws": 3,
  "automaton-pick": true
}
```

The idea is to let players choose their favorite numbers, as is the case in the preceding sample. More complex rules, like checking whether all numbers are properly given if automaton-pick is false, require general-purpose code.

Version 2.0.0: Multigame Lottery Ticket

An internationally renowned company cannot afford to offer only a single-game lottery coupon. Consequently, the sales department has decided that it is time for a major improvement of the system, combining multiple lottery games on a single ticket. Most clients have already upgraded their software to version 1.2.0. Moreover, they were ready for another upgrade. This time it was okay to break compatibility, so the version number got bumped up to 2.0.0.

Each major upgrade should be a perfect opportunity to improve the maintainability of the current solution. This is also a chance to reassess what the expected vectors of change are; that is, what parts of the system should be flexible enough to quickly accommodate new change requests. We can identify new games in the future as one such possible direction of change. The new version of the schema is presented here.

```
{
  "id": "http://example.com/schemas/2.0.0/multi-lotto-schema#",
  "$schema": "http://json-schema.org/draft-04/schema#",
  "title": "Multi Lotto Ticket",
  "description": "A player's betting data for our on-line lottery service",

  "definitions": {
    "price-model": {
      "title": "Price model",
      "oneOf": [{
        "description": "A price of a game or ticket in USD",
        "type": "integer",
        "minimum": 1
      },
      {
        "description": "A price of a game or ticket in the chosen currency",
        "type": "object",
        "properties": {
          "currency": { "enum": ["USD", "EUR", "CAD", "RSD", "HUF"] },
          "amount": {
            "description": "An amount in 1/1000 units",
            "type": "integer",
            "minimum": 1000
```

```
        },
        "exchange-rate": {
          "description": "A fixed exchange rate > 0.0 to convert the amount into USD",
          "type": "number",
          "minimum": 0.0,
          "exclusiveMinimum": true,
          "default": 1.0
        }
      },
      "required": ["currency", "amount"],
      "additionalProperties": false
    }]
  },

  "lotto-game": {
    "type": "object",
    "properties": {
      "name": {
        "description": "The unique name of the game",
        "type": "string"
      },
      "selection": {
        "description": "A player's selection of numbers",
        "type": "array",
        "items": {
          "type": "integer",
          "minimum": 1,
          "maximum": 100
        },
        "minItems": 0,
        "uniqueItems": true
      },
      "number-of-draws": {
        "description": "The number of draws in which a ticket should participate",
        "type": "integer",
        "minimum": 1,
        "maximum": 10
      },
      "automaton-pick": {
        "type": "boolean",
        "default": false
      }
    },
    "required": [
      "name",
      "number-of-draws"
    ],
    "additionalProperties": false
  }
},

"type": "object",
```

```
"properties": {
  "version": {
    "description": "The unique semantic version number (X.Y.Z) of the document",
    "type": "string",
    "pattern": "^\\d{1,2}\\.\\d{1,2}\\.\\d{1,3}$"
  },
  "games": {
    "type": "array",
    "items": {
      "type": "object",
      "properties": {
        "game": { "$ref": "/definitions/lotto-game" },
        "game-price": { "$ref": "/definitions/price-model" }
      },
      "additionalProperties": false
    }
  },
  "ticket-price": { "$ref": "/definitions/price-model" }
},
"required": [
  "version",
  "games",
  "ticket-price"
],
"additionalProperties": false
}
```

The resulting instance document containing two different lottery games is presented here.

```
{
  "version": "2.0.0",
  "games": [
    {
      "game": {
        "name": "Wednesday Lotto",
        "selection": [4, 12, 22, 44, 45, 46],
        "number-of-draws": 1
      },
      "game-price": 2
    },
    {
      "game": {
        "name": "Saturday Lotto",
        "selection": [4, 12],
        "number-of-draws": 1,
        "automaton-pick": true
      },
      "game-price": 1
    }
  ],
  "ticket-price": 3
}
```

The major new JSON Schema feature that we have introduced here is the `definitions` section. This is a container for reusable schema chunks. Other parts of the schema reference these via JSON Pointers[13] (notice those $ref members). This is the principal reuse mechanism in JSON Schema.

The `id` member, besides versioning our schema, also defines the schema's base URL. The value of a relative JSON Pointer is then attached to this base URL to get a full address of the referenced entity. This is useful if you want to point to definitions, which are located outside of your schema. The JSON Pointer can also be an absolute URL; for example, `http://json-schema.org/geo` (this points to the schema definition specifying a geographical location).

You should notice that we have a separate price for each game as well as a total price for a ticket. Nevertheless, the same `price-model` definition was reused in both situations.

Version 2.1.0: Separate Game Start Times

Players are not quite satisfied with the multigame ticket. They would like to control the draw date for each game separately. Currently, all of them are scheduled for the next available draw event, as dictated by game rules. Therefore, an additional property must be introduced in a backward-compatible fashion for players to select a draw date for each game (by default game purchases will be scheduled as before). The necessary patch for the schema is presented here (the `lotto-game` definition is expanded with this new optional property).

```
"start-date": { "format": "date-time" }
```

The resulting instance document now looks like this.

```json
{
  "version": "2.0.0",
  "games": [
    {
      "game": {
        "name": "Wednesday Lotto",
        "selection": [4, 12, 22, 44, 45, 46],
        "number-of-draws": 1,
        "start-date": "2016-06-03T20:00:00.00Z"
      },
      "game-price": 2
    },
    {
      "game": {
        "name": "Saturday Lotto",
        "selection": [4, 12],
        "number-of-draws": 1,
        "automaton-pick": true,
        "start-date": "2016-06-04T20:00:00.00+03:00"
      },
      "game-price": 1
    }
  ],
  "ticket-price": 1
}
```

---

[13]Serves the same purpose as XPath in XML.

The main thing to notice here is that even though the schema became quite complex, it was still easy to perform the change. We knew exactly where to put that extra property. Modularizing your schema is the principal enabler to achieve high maintainability.

Summary

Through this simulated evolution of a hypothetical lottery organization's online service, we have gained several insights regarding JSON Schema and its features related to software maintenance. Schema-based messages are just the first step toward putting changes under our control. There are lots of other JSON Schema features that can help you in everyday professional practice. Nonetheless, those presented here are of central importance to creating evolvable message structures.

CONDENSED OUTPUT

In version 2.0.0, the schema has introduced a quite verbose way to enroll games. Try to modify the schema, while keeping it tidy, to support the following message structure:

```
{
  "version": "2.0.0",
  "games": [{
    "name": "Wednesday Lotto",
    "selection": [4, 12, 22, 44, 45, 46],
    "number-of-draws": 1,
    "start-date": "2016-06-03T20:00:00.00Z"
    "game-price": 2
  }],
  "ticket-price": 1
}
```

In other words, get rid of those superfluous game "wrappers." You need to know that this change is definitely not going to be backward compatible. This is the reason why extra care should be taken before releasing anything to the public (especially an API).

References

1. Bau, David. "Theory of Compatibility (Part 1)." http://davidbau.com/archives/2003/12/01/theory_of_compatibility_part_1.html

2. Droettboom, Michael. "Understanding JSON Schema." http://spacetelescope.github.io/understanding-json-schema/

CHAPTER 15

The Core JSON API

Conventional interfaces represent one of the most powerful design principles for working with message payloads, or data structures in general. In nearly all functional programming languages, sequences[1] play this role. The idea is simple: Use a common facility to interconnect modules, and implement program features by combining multiple, independent modules into a unified system. Instead of changing existing modules for each new change request, just combine them in a different way to provide a different behavior. The modules themselves should be self-contained, reusable entities with a single well-specified responsibility. This quote nicely illustrates the idea behind the concept of a conventional interface:

> *In Pascal the plethora of declarable data structures induces a specialization within functions that inhibits and penalizes casual cooperation. It is better to have 100 functions operate on one data structure than to have 10 functions operate on 10 data structures.*
>
> —Alan Perlis, Foreword to *Structure and Interpretation of Computer Programs*

The conventional interface principle has many reincarnations at various levels of scope. If used as an architectural style, it is commonly known as *Pipe and Filter* (see the sidebar "Word Frequency Counter" later in this chapter for an example of how this works in practice). Because JSON API relies on JSON, which is rarely used as a message format for local interprocess communication, our focus will be on JSON API's role as a conventional interface for open distributed systems. JSON API implements the Collection pattern, which is also embodied inside the Collection+JSON hypermedia type.

Openness is an important goal of distributed systems. An open distributed system mandates certain rules regarding how services should be implemented and interconnected. An open system can easily interoperate with another open system. Likewise, services may be easily ported between different implementations of the same open system (behind a single well-described open API, many implementations may exist). We will see how JSON API's rules play a crucial role in realizing the vision of an open distributed system.

WORD FREQUENCY COUNTER

For a good introduction about this pattern you may visit `http://www.tutorialspoint.com/unix/unix-pipes-filters.htm`. The pipe is a standardized communication interface and the filter is a processing node. Perhaps a Unix shell is the best testimony about this style's flexibility, robustness, and power. In this example we would like to count the number of unique occurrences of each word in the input. The program should ignore punctuation, convert all text from lowercase to uppercase, use a

---

[1]Most commonly implemented as lists.

© Ervin Varga 2016

E. Varga, *Creating Maintainable APIs*, DOI 10.1007/978-1-4842-2196-9_15

space as a word separator, and print the result sorted by words. The output for each word should be formatted as a pair (word, frequency). Here is the chain of Unix programs connected via pipes:

```
(tr -d "[:punct:]" | tr -s "[:space:]" | tr "[:space:]" '\n' | tr "[:upper:]"
"[:lower:]" |
 sort |
 uniq -c |
 awk '{print "("$2", "$1")"}')<<EOF
```

For the following input:

The solution is made up of the following Unix programs: 'tr', 'sort', 'uniq', and 'awk'!

These Unix programs are generic, and know only about Unix-related stuff (input and output pipes, environment variables, configuration files, etc.).

This is the power of a conventional interface principle!

EOF

The program outputs the next list of pairs (the output is reformatted to save space; that is, the pairs are put on the same line):

```
(a, 1) (about, 1) (and, 3) (are, 1) (awk, 1) (comprised, 1) (configuration, 1)
(conventional, 1)
 (environment, 1) (etc, 1) (files, 1) (following, 1) (from, 1) (generic, 1) (input, 1)
(interface, 1) (is, 2) (know, 1) (of, 1) (only, 1) (output, 1) (pipes, 1) (power, 1)
(principle, 1) (programs, 2) (related, 1) (solution, 1) (sort, 1) (stuff, 1) (the, 3)
(these, 1) (this, 1) (tr, 1) (uniq, 1) (unix, 3) (variables, 1)
```

Note how each Unix program in this solution is totally generic. None of them were modified here. They were just configured and then composed in a specific way to provide the desired functionality. If you imagine that each of them is run on a separate node of a distributed system, and the pipe is replaced with its distributed counterpart, then you basically get interoperable microservices. Finally, if you reshape `tr` into a mapper, transform `uniq` into a reducer, and put them inside a *Hadoop* ecosystem (it will provide sorting, outputting, and management of components) then you get a *MapReduce* program.

The next list briefly enrolls the most salient features and benefits of JSON API:

- *It is a conventional interface:* This is fundamental to remember to understand the difference between pure message formats and JSON API. The JSON API, besides establishing a shared convention regarding message formats, also encompasses rules for how to interact with messages. For example, it contains instructions on how services should fetch, create, update, and delete resources, specify pagination, pass query parameters, and so on.

- *Enables generalized tooling support.*

- *Actively promotes the Open/Closed principle:* With JSON API, distributed services can be realized as reusable, independent, and self-contained entities. They should be easily composable without a need to alter them (we aren't taking into account bugs here, as they would entail changes in the services). Hence, the resulting system would be open for extension and closed for modification.

- *Increases the productivity of teams:* Software engineers should learn a single standard for message payloads together with a common set of development frameworks and tools. The JSON API helps increase productivity in a similar vein as software patterns. Instead of solving recurring problems multiple times in different ways, it gives immediate answers to the most frequently encountered concerns pertaining to message payloads.

- *Increases performance:* This occurs because services built around JSON API can circumvent data transfer overheads by efficiently caching responses.

- After all it is JSON, which is nowadays a default data serialization format of the Web.

At the time of this writing, the JSON API's version number is 1.0. It is its first stable release, and the upcoming version 1.1 should appear soon. The JSON API has a registered media type of `application/vnd.api+json` issued by the Internet Assigned Numbers Authority (IANA).

■ **Caution**   Never put the official JSON API media type in a request/response to or from a server without fully obeying the specification. This would simply break all clients (including development frameworks) expecting a proper JSON API document. The JSON API is very flexible, and there is no reason to concoct some curtailed version of it to "simplify" matters. You will just make your life more complicated.

■ **Note**   The JSON API is envisioned to always evolve in a backward-compatible manner. This is achieved by incrementally extending the specification, and never altering existing material. This is a fine example of how the specification itself adheres to the same principles that it advocates to the public; that is, the Open/Closed principle.

This chapter should complement the JSON API specification, not replace it. The aim here is to put JSON API into a proper context, and explain how it helps in creating maintainable APIs in regard to message payloads. We start our journey with a bit of a detour by first studying an established industry standard message format. This serves as a starting point to gradually introduce JSON API elements in a comparative fashion. Moreover, the case study emphasizes the pragmatic traits of JSON API; that is, how it addresses real-world problems. After all, JSON API was extracted from a library used in many production systems, so its origin is in the software industry, as is the case with design patterns.

Case Study of an Industry Standard Message Format

This section presents a case study of designing message payloads, and exchanging messages using a domain specific message format. We analyze the operation of an electrical power system, and what kind of issues arise there from the perspective of data exchange. The beauty of this example is that it will introduce some concepts that are extremely important from the viewpoint of JSON API. Of course, it isn't so important to understand all the details of a power system to grasp the content of this section. Therefore, I keep the details to a minimum, sometimes even at the expense of accuracy (see the References at the end of this chapter for an excellent book about this topic).

■ **Tip**   The case study is by itself a useful tutorial about designing a powerful maintainable message format, if for some reason you cannot use JSON API. The message format presented here is battle tested over years of production use by power system organizations.

Common Information Model of a Power System

An electrical power system is made up of production and distribution facilities on one side and consumers of electrical energy on the other. These sides need to be balanced (the amount of energy produced should equal the consumption rate) to have a stable situation in an electrical power grid.

This is a very dynamic system. Some changes are planned, but many of them are exceptional situations caused by all sorts of malfunctions. At any rate, all kinds of changes in the system must be promptly addressed. To achieve smooth operation, production facilities and electrical utility organizations need to exchange system modeling information with one another. Most analysis functions cannot be performed by relying solely on data acquired by a single organization. This is the reason data from neighboring systems must be included, too. Hence, the principal demand for an extensive data exchange.[2]

To cope with the diversity of systems deployed by each organization EPRI in North America developed the Common Information Model (CIM). Today it is a series of standards, collectively known as *CIM for power systems*, under the International Electrotechnical Commission (IEC), IEC 61970, IEC 61968, and IEC 62325. CIM ensures a standard way for representing resources of an electrical power system as classes, attributes, and associations between them. In other words, CIM is a conceptual model in UML for the domain of an electrical power system. This type of a domain model is imperative to establish a common vocabulary between various independent parties. Figure 15-1 shows the CIM connectivity model to illustrate what sort of entities are situated inside CIM. The connectivity model contains elements to describe physical connections inside a power network.

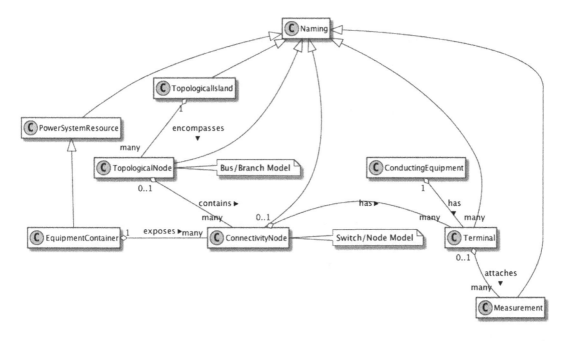

Figure 15-1. *CIM connectivity model (we will use the switch/node model intended for distribution networks).*

---

[2]The amount and granularity of data is vastly bigger in distribution networks than in transmission ones (between power generators and utility companies). This is also true for the frequency of changes in the network. I'll not delve into another reason to trade data between utility organizations, which is related to the regulation of an electrical power market.

To express how equipment of a network is interconnected you can use instances of Terminal and ConnectivityNode classes. A piece of conducting equipment usually has two terminals (e.g., a regular disconnector), or just one (e.g., the ground disconnector). Equipment terminals are joined via an instance of a ConnectivityNode. Figure 15-2 shows a simplified network model (e.g., the busbar sections are omitted), and its translation into CIM.

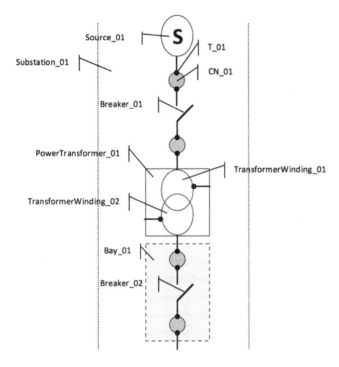

Figure 15-2. *Simplified network diagram with the corresponding CIM classes in abbreviated form.*

Serialization of a Power Network with CIM/XML

UML diagrams are not amenable for a direct machine processing. Therefore, it is necessary to specify the set of rules and message structures to encode the CIM model into a form understandable by computers. The Knowledge Representation concept proved to be a good match here. Leveraging the Resource Description Framework (RDF) and its associated schema (contains instructions about valid statements inside an RDF document) enables CIM models to be represented in a desired format. We will see shortly that comprehending the basics of RDF is crucial to grasp how JSON API handles resources.

In the RDF's data model, a *resource* is any identifiable entity. RDF relies on the URI for resource identification. A *property* of a resource is its characteristic, which can be designated by a *value*. To avoid ambiguities in the vocabulary (naming of properties), a *property* is also associated with a URI. An ordered triple[3] (*resource, property, value*) is the unit of information in RDF, and it is called a *statement*. We can also portray this triple as (*subject, predicate, object*). The *object* may be a raw value (e.g., string, number, etc.), or a reference to another resource.

---

[3]These triples can be easily visualized as a graph.

The serialization format of CIM is CIM/XML.[4] It is an application of RDF on CIM using XML as a backbone message format. A valid CIM/XML document conforms to the CIM/XML schema (much like valid XML conforms to the matching XML schema). There are three possible approaches to serializing a CIM network model into CIM/XML:

1. Using a flat structure.

2. Embedding resources inside each other; that is, applying a recursive style.

3. Using a hybrid variant.

Here is the abridged CIM/XML document representing the network shown in Figure 15-2 (the boilerplate XML is omitted to reduce space, the equipment's electrical properties are left out, and almost all connectivity data is removed). This document is produced using the third approach from the preceding list.

```
<cim:Company ID="Company_01" CompanyName="Example Electrical Company, Inc.">
  <cim:CompanyDescription>
    Learner's electrical utility organization.
  </cim:CompanyDescription>
</cim:Company>

<cim:Substation rdf:ID="Substation_01">
  <cim:IdentifiedObject.name>HV/MV 1</cim:IdentifiedObject.name>
  <cim:MemberOfCompany rdf:resource="#Company_01">
  <cim:Contain>
    <cim:Breaker rdf:ID="Breaker_01">
      <cim:IdentifiedObject.name>High Voltage Breaker 1</cim:IdentifiedObject.name>
      <cim:Switch.open>NO</cim:Switch.open>
    </cim:Breaker>
  </cim:Contain>
</cim:Substation>

<cim:EquivalentSource rdf:ID="Source_01">
  <cim:IdentifiedObject.name>High Voltage Source 1</cim:IdentifiedObject.name>
  <cim:Equipment.MemberOf_EquipmentContainer rdf:resource="#Substation_01" />
</cim:EquivalentSource>

<cim:Terminal rdf:ID="T_01">
  <cim:Terminal.ConnectivityNode rdf:resource="#CN_01" />
  <cim:Terminal.ConductingEquipment rdf:resource="#Source_01" />
</cim:Terminal>

<cim:ConnectivityNode rdf:ID="CN_01">
  <cim:ConnectivityNode.MemberOf_EquipmentContainer rdf:resource="#Bay_XXX" />
</cim:ConnectivityNode>

<cim:PowerTransformer rdf:ID="PowerTransformer_01">
  <cim:ConductingEquipment.phases>ABC</cim:ConductingEquipment.phases>
  <cim:Equipment.MemberOf_EquipmentContainer rdf:resource="#Substation_01" />
  <cim:Contain>
    <cim:TransformerWinding rdf:ID="TransformerWinding_01">
      <cim:TransformerWinding.windingType>PRIMARY</cim:TransformerWinding.windingType>
      <cim:TransformerWinding.connectionType>WYE (Y)</cim:TransformerWinding.connectionType>
```

```
     <cim:TransformerWinding.grounded>YES</cim:TransformerWinding.grounded>
    </cim:TransformerWinding>
    <cim:TransformerWinding rdf:ID="TransformerWinding_02">
     <cim:TransformerWinding.windingType>SECONDARY</cim:TransformerWinding.windingType>
     <cim:TransformerWinding.connectionType>Delta (D)</cim:TransformerWinding.
connectionType>
     <cim:TransformerWinding.grounded>NO</cim:TransformerWinding.grounded>
    </cim:TransformerWinding>
   </cim:Contain>
</cim:PowerTransformer>

<cim:Bay rdf:ID="Bay_01">
  <cim:IdentifiedObject.name>Breaker Bay</cim:IdentifiedObject.name>
  <cim:Bay.MemberOf_Substation rdf:resource="#Substation_01" />
</cim:Bay>

<cim:Breaker rdf:ID="Breaker_02">
  <cim:IdentifiedObject.name>High Voltage Breaker 2</cim:IdentifiedObject.name>
  <cim:Switch.open>NO</cim:Switch.open>
  <cim:ConductingEquipment.phases>ABC</cim:ConductingEquipment.phases>
  <cim:Equipment.MemberOf_EquipmentContainer rdf:resource="#Bay_01" />
</cim:Breaker>
```

The elements and attributes in this document are designated with proper namespaces (cim and rdf).[5] For example, cim:Substation represents a substation in the CIM model, and rdf:ID is an RDF resource identifier. Namespaces are crucial here to separate different vocabularies inside the same XML document. Moreover, a namespace is useful to specify the version number of a vocabulary. The cim namespace can be defined as xmlns:cim="http://iec.ch/TC57/2006/CIM-schema-cim10#" (often this URI is also a URL with retrievable content describing the matching vocabulary). Versioning is an important topic in JSON API, too.

Every CIM/XML document has a URI denoting its base "address." It could be implicitly defined via the server's URL that created it, or it may contain an explicit xml:base attribute at the top.[6] An rdf:ID attribute's value is then attached to this base address to produce a global resource URI. To reference resources locally (inside the same document) you can use rdf:resource with a relative reference. The same resource identification machinery is also present in JSON API.

Relationships between resources are specified via explicit references (e.g., cim:Equipment.MemberOf_ EquipmentContainer) or by using the cim:Contain construct. A consumer of a CIM/XML document must be prepared for all possibilities. This complicates the document parsing process, and prevents efficient caching of responses. For this reason, most servers generate flat CIM/XML documents to avoid these issues.

Extending the CIM/XML Schema

Suppose we would like to extend the CIM vocabulary by a new element to associate an oil capacity with an oil-filled power transformer. This is straightforward to do in CIM/XML thanks to the distributed nature of RDF, and that it is descriptive and not prescriptive.[7] We need to introduce a separate vocabulary with a

---

[4]CIM/JSON also starts to gain traction, and there are scientific papers published on this topic.
[5]The CIM/XML approach is in some way reminiscent of MOF (meta-object facility). See https://en.wikipedia.org/ wiki/Meta-Object_Facility.
[6]You can consult the *XML Base* specification at http://www.w3.org/TR/xmlbase/ for more details.
[7]A class definition in most OO languages is prohibitive regarding unknown elements. You cannot simply add an attribute to a class without chaning the class definition. RDF tolerates such new additions. If something is not constrained, then it is free content. Clients can deal with them in any way they want. RDF and OWL are about inference.

designated URI. The vocabulary is actually a CIM/XML schema describing our extension. We also need to publish it with a stable URI (there are lots of publicly available vocabularies on the Web for various domains). Once this is done, we can incorporate our new element into a CIM/XML document just by referencing our vocabulary's URI in the corresponding namespace.[8]

If the new namespace is denoted by cim-ext, then we can describe a power transformer in the following manner:

```
<cim:PowerTransformer rdf:ID="PowerTransformer_XY">
    <cim:ConductingEquipment.phases>ABC</cim:ConductingEquipment.phases>
    <cim:Equipment.MemberOf_EquipmentContainer rdf:resource="#Substation_YYY" />
    <cim-ext:PowerTransformer.OilCapacity>100</cim-ext:PowerTransformer.OilCapacity>
</cim:PowerTransformer>
```

By convention, clients who don't "speak" the new language will ignore elements coming from an unknown namespace (vocabulary). This same principle is also used in JSON API. These conditions allow the schema to evolve through additive changes.

Practical Guide to JSON API

In this chapter we systematically introduce JSON API's features starting with a simple construct, and gradually boosting it up. We convert the CIM/XML document of a small power network into JSON API step by step. You will notice how JSON API governs the interaction between a client and a server, and solves recurring concerns in a systematized way. These aspects of JSON API are what differentiates it from bare message format standards. CIM/XML doesn't try to suggest, for example, how to request pagination, filter results, update resources, and so on. Moreover, with JSON API a server fully controls what is exposed to clients, and clients can learn the service graph by parsing what links are available in the response document. A JSON API client is able to decipher the interaction patterns with a server even if it knows nothing about the particular content provided by a server. A server might even support HEAD requests on resources, and can return allowed actions inside the HTTP Allow response header (e.g., Allow: GET,PATCH).

The following subsections are organized as user stories. Each one has a clear goal, and introduces a new feature of JSON API. The assumption is that we have a server available at http://example.com.

Fetching an Individual Resource

The goal is to fetch a JSON API document containing only a company information. A client needs to create the following HTTP request:[9]

```
GET /companies/Company_01 HTTP/1.1
Accept: application/vnd.api+json
```

The server should return the following response:

```
HTTP/1.1 200 OK
Content-Type: application/vnd.api+json
```

---

[8]Version 1.1 of JSON API will use extension registries with URIs to introduce extensions, very similar to the way in which RDF vocabularies are entered into a picture.
[9]We could also use HTTP 2.0 in our examples, but HTTP 1.1 is still prevalent at the time of this writing.

```
{
  "jsonapi": {
    "version": "1.0"
  },
  "links": {
    "self": "http://example.com/companies/Company_01"
  },
  "data": {
    "type": "companies",
    "id": "Company_01",
    "attributes": {
      "CompanyName": "Example Electrical Company, Inc.",
      "CompanyDescription": "Learner's electrical utility organization."
    }
  }
}
```

It is very important both for a client and a server to reference the JSON API's media type `application/vnd.api+json` while exchanging data. The current version of JSON API doesn't allow any additional parameters inside this media type. Future versions of JSON API might use these parameters for versioning.

A JSON API document used in requests and responses must be a valid JSON document,[10] with a JSON object at its root. This JSON object is a *top-level* entity. It must contain at least one of the following members:

- `data`: is a representation of the returned resource (or collection of resources), usually termed the document's *primary data*.

- `errors`: is an array of error objects.

- `meta`: is a meta object that contains nonstandard meta-information (this is a topic in Chapter 16).

In our case we only have a `data` member. The `errors` member would be present in case of some error. However, in this scenario no primary data would be returned. Besides the mandatory `data` member, our document also contains some optional members:

- `jsonapi`: An object describing the server's implementation and its capabilities.

- `links`: A links object related to the primary data.

Our top-level `links` member contains a `self`-pointer. This contains a URL, which generated the current response document. The self-link provides valuable historical data about the document's origin.

The primary data in our response document is a single *resource object*. It is identified by its `type` and `id` members. We don't directly use the CIM class `Company` here for a `type`. A namespace designator cannot be part of the type.[11] Moreover, to comply with JSON API's recommended practice of URL design, we set `type` in plural form using lowercase letters. This translation technique will be used for all the other CIM classes, too.

The pair (`type`, `id`) uniquely identifies a resource inside a document served from the same URL; that is, belonging to the same *base*. JSON API calls all servers associated with the same base simply *API*. This is again similar to what we have seen in CIM/XML.

---

[10]The JSON API has an associated JSON schema available at `http://jsonapi.org/schema`.
[11]Chapter 16 shows how to extend JSON API to include RDF constructs. It is not possible to just use `"cim:Company"`, because the `type` name must adhere to the same rules as member names in general (the colon is not allowed in member names).

The `attributes` member contains an *attributes object* representing the company's data (the attribute names are reused from CIM). Individual members of an attributes object are called its *fields*. Although in our document the fields are simple strings, they can be any valid JSON documents. The only restriction is that those JSON documents must not contain `relationships` or `links` members, as these are reserved for future use.

■ **Caution**   If you catch fields representing foreign keys then it is a sign that the corresponding document only looks like JSON API (e.g., if a company would reference its owner as "`owner_id`" rather than using the `relationships` link). Moreover, you should be very careful when embedding a huge JSON document as an attribute's value. JSON API cannot help you access resources inside such monoliths.

Fetching Related Resources with Autoinclusion

The goal is to fetch a JSON API document containing data about a power transformer. This data should include information about the transformer's windings. A client needs to create the following HTTP request:

```
GET /power-transformers/PowerTransformer_01 HTTP/1.1
Accept: application/vnd.api+json
```

The server should return the following response:[12]

```
HTTP/1.1 200 OK
Content-Type: application/vnd.api+json

{
  "jsonapi": {
    "version": "1.0"
  },
  "links": {
    "self": "http://example.com/power-transformers/PowerTransformer_01"
  },
  "data": {
    "type": "power-transformers",
    "id": "PowerTransformer_01",
    "attributes": {
      "ConductingEquipment-phases": "ABC"
    },
    "relationships": {
      "member-of": {
        "data": { "type": "substations", "id": "Substation_01" }
      },
      "windings": {
        "links": {
          "self":
            "http://example.com/power-transformers/PowerTransformer_01/relationships/windings",
```

---

[12]We are encoding CIM attributes by using a hyphen minus instead of a period, which is not allowed in member names. The low line is still retained to be closer to CIM names, but JSON API recommends hyphen minus as a word separator.

```
          "related": "http://example.com/power-transformers/PowerTransformer_01/windings"
        },
        "data": [
          { "type": "transformer-windings", "id": "TransformerWinding_01" },
          { "type": "transformer-windings", "id": "TransformerWinding_02" }
        ]
      }
    }
  },
  "included": [{
    "type": "transformer-windings",
    "id": "TransformerWinding_01",
    "attributes": {
      "TransformerWinding-windingType": "PRIMARY",
      "TransformerWinding-connectionType": "WYE (Y)",
      "TransformerWinding-grounded": "YES"
    },
    "relationships": {
      "member-of": {
        "data": { "type": "power-transformers", "id": "PowerTransformer_01" }
      }
    },
    "links": {
      "self": "http://example.com/transformer-windings/TransformerWinding_01"
    }
  }, {
    "type": "transformer-windings",
    "id": "TransformerWinding_02",
    "attributes": {
      "TransformerWinding-windingType": "SECONDARY",
      "TransformerWinding-connectionType": "Delta (D)",
      "TransformerWinding-grounded": "NO"
    },
    "relationships": {
      "member-of": {
        "data": { "type": "power-transformers", "id": "PowerTransformer_01" }
      }
    },
    "links": {
      "self": "http://example.com/transformer-windings/TransformerWinding_02"
    }
  }]
}
```

The first new JSON API element here is the relationships member, the value of which is a *relationships object* describing relationships between the primary resource and its related resources. In our case, the power transformer has two relationships: member-of and windings. The former is a *to-one*, whereas the latter is a *to-many* type of a relationship (our power transformer belongs to a single substation and has two windings).

Inside the windings relationships object we have two additional members: links and data. The self-pointer is the *relationships link*. Through this URL a client can manipulate the relationship; for example, fetch related resources (in our case windings), add new resources to the relationship (like adding a third winding to a transformer), remove resources, and so on. The related pointer is the URL through which related resources are retrieved, if a client decides to issue a fetch request using the given link. The `member-of` relationship only has a `data` member with a reference to the containing substation. Referencing resources using a data member only consisting of a pair (`type`, `id`) is called a *resource linkage*. The pair itself is known as a *resource identifier object*.

The `data` member inside the `windings` relationships object is an array of *resource identifier objects*. Each element references a specific transformer winding. Each winding is situated inside an array associated with the `include` top-level member. The idea here is to automatically return all the windings of a power transformer inside a single document: This approach saves a client from the burden of fetching them via a separate GET request. On the other hand, if the number of related resources is vast then it is better to let a client decide when and how to get them.

A JSON API document that bundles the primary data with related resources is called a *compound document*. In such a document all included (related) resources must be represented as an array of resource objects in a top-level `include` member. Each included resource must be referenced inside the same document (either from primary data or indirectly through the relationship objects). In our example, the `windings` relationship object contains two resource identifiers referencing the primary and the secondary winding of a power transformer.

Each transformer winding has a relationship with a resource identifier object pointing back to the containing power transformer. In CIM/XML the windings were embedded inside a power transformer, but in JSON API the structure is flat. Also, each winding has a resource link with a `self`-pointer. A client may hit the server with the provided URL to get details about the given winding only.

Fetching Relationships

The goal is to fetch a JSON API document containing data about the `windings` relationship of a power transformer. The response should contain as its primary data an array of resource identifier objects. A client needs to create the following HTTP request (notice that the URL is the one given in the JSON API document listed in the previous section).

```
GET /power-transformers/PowerTransformer_01/relationships/windings HTTP/1.1
Accept: application/vnd.api+json
```

The server should return the following response:

```
HTTP/1.1 200 OK
Content-Type: application/vnd.api+json

{
  "jsonapi": {
    "version": "1.0"
  },
  "links": {
    "self": "/power-transformers/PowerTransformer_01/relationships/windings",
    "related": "/power-transformers/PowerTransformer_01/windings"
  },
  "data": [
    { "type": "transformer-windings", "id": "TransformerWinding_01" },
    { "type": "transformer-windings", "id": "TransformerWinding_02" }
  ]
}
```

A client may now retrieve data about each winding by issuing the following GET request:

```
GET /transformer-windings/TransformerWinding_XY HTTP/1.1
Accept: application/vnd.api+json
```

Fetching a Collection of Resources

The goal is to fetch a JSON API document containing all substations present in the system (let us presume that a company owns more than 100 various substations). The response should contain as its primary data an array of resource identifier objects.[13] A client needs to create the following HTTP request:

```
GET /substations HTTP/1.1
Accept: application/vnd.api+json
```

The server should return the following response:

```
HTTP/1.1 200 OK
Content-Type: application/vnd.api+json

{
  "jsonapi": {
    "version": "1.0"
  },
  "meta": {
    "count": "100"
  },
  "links": {
    "self": "http://example.com/substations",
    "next": "http://example.com/substations?page[offset]=10&page[limit]=10",
    "last": "http://example.com/substations?page[offset]=90&page[limit]=10"
  },
  "data": [
    { "type": "substations", "id": "Substation_01" },
    { "type": "substations", "id": "Substation_02" },
    { "type": "substations", "id": "Substation_03" },
    { "type": "substations", "id": "Substation_04" },
    { "type": "substations", "id": "Substation_05" },
    { "type": "substations", "id": "Substation_06" },
    { "type": "substations", "id": "Substation_07" },
    { "type": "substations", "id": "Substation_08" },
    { "type": "substations", "id": "Substation_09" }
  ]
}
```

Due to a large number of substations the server has decided to apply pagination. In each round it delivers nine references with pagination links. The next link tells how to request the next batch of data. The last is a pointer to the last batch of data. The server might also provide two additional links: first and prev. These are useful when a client is in the middle of a collection.

---

[13]The response could also contain a full-blown representation of each entity. We are just hinting here at what we expect from our fictitious server.

The meta member contains the count field, which is an indicator of the collection's size. It is convenient to introduce such implementation-specific additions (outside of JSON API's jurisdiction).

A client might decide to ask a server for a specific batch of data using the page query parameter. For example, this request would ask for substations at offset 50, with a batch size of 20:[14]

```
GET /substations?page[offset]=50&page[limit]=20 HTTP/1.1
Accept: application/vnd.api+json
```

This pagination is offset-based. However, a server might also support page-based as well as cursor-based methods.

Fetching Related Resources with Explicit Inclusion

The goal is to fetch a JSON API document containing basic data about a substation. This data should include information about bays.[15] A substation can contain multiple bays, and usually it is impossible to predict whether a client will always want to receive these when requesting a substation. Therefore, it is left to a client to explicitly ask for an inclusion of bays in a response. A client needs to create the following HTTP request (notice the usage of the include parameter):

```
GET /substations/Substation_01?include=bays HTTP/1.1
Accept: application/vnd.api+json
```

The server should return the following response:

```
HTTP/1.1 200 OK
Content-Type: application/vnd.api+json

{
  "jsonapi": {
    "version": "1.0"
  },
  "links": {
    "self": "http://example.com/substations/Substation_01?include=bays"
  },
  "data": {
    "type": "substations",
    "id": "Substation_01",
    "attributes": {
      "IdentifiedObject-name": "HV/MV 1"
    },
    "relationships": {
      "member-of": {
        "data": { "type": "companies", "id": "Company_01" }
      },
```

---

[14]The [and] characters need to be URL encoded, but it is not done here to increase readability.

[15]A bay is a container for grouping equipment connected in some predefined manner. Inside a typical substation you will encounter many instances of bays, but most of them are of the same type. In other words, the number of topologically different bays is not that big. Using bays could reduce the complexity of a network, hence, they are kind of an abstraction to reason about a power grid.

```
      "bays": {
        "links": {
          "self": "http://example.com/substations/Substation_01/relationships/bays",
          "related": "http://example.com/substations/Substation_01/bays"
        },
        "data": [
          { "type": "bays", "id": "Bay_01" }
        ]
      }
    }
  },
  "included": [{
    "type": "bays",
    "id": "Bay_01",
    "attributes": {
      "IdentifiedObject-name": "Breaker Bay"
    },
    "relationships": {
      "member-of": {
        "data": { "type": "substations", "id": "Substation_01" }
      }
    },
    "links": {
      "self": "http://example.com/bays/Bay_01"
    }
  }]
}
```

Notice that the other associated equipment (power transformer, breaker, etc.) is not included here, because a client only asked for inclusion of bays. To also include a power transformer a client would need to issue the next request:

```
GET /substations/Substation_01?include=bays,power-transformers HTTP/1.1
Accept: application/vnd.api+json
```

Fetching a Partial View of an Individual Resource

The goal is to fetch a JSON API document containing only data about a specified breaker. However, we are only interested in seeing the status of a breaker; that is, is it ON or OFF. A client needs to create the following HTTP request:[16]

```
GET /breakers/Breaker_2300?fields[breakers]=Switch-open HTTP/1.1
Accept: application/vnd.api+json
```

The server should return the following response:

```
HTTP/1.1 200 OK
Content-Type: application/vnd.api+json
```

---

[16]The [and] characters need to be URL encoded, but it is not done here to increase readability.

```
{
  "jsonapi": {
    "version": "1.0"
  },
  "links": {
    "self": "http://example.com/breakers/Breaker_2300?fields[breakers]=Switch-open"
  },
  "data": {
    "type": "breakers",
    "id": "Breaker_2300",
    "attributes": {
      "Switch-open": "NO"
    }
  }
}
```

Note that the member-of relationship is not listed here, as it is excluded (relationship names are also treated as fields). To include it a client would need to make the following request:

```
GET /breakers/Breaker_2300?fields[breakers]=Switch-open,member-of HTTP/1.1
Accept: application/vnd.api+json
```

Creating a New Resource

The goal is to create a new substation with a reference to the owner. The request should be processed in a synchronous manner. A client needs to create the following HTTP request:

```
POST /substations HTTP/1.1
Content-Type: application/vnd.api+json
Accept: application/vnd.api+json

{
  "data": {
    "type": "substations",
    "attributes": {
      "IdentifiedObject-name": "HV/MV 101"
    },
    "relationships": {
      "member-of": {
        "data": { "type": "companies", "id": "Company_01" }
      }
    }
  }
}
```

The server should return the following response:

```
HTTP/1.1 201 Created
Location: http://example.com/substations/Substation_101
Content-Type: application/vnd.api+json

{
```

```
  "jsonapi": {
    "version": "1.0"
  },
  "links": {
    "self": "http://example.com/ substations/Substation_101"
  },
  "data": {
    "type": "substations",
    "id": "Substation_101",
    "attributes": {
      "IdentifiedObject-name": "HV/MV 101"
    },
    "relationships": {
      "member-of": {
        "data": { "type": "companies", "id": "Company_01" }
      }
    }
  }
}
```

The request doesn't contain an `id` member, because a client leaves the job of generating a resource identifier to a server. Of course, a client can provide an identifier, but in this case it would be a client's responsibility to make it globally unique. In the case when a server creates an identifier (like in our case) then it must respond with a full resource object. It would be silly to respond with `204 No Content`. At any rate, the request must be processed in an atomic fashion by a server. It cannot happen, for example, that the new substation is created without the specified relationship (as given in the HTTP request body).

Updating a Resource

The goal is to update the owner for a substation. It is assumed that the server will not alter attributes except those specified in the request. A client needs to create the following HTTP request:

```
PATCH /substations/Substation_01 HTTP/1.1
Content-Type: application/vnd.api+json
Accept: application/vnd.api+json

{
  "data": {
    "type": "substations",
    "id": "Substation_01",
    "relationships": {
      "member-of": {
        "data": { "type": "companies", "id": "Company_02" }
      }
    }
  }
}
```

The server should return a `204 No Content` status code without a response document. All omitted fields in the request should retain their current value; that is, the server cannot treat them as `null`.

The preceding request has updated the `member-of` relationship by updating the resource itself. However, relationships can be managed by directly hitting the relationships link with PATCH (update), POST (create), and DELETE (remove) requests. A change in the relationship doesn't affect the target resource(s); that is removing a related resource from a relationship will not automatically delete that resource.

When updating a `to-many` relationship, a client could specify multiple resources at once. The HTTP PATCH request must be executed in an atomic fashion, so the whole bulk update must either completely succeed or fail. This is the reason servers may choose to disallow such bulk updates. In this case a server will return a response with a `403 Forbidden` status code.

Deleting a Resource

The goal is to delete a substation. The request should be processed in a synchronous manner. A client needs to create the following HTTP request:

```
DELETE /substations/Substation_01 HTTP/1.1
Accept: application/vnd.api+json
```

If the deletion is successful, then the server responds with a `204 No Content` status code.

Summary

We have seen that JSON API = message format + interaction rules, which combined offers a unified way to work with resources. There are many aspects of JSON API, which are not exemplified in this chapter, such as the following:

- Sorting.
- Filtering.
- Custom query parameter handling.
- Error processing.
- Asynchronous processing.

You can find information about these in the JSON API specification. There is also an excellent discussion forum available at `http://discuss.jsonapi.org`.

■ **Tip**   To practice interaction with a sample JSON API server you can visit the following open source project: `https://github.com/endpoints/endpoints-example`.

```
┌─────────────────────────────────────────────────────────────────────┐
│                    SERVICE GRAPH CREATION                             │
└─────────────────────────────────────────────────────────────────────┘
```

Validating That JSON API Is Based on HATEOAS (Hypermedia as the Engine of Application State)

Write a JSON API client to generate a service graph (assume that it is small) for content provided by an arbitrary JSON API server. Your graph traversal should start from the server's root URL. You can serialize the output using the *GraphML File Format* (visit `http://graphml.graphdrawing.org` for more information). You could use the sample server mentioned in the summary section to test your client.

The graph should be made up of nodes and directed links. A node would be a resource identifier object. Two nodes are connected if there is a link between them; that is, a resource object representation of the first node points to the second one. A link has to be labeled with a (relationship name, URL) pair extracted from the resource object associated with the first node. Additionally, you can attach allowed actions on resources (nodes), in case a server supports the HTTP `HEAD` request.

If your client really rocks, then don't forget to publish it as well as make an announcement on the JSON API's discussion forum!

References

1. Uslar, M., M. Specht, S. Rohjans, J. Trefke, and J. M. González. *The Common Information Model CIM IEC 61968/61970 and 62325: A Practical Introduction to the CIM.* New York: Springer, 2012.

2. JSON API Specification 1.0. `http://jsonapi.org/format/`

3. Abelson, Harold, Gerald Jay Sussman, and Julie Sussman. *Structure and Interpretion of Computer Programs, Second Edition.* Cambridge, MA: MIT Press, 1999.

4. deVos, A., S. E. Widegren, and J. Zhu. "XML for CIM Model Exchange." Paper presented at the Power Ind. Comput. Applicat. Conference, Sydney, Australia, 2001. `http://www.langdale.com.au/PICA/CIMXML.pdf`

5. Popović, Dragan, Ervin Varga, and Zvezdana Perlić. "Extension of the Common Information Model with a Catalog of Topologies." *IEEE Transactions on Power Systems,* Volume 22, Number 2, May 2007.

6. Tanenbaum, Andrew S., and Maarten Van Steen. *Distributed Systems: Principles and Paradigms, Second Edition.* Upper Saddle River, NJ: Pearson, 2007.

■ ■ ■

CHAPTER 16

Evolving the JSON API

There is no one-size-fits-all solution,[1] as every specification eventually needs to evolve. There are many reasons for this,[2] but the most prominent one is that software needs to adapt to a changing environment, and has to support new use cases. A message format is "something others can depend on" and as such it is part of the API of one's system.[3] Hence, it needs to be flexible enough to address the demands for new kinds of data. To make a message specification reusable across disparate business and technology domains, it must be designed for extension and evolution. This is very similar to the notion of a reusable class in OOP, where reusability doesn't happen by chance, and requires a careful approach (the class has to be designed for reuse). Besides the reasons related to new messages, the JSON API could also expand due to new interaction models and features. We have seen in the previous chapter that the JSON API is a conventional interface rather than a simple message specification.

A Case Study of Integrating Disparate Data Sources

This example tries to answer the question of whether you need anything more advanced than the core JSON API. Suppose we would like to implement a blog portal that consumes blog posts from different sites (we will assume that example1.com and example2.com are independent blog sources). Our goal is to try to coalesce posts according to some criteria. We presume that the messages from those sites are already delivered in the JSON API format. The following is the contrived message received from example1.com.

```
{
  "links": {
    "self": "http://example1.com/posts",
    "next": "http://example1.com/posts?page[offset]=2",
    "last": "http://example1.com/posts?page[offset]=10"
  },
  "data": [{
    "type": "posts",
    "id": "1",
    "attributes": { "content": "It is easy to extend the JSON API!" },
```

---

[1]There are unisex eyeglass frame designers who think that this is feasible. This is the principal reason why I always have a hard time finding myself a comfortable frame.
[2]For a more rigorous treatment of this topic consult the "Program Evolution Dynamics" article at http://iansommerville.com/software-engineering-book/web/program-evolution-dynamics/.
[3]Of course, we need to be careful to avoid including everything as an API. Protocols are definitely part of it, and in this respect JSON API plays an important role in specifying interaction patterns between services.

© Ervin Varga 2016

E. Varga, *Creating Maintainable APIs*, DOI 10.1007/978-1-4842-2196-9_16

```
    "relationships": {
      "author": {
        "links": {
          "self": "http://example1.com/posts/1/relationships/author",
          "related": "http://example1.com/posts/1/author"
        },
        "data": { "type": "people", "id": "10" }
      },
      "comments": {
        "links": {
          "self": "http://example1.com/posts/1/relationships/comments",
          "related": "http://example1.com/posts/1/comments"
        },
        "data": { "type": "comments", "id": "1" }
      }
    },
    "links": { "self": "http://example1.com/posts/1" }
  }],
  "included": [{
    "type": "people",
    "id": "10",
    "attributes": {
      "first-name": "Ervin",
      "last-name": "Varga",
      "username": "ervin.varga"
    },
    "links": {
      "self": "http://example1.com/people/10"
    }
  },
  {
    "type": "comments",
    "id": "1",
    "attributes": { "body": "I like this post!" },
    "relationships": {
      "author": { "data": { "type": "people", "id": "11" } }
    }
  },
    "links": {
      "self": "http://example1.com/comments/1"
    }
  }]
}
```

Next is the contrived message received from example2.com.

```
{
  "links": {
    "self": "http://example2.com/articles",
    "next": "http://example2.com/articles?page[number]=2",
    "last": "http://example2.com/articles?page[number]=7"
```

```
  },
  "data": [{
    "type": "articles",
    "id": "1",
    "attributes": { "text": "We use JSON API to gain flexibility!" },
    "relationships": {
      "author": {
        "links": {
          "self": "http://example2.com/articles/1/relationships/author",
          "related": "http://example2.com/articles/1/author"
        },
        "data": { "type": "persons", "id": "5" }
      },
      "comments": {
        "links": {
          "self": "http://example2.com/articles/1/relationships/comments",
          "related": "http://example2.com/articles/1/comments"
        },
        "data": { "type": "comments", "id": "1" }
      }
    },
    "links": { "self": "http://example2.com/articles/1" }
  }],
  "included": [{
    "type": "persons",
    "id": "5",
    "attributes": {
      "name": "Ervin Varga",
      "user-id": "evarga"
    },
    "links": {
      "self": "http://example2.com/persons/5"
    }
  },
  {
    "type": "comments",
    "id": "1",
    "attributes": { "text": "We also use JSON API!" },
    "relationships": {
      "author": { "data": { "type": "persons", "id": "21" } }
    }
  },
    "links": {
      "self": "http://example2.com/comments/1"
    }
  }]
}
```

These messages appear to follow the same structure, and have a common subject. If humans would need to parse them, this statement would be absolutely true. Unfortunately, what is intuitive and straightforward for us doesn't mean that it is understandable for machines, too. Table 16-1 contains a list of all semantic differences; that is, all variations excluding the values of fields (e.g., a concrete content of a post, comment, identifier values of entities, etc.). In a real-world scenario, these messages would diverge even more (e.g., comments as a type would be probably denoted differently, the name of the relationships will differ, etc.).

Table 16-1. *The List of Semantic Differences Between Messages*

Example1.com	Example2.com
Uses the `offset` field for pagination	Uses the `number` field for pagination
The type of a blog post is `posts`	The type of a blog post is `articles`
The content of a post is denoted as `content`	The content of a post is denoted as `text`
The content of a comment is denoted as `body`	The content of a comment is denoted as `text`
The type of an entity associated with the author relationship is `people`	The type of an entity associated with the author relationship is `persons`
The first name of an author is denoted as `first-name`	The first name of an author is bundled inside a `name` field
The last name of an author is denoted as `last-name`	The last name of an author is bundled inside a `name` field
The username of an author is denoted as `user-name`	The username of an author is denoted as `user-id`

Except for the disparity in the pagination mechanism, all other variations do degrade our ability to efficiently combine these messages. For example, we need to somehow convey the information to our program that `name` is a composite field, and that the first name and the last name are separated by a space.[4] Obviously, the JSON API specification doesn't encompass all message instances, consequently can't support all of them in a unified manner. Let's analyze our options here.

1. Coordinate the effort to unify the message formats produced by the blog sites. This is not a realistic endeavor. Usually, those sites are external entities out of our control. Even if we could by some magic succeed in this mission, it would be a matter of time before we would encounter a new blog source.

2. Incorporate the specifics of each blog site into the blog portal. This is again a troublesome approach, as it will introduce hidden couplings between the portal and external blog sites. Moreover, this approach cannot scale.

3. Enrich the input messages with additional information. The idea is to attach a kind of a dictionary to each message to translate foreign terms into a common vocabulary.[5] It is much faster to append additional data than to perform a full translation. The portal could be devised to expect such a dictionary irrespective of who created it (the remote site or the site-specific interceptor).

---

[4]At this moment, we can't even be sure whether this assumption will always hold. Can the `name` field contain a middle name, as well? Is it always the case that a single space character will delimit parts of a name?
[5]This message preprocessing could be implemented using the *Interceptor* design pattern.

The core JSON API allows us to insert meta information into a message via the `meta` member, which may contain an arbitrary number of custom fields. The final question is how to structure the dictionary (we will keep the elaboration comprehensible, without bringing in RDFS constructs like <term 1> rdsf:subPropertyOf <term 2>). One solution is to leverage Semantic Web technologies (it is an enabler of a vision to interlink web data through data stores, common vocabularies, and rules to handle data). We use here the FOAF linked data system to resolve the author's attributes.[6]

The next listing shows how such a `meta` member might look. Sticking this snippet into the original message from example1.com[7] would adorn it with a linked data vocabulary. Because our portal presumably understands the referenced FOAF vocabulary, it will be able to properly parse the matching JSON API message.

```
"meta": {
  "dictionary": [{
    "name": "FOAF",
    "context": "http://xmlns.com/foaf/spec/",
    "people": "#term_Person",
    "first-name": "#term_givenName",
    "last-name": "#term_familyName",
    "user-name": "#term_accountName"
  }]
}
```

Based on this dictionary, for example, the member `first-name` maps onto a URL http://xmlns.com/foaf/spec/#term_givenName. There is no chance now to misunderstand what `first-name` refers to. The FOAF vocabulary precisely defines the term *given name*. Note that for *people* we are mapping the term defined in a plural form onto the definition in a singular form. This is an aspect that needs additional consideration, but that is outside of scope of this book.[8]

So far, so good. We have just managed to extend the JSON API with a new construct called linked data vocabulary by introducing a member `dictionary`[9] inside a meta section. Meta information is the most rudimentary facility built into the JSON API specification to expand its capabilities (see the sidebar "What Is Meta?" later in this chapter for more information).

Nevertheless, there are some drawbacks of leveraging only the meta feature, as listed here.

- It is not clear where to put the `meta` member. Should it be a top-level element, or only associated with a specific type (in our case `people`)?

- How to interpret the dictionary element? How to publish this proprietary solution?

- How to maintain and evolve the proposal? How to version it?

Luckily, JSON API also defines more advanced constructs to enrich its capabilities. Figure 16-1 gives a broad overview of JSON API's built-in mechanisms governing its evolution. We have just seen the `meta` information in action (this is part of the core specification).

---

[6]Essentially, we refer to a public vocabulary defining terms related to persons. The idea is to associate a URI for each term. In this manner, the first name will not be a bare field anymore, but a URI. The uniqueness of URIs guarantees the exactness of terms. For more information about the FOAF project, visit www.foaf-project.org. There is also a JSON linked data project called JSON-LD (json-ld.org).

[7]Similar content could be attached to example2.com.

[8]You can find more information about linked data at linkeddata.org.

[9]It is a dictionary because it maps one term onto another (using FOAF as the target vocabulary).

Figure 16-1. *The JSON API'S mechanisms governing its evolution.*

▪ **Note**   The rest of the chapter describes some extension mechanisms that were available with the 1.0 version of JSON API. These were experimental features, and will not be accessible in the future version of JSON API (at the time of this writing they are marked as deprecated[10]). Nonetheless, there are systems using the currently offered facilities, and it is instructional to describe them anyhow (you might find them useful as ideas in other contexts). Moreover, some features, like the Bulk extension, will probably reappear in a similar form.

WHAT IS META?

The JSON API specification only mentions that a meta information is any nonstandard element. However, this is a pretty vague definition. Consider the case of a composite identifier, which is made up of an entity's relative key and a foreign key. Should the foreign key be a meta element or an attribute? To answer such questions, you always need to consider the business viewpoint. If the foreign key is an important part of an entity's description, then it should be put into an attributes section.

Another example is arbitrary content attached to an entity, which only needs to be stored without being interpreted in any other way. This extra content could serve as a generic data placeholder for ad-hoc extensions. Should this extra payload[11] be an attribute, or should it be treated as a nonstandard thing (kind of an extension)? If it doesn't possess a business value for the matching entity, then it is better handled as a `meta` element.

Whatever you choose as your guiding principle to declare something as a nonstandard and nonmeta element, you need to be consistent. The worst situation is being inconsistent.

---

[10]*Deprecated* doesn't mean something is worthless to know about!
[11]You might even want to have a meta element called `payload` to play this role.

Finally, there is no point of entering a dreadful *analysis paralysis* state regarding some feature of the JSON API. If you don't contradict the specification in some rude fashion, then just make a decree, and move on!

Main Directions to Evolve the JSON API

The JSON API is made up of separate independent parts as depicted in Figure 16-1. The core represents the stable 1.0 specification of JSON API. The *Extensions* facility is similar in concept to a software module, and the *Profiles* feature is based on RFC[12] 6906. The main difference between an extension and a profile is that the former could alter the semantics of the base specification.[13]

At this point, it is worthwhile to cite again the JSON API specification regarding its future versions: "New versions of JSON API will always be backward-compatible using a never remove, only add strategy."

This is an extremely sound principle to follow in general. It tells us that we can rest assured, that any addition to the JSON API will not break our current system. As a consequence, it will be always wise to switch to the latest version, as it might deliver some useful novelty. Who knows? Maybe the next version will support linked data out of the box.

Extensions

An extension can be imagined as a plug-in module (abbreviated as plug-in), which once "installed," extends JSON API's capabilities in some particular way. This could be a pure incremental change (only adding new stuff), or a combination of additions and updates with respect to the base specification. There are two types of extensions: official and custom. Official extensions are publicly announced on the JSON API's web site, whereas custom ones are kept private, or simply not recognized by the JSON API's maintainers.

Anyone willing to effectively introduce a JSON API extension should do the following.

- Assign a unique identifier to the new extension.

- Offer a server, which implements the new extension.

- Offer a client library capable of consuming a JSON API message with the new extension.

For custom extensions it is important to avoid name collisions. To achieve this, you might want to prefix your extension's name with your organization's unique identifier (e.g., my-organization-name.dictionary). This is the same approach you would use to name packages in Java. Only official extensions are expected to be without a prefix; that is, to belong to the "default" namespace.

■ **Caution**   Here is the warning from the JSON API's web site regarding considerations about supported extensions by servers: "Since extensions can contradict one another or have interactions that can be resolved in many equally plausible ways, it is the responsibility of the server to decide which extensions are compatible, and it is the responsibility of the designer of each implementation of this specification to describe extension interoperability rules which are applicable to that implementation."[14]

---

[12]The Request for Comments (RFC) is a set of publicly available documents related to Internet-connected systems describing communication protocols, message formats, best practices, and so on.
[13]This is the major design concern that motivated the authors of JSON API to change the extension mechanism in the next version.
[14]You definitely don't want to come up with a "bright" idea of creating a custom extension for content negotiation (the topic discussed in the next section). This setting would be reminiscent of the scenario of putting a can opener inside a can.

The best strategy is always to create extensions without altering the semantics of the base specification. Also, you should never create an extension having another extension as a required dependency; that is, each extension should be self-contained.

Content Negotiation for HTTP-Based Services[15]

When two parties want to communicate, they need to understand each other. In this discussion, we would like to see how a client and a server could successfully exchange JSON API messages possibly containing extension(s). The sole preconditions are that both of them adhere to the JSON API specification, and that they know how to negotiate JSON API extensions. Usually, the capabilities of the clients and servers will be different, especially if they are developed by independent organizations.

Figure 16-2 shows why is it important to know how to negotiate what is going to be delivered over the wire in both directions. The server can't offer to the client content containing a custom extension 3. Similarly, the client can't send bulk requests to the server using the official Bulk extension. Both of them need to establish a common agreement about what content is acceptable. In our case, the common denominator is the following set of extensions: JSON Patch and custom extension 1. We are assuming here that the parties will always refer to the latest version of such extensions. The version handling is outside the scope of this book and the JSON API specification. Versioning should be implemented as part of the extension itself.

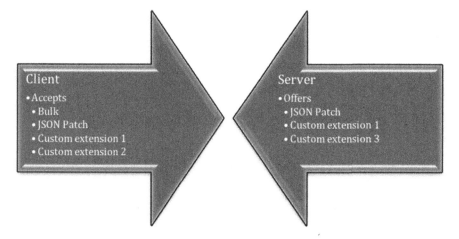

Figure 16-2. The importance of a content negotiation

A possible way to support content negotiation is by using the `supported-ext` and the `ext` media type parameters. The `supported-ext` is used by a server to advertise what it can offer, and the `ext` is an indicator that what is inside the delivered message can be used by both parties, or what is mandated to be included in a response (used by a client to tell the server what kind of message it expects). In our case, the server must always return in the `Content-Type` HTTP response header the following content:

```
application/vnd.api+json; supported-ext="jsonpatch,myOrg.ext1,myOrg.ext3"
```

---

[15]HTTP is the most prevalent protocol on the Web, but essentially any protocol could apply here, where a client and a server can establish a bidirectional communication path (in this case the HTTP request/response headers would be emulated by another means). In other cases, the mutual expectations will have to be arranged in advance, or over a separate channel. Even though extensions in the next version will not use content negotiation, it is interesting to see how such negotiation might work. After all, a much simplified content negotiation does constitute part of the core JSON API specification.

In this way, the client will receive information about what the server supports. A well-behaved client will not try to push over content with an unknown extension (from the server's perspective).

If a request or a response message is formatted according to some set of extensions, then these must be specified in the matching `Content-Type` HTTP header. For example, if a client sends a message using the custom extension 1 then the `Content-Type` HTTP request header must contain the following:

```
application/vnd.api+json; ext=myOrg.ext1
```

Correspondingly, if a server sends a message using the custom extension 1 then the `Content-Type` HTTP response header must contain the following:

```
application/vnd.api+json; ext=myOrg.ext1;
                       supported-ext="jsonpatch,myOrg.ext1,myOrg.ext3"
```

A client might inform a server that it wants the response to be formatted according to some set of extensions. A client specifies this inside the `Accept` HTTP header using the `ext media type` parameter. For example, a client can ask a server to use the custom extension 1 by putting the following content into the previously mentioned header:

```
application/vnd.api+json; ext=myOrg.ext1
```

Error Handling

If a server doesn't recognize at least one extension inside the `Accept` HTTP header, then it must return a message with a `406 Not Acceptable` status code.

If a server doesn't recognize at least one extension inside the `Content-Type` HTTP header (although it is happy with the list given inside the `Accept` HTTP header), then it must return a message with a `415 Unsupported Media Type` status code.

A server must be conservative toward clients. This means that a server is not allowed to format a message with an extension not specifically requested by a client.

Example Content Negotiation Scenario

Figure 16-3 shows a sample session[16] between a client and a server including the erroneous attempts. To reduce visual clutter, the JSON API media type `application/vnd.api+json` was removed from all HTTP headers. The same remark applies to the concrete JSON API messages exchanged between a client and a server.

---

[16]The sequence diagram shouldn't be treated as a reference client/server dialog; that is, your session will surely differ.

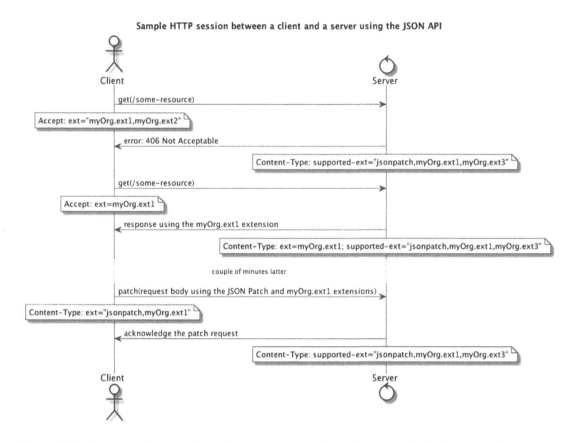

Figure 16-3. *A scenario where the client tries to get a resource from the server using both* myorg.ext1 *and* myorg.ext2 *extensions. After the server's reply, the client only requires content with known extensions from the server.*

Bulk Extension

The name of this extension is bulk. It is introduced as a convenience for a client to be able to send multiple requests at once for creating, updating, and deleting resources. Making a single call toward the server is better than making many small calls. Each call over the network introduces an additional latency, and a server might also perform better if it receives many requests in one batch.

One of the crucial traits of a bulk request is atomicity. This means that all requests bundled together have to be carried out as one atomic unit (either all succeed or all fail). The state of the server must reflect this decision; that is, it can't, for example, partially change the specified set of resources inside its own data store.

Creating Multiple Resources at Once

The client needs to send an HTTP POST request toward the server referencing the URL path for an endpoint, which denotes a collection of resources. The request must include an array of resource objects as primary data. Each resource should have at least a type member. The identifier (id member) is usually not needed, as it is assumed that it is the server's responsibility to create one automatically. However, this scheme might be altered if the external entity wants to provide and control resource identifiers. Here is the sample request to a pretend blog site for entering two new bloggers.

```
POST /persons HTTP/1.1
Content-Type: application/vnd.api+json; ext=bulk17

{
  "data": [{
    "type": "persons",
    "attributes": {
      "name": "Ervin Varga",
      "user-id": "evarga"
    }
  }, {
    "type": "persons",
    "attributes": {
      "name": "Zorica Varga",
      "user-id": "zvarga"
    }
  }]
}
```

The batch request must contain homogenous resource types. In our case all resources have the same persons type.

Updating Multiple Resources at Once

The only difference compared to the previous case (resource creation) is that the client needs to make an HTTP PATCH request. Also, each resource should at least contain a type and id members. Here is the sample request to a pretend blog site for updating the usernames of the previously created bloggers.

```
PATCH /persons HTTP/1.1
Content-Type: application/vnd.api+json; ext=bulk

{
  "data": [{
    "type": "persons",
    "id": "1",
    "attributes": {
      "user-id": "ervin.varga"
    }
  }, {
    "type": "persons",
    "id": "2",
    "attributes": {
      "user-id": "zorica.varga"
    }
  }]
}
```

---

[17]There is a shortcut in handling extensions. If a client sends a message formatted with some extension(s) (as specified in the Content-Type header), the server assumes that the client will also accept a response formatted with the referenced extension(s).

Deleting Multiple Resources at Once

The client needs to make an HTTP DELETE request. Each resource must only contain a type and id members. Here is the sample request to a pretend blog site for deleting the previously created bloggers.

```
DELETE /persons HTTP/1.1
Content-Type: application/vnd.api+json; ext=bulk

{
  "data": [
    { "type": "persons", "id": "1" },
    { "type": "persons", "id": "2" }
  ]
}
```

JSON Patch Extension

The name of this extension is jsonpatch. It is intended to implement two related RFCs: HTTP PATCH method (RFC 5789) and JSON Patch format[18] (RFC 6902). Both of these are associated with modification (create, update, and delete) of entities (collections, resource, attributes, and relationships). The JSON Patch extension also incorporates bulk operations. Because the HTTP PATCH method is atomic, this means that all operations must succeed or fail without causing any state change on the server. Figure 16-4 demonstrates the basic idea behind this extension (a variant of the *Interpreter* design pattern).

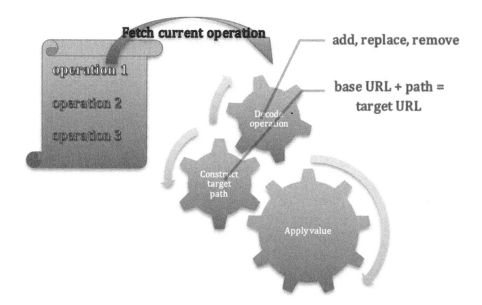

Figure 16-4. *Processing JSON PATCH operations*

---

[18]The move, copy, and test operations are not yet supported.

■ **Note**   It is advisable to cite the Abstract section of RFC 6902: "JSON Patch defines a JSON document structure for expressing a sequence of operations to apply to a JavaScript Object Notation (JSON) document; it is suitable for use with the HTTP PATCH method. The "application/json-patch+json" media type is used to identify such patch documents."

A JSON Patch request is made up of an array of heterogeneous operations. A server is free to impose limits on the type, order, and count of operations. Each operation is a triple (op-code, relative path, value). The relative path is combined with the base URL (the endpoint on the server hit by the HTTP PATCH request) to form a target URL. This target URL must point to a valid server endpoint for handling collections, resources, attributes, or relationships.

It is also vital to note that the JSON Patch extension uses the JSON API's media type instead of the one referred to in RFC 6902. This highlights the nonscalability of media types and the importance of *profiles*.[19]

In the subsections that follow, we exhibit the same create, update, and delete actions as for the Bulk extension, but this time using the JSON Patch extension.

Creating Multiple Resources at Once

The operation is add, the target path[20] must point to the end of a resource's corresponding collection, and the value is the resource itself.

```
PATCH /persons HTTP/1.1
Content-Type: application/vnd.api+json; ext=jsonpatch

[
  {
    "op": "add",
    "path": "/-",
    "value": {
      "type": "persons",
      "attributes": {
        "name": "Ervin Varga",
        "user-id": "evarga"
      }
    }
  },
  {
    "op": "add",
    "path": "/-",
    "value": {
      "type": "persons",
      "attributes": {
        "name": "Zorica Varga",
        "user-id": "zvarga"
      }
    }
  }
]
```

---

[19]See the References at the end of this chapter for more information about profiles and why media types cannot scale.
[20]In this example, the base URL is /persons and the relative path is /-, so the target URL is /persons/-.

261

Updating Multiple Attributes at Once

The operation is replace, the target path must point to the matching resource's attribute, and the value is the attribute itself.

```
PATCH /persons HTTP/1.1
Content-Type: application/vnd.api+json; ext=jsonpatch

[
  {
    "op": "replace",
    "path": "/1/user-id",
    "value": "ervin.varga"
  },
  {
    "op": "replace",
    "path": "/2/user-id",
    "value": "zorica.varga"
  }
]
```

Deleting Multiple Resources at Once

The operation is remove, the target path must point to the matching resource, and the value must be omitted.

```
PATCH /persons HTTP/1.1
Content-Type: application/vnd.api+json; ext=jsonpatch

[
  {
    "op": "remove",
    "path": "/1"
  },
  {
    "op": "remove",
    "path": "/2"
  }
]
```

Updating To-One Relationships

The operation is replace, the target path must point to the matching relationship, and the value is a resource identifier object for an update, or null for a reference deletion. Here, we refer back to the content received from the example1.com blog site. The author relationship for the post with id=1 references the person with id=10. We first change it to 11, and afterward remove it from the relationship.

```
PATCH /posts/1/relationships/author HTTP/1.1
Content-Type: application/vnd.api+json; ext=jsonpatch

[
  {
    "op": "replace",
    "path": "",
    "value": { "type": "persons", "id": "11" }
  },
  {
    "op": "replace",
    "path": "",
    "value": null
  }
]
```

Updating To-Many Relationships

The operation can be add, replace,[21] or remove, the target path must point to the matching relationship, and the value is an array of resource identifier objects, or an empty array to remove all references at once. Here, we refer back to the content received from the example1.com blog site. The comments relationship for the post with id=1 has a single comment with id=1. We first change it to 5, then add two new comment references, and finally remove one comment from the relationship.

```
PATCH /posts/1/relationships/comments HTTP/1.1
Content-Type: application/vnd.api+json; ext=jsonpatch

[
  {
    "op": "replace",
    "path": "",
    "value": [{ "type": "comments", "id": "5" }]
  },
  {
    "op": "add",
    "path": "/-",
    "value": [
      { "type": "comments", "id": "8" },
      { "type": "comments", "id": "9" }
    ]
  },
  {
    "op": "remove",
    "path": "",
    "value": [{ "type": "comments", "id": "9" }]
  }
]
```

---

[21]In case of a replace operation the server could refuse to carry it out with an error response 403 Forbidden. Otherwise, all replacements must succeed, or the server will return an error to the client.

Responses from the Server

If the result of an operation doesn't change anything on the client side, then the server must return a 204 No Content status code. Otherwise, it must return a 200 OK status code, and pass in the HTTP response body the representation of the altered resources. The ordering of resources must be the same as the ordering of the operations in a client's request. This case is especially important when creating resources without explicitly providing identifiers; that is, when the server creates them.

Suppose that the server has successfully executed the request from the earlier section "Creating Multiple Resources at Once." Apparently, the client will not know what the IDs of these newly created resources are. This is the reason the server responds with the following content.

```
HTTP/1.1 200 OK
Content-Type: application/vnd.api+json; ext=jsonpatch

[
  {
    "data": [{
      "type": "persons",
      "id": 100,
      "attributes": {
        "name": "Ervin Varga",
        "user-id": "evarga"
      }
    }]
  }, {
    "data": [{
      "type": "persons",
      "id": 101,
      "attributes": {
        "name": "Zorica Varga",
        "user-id": "zvarga"
      }
    }]
  }
]
```

If the server experiences an error while executing the operations, then it might return error objects that correspond to each operation. The ordering of these objects must match those of the operations. Inside the status member of each error object, the server can put the corresponding status code. Of course, if the server returns an error then it is the only content passed back to a client (this is according to the core JSON API specification).

Profiles

There is support for the 'profile' link relation type, as described in RFC 6906. The main motivation behind the profile is to prevent the proliferation of custom media types, as the media type has a limited flat structure.

■ **Note**   Here is the full Abstract section from this RFC explaining the purpose of profiles: "This specification defines the 'profile' link relation type that allows resource representations to indicate that they are following one or more profiles. A profile is defined not to alter the semantics of the resource representation itself, but to allow clients to learn about additional semantics (constraints, conventions, extensions) that are associated with the resource representation, in addition to those defined by the media type and possibly other mechanisms."

A profile link should be put inside the links object of the dictionary resource. The main advantage of a profile over ad-hoc meta information is that its link can be dereferenced for additional information. Moreover, profiles are composable, because each profile is identified by a URL, and it is easy to create a new profile based on a parent one. It is also straightforward to create mix-ins by including multiple profiles inside the same JSON API message.

Our dictionary meta information is a perfect candidate to be transformed into a profile. Here are the steps needed to make it a reality:

1. Create a public profile page on the Web documenting its purpose.

2. Include the profile link in every message based on it.

Assuming that we have published our profile on the Web, the links object of a blog resource's relationship called dictionary should look like what follows (we omit the self-link for brevity).

```
"links": {
  "related": "http://my-organization/dictionaries/blog"
}
```

Now, the `dictionary` member is precisely defined, and the extension can be freely shared with the JSON API community.

Summary

This chapter has introduced various ways to extend the JSON API's capabilities and also explained the necessity of doing that. You should be very careful not to abuse any of the presented mechanisms. Meta information is the most susceptible part for such a misapplication. After all, everything can be put inside a meta object, but then you will mimic those all-purpose procedures from the old days of C programming.[22]

In deciding whether to extend the JSON API or not, and how to do that once you decide to extend it, I would suggest the following procedure:

1. Check the latest JSON API specification, as it might already contain what you are looking for. You should never reinvent the wheel. For example, JSON API already has a solution for pagination, filtering, passing back errors, and so on.

---

[22]Many early C database libraries had a single procedure as their entry point. The signature was something like `STATUS process(void* rec, RECORD_TYPE rec_type)`. You invoked different parts of the library by passing records of different types. At least, nobody can question the achieved abstraction level here. Yeah, before you wonder, the `STATUS` (and similarly the `RECORD_TYPE`) was just `#define STATUS int`.

2. Start with the simplest approach; that is, using meta information. If the extension proves to be useful in a broader context, then you can create more advanced constructs, like a profile or a custom extension.

3. If your idea is rather complex, then it might deserve a full-blown JSON API custom extension. Try to avoid changing the semantics of the base specification, as your extension will not be reusable, nor easily composable with other extensions. At least, properly document all compatibility aspects, and which publicly known extensions might be affected by yours.

JSON API-BASED LOG MESSAGES

In a complex distributed system based on the service-oriented architectural style you will have a mixture of services of different kinds: HTTP REST, RPC, and message queue based. To trace what is happening across all these services you will definitely need to produce log messages (more precisely machine-processable structured log events). The first step to have control is to collect all these logs in a central place.[23] However, having all logs lumped together will not be of much use if you can't correlate them. In other words, you would like to have the ability to see for a particular business use case what log events were generated in the system. For this you will need a log correlation identifier.

One possible solution is to create a unique correlation ID at the use case entry service; that is, the service initiating the matching use case. When this service calls another one, it will pass this correlation ID further along the call chain. The principle is that each service will put this correlation ID inside every log message. Now the conundrum is how to pass this data between services using disparate technologies.[24] If we assume that all services use the JSON API message format, then this identifier can be put inside JSON API messages. Your task is to figure out what the options would be here: meta information, profile, or custom extension. Discuss what the benefits and drawbacks of each approach would be.

DOMAIN-SPECIFIC JSON API

Extend JSON API's capabilities by integrating a Jsonnet (`jsonnet.org`) templating engine. It would give you the possibility to define dynamic constructs inside your JSON API document. The Jsonnet web site contains lots of good examples of how the framework works. This extension of JSON API would likely require a custom extension.

---

[23]There are multiple tools for this, like Elasticsearch/Logstash/Kibana stack, Loggly, Splunk, and so on.
[24]If all services are HTTP based, you might choose to use a custom HTTP request header; for example, `X-log-correlation-id`.

References

1. Heath, Tom, and Christian Bizer, *Linked Data: Evolving the Web into a Global Data Space*.http://linkeddatabook.com/book

2. "JSON API Extensions." http://jsonapi.org/extensions/

3. Nottingham, Mark. "Profiles." www.mnot.net/blog/2012/04/17/profiles

CHAPTER 17

■ ■ ■

Katharsis

This chapter is a real catharsis: By backing the ideas of previous chapters with a real framework and a sample application, one gets a much clearer vision of what the JSON API can do. Moreover, by leaving the REST API to be implicitly driven by JSON API, you can appreciate the level of consistency achieved in our tutorial service. The best thing to note here is how much all this happens in the background, enabling true cluelessness regarding aspects not directly associated with our problem domain. This chapter also demonstrates how JSON API reuses concepts from the resource-oriented architecture style (see [1] for more details).

There are three key enablers for achieving uniform REST APIs.

1. HATEOAS as a characteristic of a Level 3 REST API, which allows a client to learn[1] dynamically the capabilities of the server. A client can create a complete service graph offered by the server, using hypermedia links provided in responses. A client doesn't need to know in advance all the resource URLs, nor what actions are permitted on those resources. Similarly, the server might choose to provide customized offerings of resources based on the identity of the requester or state of the resources. The interaction usually begins when a client hits the entry point of a server to receive the first batch of links. In some sense, the server can impose flow control over clients, as changes in links would dynamically alter the actions and routes taken by clients.

2. *Demand-driven programming* as a principle by which clients demand computation according to their need (an example for this paradigm is the Java 8 Stream API, or for that matter, the *streams* computational model in functional programming languages). In the case of a REST API this is tightly associated with HATEOAS. JSON API's support for caching relies on the fact that clients can build up data about resources, and issue requests only for unknown ones.

3. *Elegant and powerful framework* as a means to make this a reality; that is, to efficiently support creating Level 3 REST APIs in Java using JSON API. The focus of this chapter is the Katharsis framework[2] and how to leverage it to create services providing homogeneous REST APIs.

Besides directly supporting the goal of producing Level 3 REST APIs with JSON API, the designated framework, in this case Katharsis (another good choice for Java is Elide), should also possess the following traits:

- *Has to easily interplay with other established Java frameworks:* Katharsis integrates smoothly with Spring, and Dropwizard, with other frameworks leveraging the Java Servlet API, JAX-RS, and so on.

---

[1]This is related to the conundrum *teach vs. learn*. Instead of teaching clients how to interact with a system, through extensive documentation, we simply let them learn themselves what is doable via hypermedia links.
[2]Katharsis requires at least Java 7.

© Ervin Varga 2016
E. Varga, *Creating Maintainable APIs*, DOI 10.1007/978-1-4842-2196-9_17

- *Needs to be performant in handling JSON:* Katharsis internally uses Jackson for JSON manipulation and resource definition.

- *Should support integration with both SQL and NoSQL data stores:* This is especially important for implementing resource repositories.

- *Must have a vibrant supportive community*: The best testimony for this is my own bug report (`https://github.com/katharsis-project/katharsis-core/issues/345`) on setting a relationship of a resource. In about an hour, one community member responded with the patch, and sent back a pull request toward the maintainers of Katharsis. There is nothing more frustrating than working with an abandoned open source system, so having a community like the one gathered around Katharsis is crucial.

By relying on JSON API, services developed with Katharsis can effortlessly interoperate with other JSON API-capable clients. It doesn't even matter in what programming languages those clients are developed. To showcase the various features of Katharsis, we use a pragmatic approach, and build a full-fledged HATEOAS REST service using JSON API.

■ **Tip**   You might want to go through the "Getting Started" guide of Katharsis (available at `http://katharsis.io/start`) before proceeding with the rest of this chapter. It will introduce you to the very basics of this framework, and show how to set up a project using the Maven build tool.

Community Game Service

We develop here a very simplified Community Game service supporting games like Warcraft. The aim is to give a demonstration of how Katharsis handles resources and their relationships through the usage of JSON API. The resource manipulation use cases revolve around CRUD operations with master, details, and subdetails views. This is exactly where JSON API shines the most. Moreover, we will see how a generic JSON API-aware client could figure out which resources and relationships are offered by our service, and what actions are permitted on those resources.

Figure 17-1 shows the conceptual model of our service using a UML class diagram. We are only concerned for now with structural descriptions; that is, we are not modeling methods. Each entity (stereotyped as `resource`) is inherited from the `NamedEntity` class, which contains the mandatory fields `id` and `name`. The `id` is a globally unique identifier of a resource. At this level we don't care how we are going to produce such identifiers. The name of a resource is any arbitrary string, and it doesn't need to be unique (although usually it is). Using names is more user friendly than referencing identifiers.

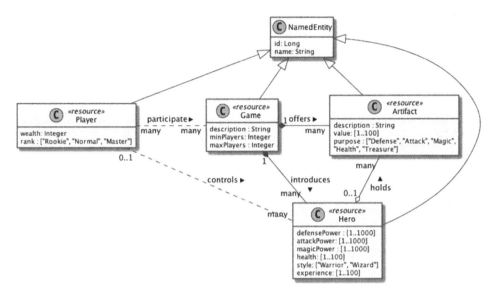

Figure 17-1. *The conceptual model of our Community Game service[3]*

The Game is the central entity, and serves as a domain (namespace) for artifacts (Artifact) and heroes (Hero). These contained elements are not shared among games; that is, they are existentially bound to one specific game. A game could contain multiple artifacts and heroes, and have some number of registered players (denoted by an interval [minPlayers, maxPlayers]).

An Artifact is something heroes can collect in a game. A hero will boost its strength or health each time it picks up an artifact. If an artifact is a treasure, then the player (Player) who controls the corresponding hero will accrue wealth. This wealth could be used, for example, to buy artifacts from other players.

A Hero possesses artifacts and participates in battles. The next three parameters dictate the overall power of a hero: the number and types of artifacts, experience, and style. The attack, defense, and magic power of a hero is equal to the sum of the attack, defense, and magic value of artifacts it owns. These three types of powers constitute the base power of a hero, which is limited. A hero cannot pick up weapons, which would theoretically increase its power beyond limits. A hero accumulates experience by participating in battles. Experience denotes the hero's level of efficiency in using weapons. Finally, the style alters the base power of a hero. For example, a warrior's defense and attack power will prevail over the same defense and attack power of a wizard (assuming they both have the same base power and experience). If a hero dies, then it is resurrected with all artifacts lost. Both the artifacts and the hero again become freely available to all players.

Finally, a Player is someone playing a game by controlling her or his heroes (a player may procure only free heroes). The player must first register in a game to be able to play. If a player chooses to leave the game, all of her or his heroes will "drop" their artifacts and become free.

The model nicely segregates duties. Players accumulate wealth and control heroes, who further possess weapons and health packs. The game provides the terrain where actions take place. A game is also a kind of a container for artifacts and heroes. Apparently, the model allows having wealthy players who don't currently control a single hero. However, such wealthy players could become formidable by buying potent artifacts for their heroes (once they find some in a game).

There is another powerful trait of the model. It provides the backbone (core functionality) of a community game. Concrete games can be instantiated by applying different configurations. Even the algorithm to calculate the total power of a hero is outside the scope of the presented model.

---

[3]See the sidebar "How to Maintain an API Documentation with Diagrams?" later in this chapter for more information about how this and the other UML diagrams in this book were produced.

This minimalistic approach is the cornerstone in achieving a high level of reusability. Instead of trying to squeeze every game-specific detail into the core service, we just let other services build on this one. A custom game would delegate the basic resource (game, player, hero, or artifact) requests to the core Community Game service; it would therefore just need to handle its own game-specific rules. This is very similar to the principle of using composition over inheritance in the object-oriented world. Effective composition and collaboration of services is what *microservices* architectural style tries to advocate and bring to the fore.

HOW TO MAINTAIN AN API DOCUMENTATION WITH DIAGRAMS?

The class diagram in Figure 17-1 as well as the introductory text about our service is usually part of documentation. As a high-level overview, it is related to the API documentation. After all, our service's API exposes resourceswith definitions and relationships that are best conveyed by the previously mentioned diagram. Maintaining such diagrams directly, or manually drawing them in some graphical tool, is simply out of question. The only scalable solution is to specify them in a textual format. This approach also nicely interplays with version control, because it is far easier to trace changes over a textual file than a graphical one. At any rate, the goal is to always maintain a single truth without duplication. The UML diagrams would usually represent high-level stable conceptual and behavioral models on top of which the implementation is based. This layered documentation approach is beneficial, as there are no overlaps, and so no need to worry about the issues with round-trip engineering (the biggest problem in model-driven approaches backed by case tools). Having UML material in textual format is especially handy in early phases of development, when there is a need to rapidly change models until they stabilize (until the initial architecture is created).

Here is the source code[4] to produce Figure 17-1.

```
@startuml
class NamedEntity {
  id: Long
  name: String
}
class Game << resource >> {
    description: String
    minPlayers: Integer
    maxPlayers: Integer
}

class Artifact << resource >> {
    description: String
    value: [1..100]
    purpose: ["Defense", "Attack", "Magic", "Health", "Treasure"]
}

class Hero << resource >> {
    defensePower: [1..1000]
    attackPower: [1..1000]
    magicPower: [1..1000]
```

---

[4]I've used the PlantUML open-source tool (`plantuml.com`) capable of producing all sorts of UML diagrams (Figure 16-3 is an example of a sequence diagram).

```
    health: [1..100]
    style: ["Warrior", "Wizard"]
    experience: [1..100]
}

class Player << resource >> {
    wealth: Integer
    rank: ["Rookie", "Normal", "Master"]
}

NamedEntity <|-- Game
NamedEntity <|-- Artifact
NamedEntity <|-- Hero
NamedEntity <|-- Player

Game "1" *-- "many" Hero : introduces >
Game "1" *- "many" Artifact : offers >
Hero "0..1" o-- "many" Artifact : holds >
Player "0..1" .. "many" Hero : controls >
Player "many" . "many" Game : participate >

hide methods
@enduml
```

Maintaining this source code is much easier than poking around in some GUI editor.

The Architecture of the Community Game Service

The starting point for the Community Game service was the *Dropwizard + MongoDB* example project of Katharsis (see https://github.com/katharsis-project/katharsis-examples for all examples).[5] It is an HTTP JAX-RS (Java API for RESTful Web Services) service using MongoDB as a data store. The service relies on the following major frameworks.

- *Katharsis*: Implements the JSON API convention. Katharsis has many modules, and allows integration with a JAX-RS provider, a servlet container, Spring, and Vert.x. We are using it here integrated with a JAX-RS provider through Dropwizard.

- *Morphia*: Handles the MongoDB database operations. It uses the MongoDB client and driver to communicate with the back-end data store.

- *Dropwizard*: Provides the backbone for our service (eeb server, JAX-RS support, JSON parser, etc.). It is an umbrella, which integrates all major components into a cohesive unit.

Figure 17-2 shows the main architectural layers and components of the Community Game service. The Dropwizard framework also includes many additional things not depicted here, like the logging facility, metrics collector, and so on. You can consult its documentation for more details.

---

[5]Important refactoring happened on top of this (especially to eschew duplication of code), together with additions not found in the examples shipped with Katharsis. Moreover, the service uses newer versions of libraries than the Katharsis example code base.

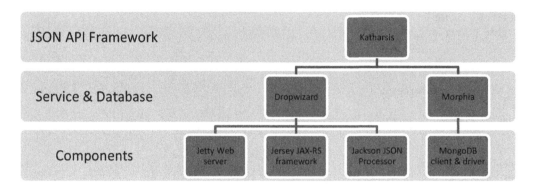

Figure 17-2. The layered architectural model of the Community Game service, which "sits" on top of Katharsis. MongoDB is assumed to be running in the background as a separate process, or on a different node.

Figure 17-3 shows the service's source folder structure, which is a Java 8 Maven project. You can take a look into the pom.xml file, located inside the root folder, to see the list of dependencies.

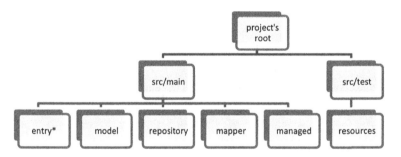

Figure 17-3. The project's source folder structure. The output of a build is created in the target folder beneath the root. The resources directory stores some JSON files for testing purposes.

The following list briefly describes what each folder contains:

- *entry**: Contains the main Dropwizard service class together with the custom configuration class.

- *model*: Holds resource definition classes as depicted in Figure 17-1.

- *repository*: Contains resource as well as relationship repository classes. These classes are data access objects (DAO) for performing database CRUD operations over resources and their relationships.

- *mapper*: Contains special exception mapper classes to produce proper error responses, as specified by the JSON API standard.

- *managed*: Holds Dropwizard managed components. Currently, it wraps the MongoDB client and driver, and sets up the Morphia instance.

To build the Community Game service, issue the following command from the project's root folder.[6]

---

[6]You must have Maven (mvn) and Java 8 JDK installed on your machine. You can also import the project into your favorite IDE, and build and run it from there. IDEs are usually bundled with Maven support.

```
mvn clean package
```

To start the service, you need access to a running MongoDB database process (local or remote). Assuming that you are running it on your local machine using the standard 27017 port number, you can start the Community Game service by executing

```
mvn package exec:exec
```

To test whether the service is properly running (besides looking at the logs printed out at a console) you can execute[7]

```
curl -v localhost:8080/community-game/games
```

You should get the following response:

```
*   Trying ::1...
* Connected to localhost (::1) port 8080 (#0)
> GET /community-game/games HTTP/1.1
> Host: localhost:8080
> User-Agent: curl/7.43.0
> Accept: */*
>
< HTTP/1.1 200 OK
< Date: Sun, 26 Jun 2016 18:18:07 GMT
< Content-Type: application/vnd.api+json
< Content-Length: 44
<
* Connection #0 to host localhost left intact
{"data":[],"included":[],"meta":{"count":0}}
```

Because the database is empty[8] we don't have any game yet. Another neat way to check what is going on with the service is to check the Administrator web page provided out of the box by Dropwizard. Just navigate to http://localhost:8080/admin in your browser, and follow the links. It is especially interesting to watch the metrics.

Configuring the Service

The mechanism to configure the service is prescribed by the Dropwizard framework. The root folder contains the configuration.yml YAML file, which has configuration sections for different parts of the system. Some of those are related to the components of Dropwizard, and some to the service itself. Here is the content of this file.

```
katharsis:
  host: http://localhost:8080
  searchPackage: rs.exproit.community_game.domain
  webPrefix: /community-game
```

---

[7]You can use any other tool to make HTTP requests, but curl is my favorite. Don't try to hit the given URL from a browser, as it would probably download the response document instead of presenting it inside a window. This is due to the fact that browsers still don't recognize the JSON API media type.

[8]If you want to clean the database used by the Community Game service, then execute mongo community_game --eval "db.dropDatabase();".

```
mongo:
  host: localhost
  port: 27017
  db: community_game
  user:
  password:

server:
  type: simple
  applicationContextPath: /community-game
  adminContextPath: /admin
  connector:
    type: http
    port: 8080

logging:
  level: ALL
  appenders:
    - type: console
```

The sections *katharsis* and *mongo* are defined by the custom Dropwizard configuration class, whereas the other two are processed automatically by the Dropwizard framework. It is instructive to see how this custom configuration class looks.

```java
package rs.exproit.community_game;

import io.dropwizard.Configuration;

import javax.validation.Valid;
import javax.validation.constraints.Max;
import javax.validation.constraints.Min;
import javax.validation.constraints.NotNull;

public class DropwizardConfiguration extends Configuration {
    @Valid
    @NotNull
    public MongoConfiguration mongo = new MongoConfiguration();

    @Valid
    @NotNull
    public KatharsisConfiguration katharsis = new KatharsisConfiguration();

    public static final class MongoConfiguration {
        @NotNull
        public String host;

        @Min(1)
        @Max(65535)
        public int port;

        @NotNull
        public String db;
```

```java
    @NotNull
    public String user;

    @NotNull
    public String password;
}

public static final class KatharsisConfiguration {
    @NotNull
    public String host;

    @NotNull
    public String searchPackage;

    public String webPrefix;
    }
}
```

The content of the YAML configuration file is mapped to class fields based on their name. Each field is associated with a set of annotations[9] to validate its content. If any constraint is violated, then the system will report an error. The @NotNull constraint is especially useful to prevent omitting a mandatory configuration parameter. Such a deed usually causes strange NullPointerExceptions to appear during runtime. Dropwizard will instantiate this configuration class and pass it as a parameter to the service's run method (see the DropwizardService class for more details, which essentially contains the service's bootstrap code).

Specifying Resources

Each resource from Figure 17-1 is represented as a separate class. Here is the snippet (imports, Javadoc, and the getters and setters are omitted) showing the base NamedEntity class.

```java
public abstract class NamedEntity {
    @Id
    @JsonApiId
    private ObjectId id;

    private String name;

    @JsonIgnore
    @Version
    private Long version;

    @JsonIgnore
    private Date createdAt = new Date();
    @JsonIgnore
    private Date updatedAt;

    @PrePersist
    void alterUpdatedAt() { updatedAt = new Date(); ...}
```

---

[9]These are part of the so-called *Bean Validation API* (http://beanvalidation.org).

277

Our conceptual model in Figure 17-1 shows only the id and name properties. At that level of abstraction it was the most prudent thing to do from the usefulness point of view.[10] Here, we see that the implementation requires more fields. Moreover, the id field's type is ObjectId, which serves globally unique identifiers. Nevertheless, the most interesting phenomenon to notice is the use of various annotations. Figure 17-4 shows the three categories of these annotations, and how they nicely interoperate to boost the matching class (see also the sidebar "Annotations vs. Interfaces" later in this chapter about how annotations can help you in creating flexible APIs).

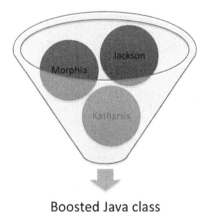

Boosted Java class

Figure 17-4. *Different categories of annotations interplay to produce a final feature-rich class. The @JsonApiId is provided by Katharsis, the @JsonIgnore is defined by Jackson, and the rest is coming from Morphia.*

Most annotations are intuitive and well documented by their implementing framework. The @Version annotation deserves an extra explanation. This is a way to signal what field should be used automatically by Morphia to implement optimistic locking. This is important when multiple clients are trying to simultaneously update the same resource. The principle is that each client needs to possess the latest version number to perform an update. Otherwise, the system will generate a ConcurrentModificationException exception. Optimistic locking is more sensible here than using coarse-grained mutual exclusion. The assumption is that most clients will work with different resources at any given moment in time. At any rate, this concurrency control is required when adding or removing multiple resources to or from a relationship. This could map to atomicity, consistency, isolation, and durability (ACID) properties of database transactions. Atomicity of updates is ensured via HTTP PATCH requests. Durability is bounded by the time it takes to handle an HTTP request. Consistency of updates is guarded by the optimistic locking. Isolation isn't fully supported, as a client could load one resource after another, cache them, and the view might not be consistent.

The @PrePersist annotation is handy to alter the date and time of the last update to a resource. The annotated method is automatically called by Morphia each time the corresponding resource is changed.

Here is the snippet that shows how the Hero resource is implemented.

```
@Entity("heroes")
@JsonApiResource(type = "heroes")
```

---

[10]Don't try to replace your programming language with UML, and start creating overly complicated "accurate" models (unless you want to publish a scientific paper or impress your boss). They rarely achieve the desired effect, and present a maintenance nightmare. Once upon a time, there was even a vision to only work through models, and leave the rest to a fully integrated computer-aided software engineering (CASE) tool.

```java
public final class Hero extends NamedEntity {
    @Min(value = 1, message = "Attack power cannot be lower than {value}.")
    @Max(value = 1000, message = "Attack power cannot be higher than {value}.")
    private short attackPower;

    @Min(value = 1, message = "Defense power cannot be lower than {value}.")
    @Max(value = 1000, message = "Defense power cannot be higher than {value}.")
    private short defensePower;

    @Min(value = 1, message = "Magic power cannot be lower than {value}.")
    @Max(value = 1000, message = "Magic power cannot be higher than {value}.")
    private short magicPower;

    @Min(value = 1, message = "Health cannot be lower than {value}.")
    @Max(value = 100, message = "Health cannot be higher than {value}.")
    private short health;

    @NotNull(message = "A hero must have a style.")
    @Pattern(regexp = "Warrior|Wizard", message = "A hero may be either a Warrior or a
    Wizard")
    private String style;

    @Min(value = 1, message = "Experience cannot be lower than {value}.")
    @Max(value = 100, message = "Experience cannot be higher than {value}.")
    private short experience;

    @Reference
    @JsonApiToOne
    private Game game;

    @Reference
    @JsonApiToMany(lazy = false)
    @JsonApiIncludeByDefault
    private List<Artifact> artifacts = new ArrayList<>();

    @JsonIgnore
    private boolean available = true; …}
```

This class has four categories of annotations (the Bean Validation API constraints are also attached to the fields). The artifacts field represents a one-to-many relationship type toward artifacts, which are always included in the definition of a hero (see the @JsonApiIncludeByDefault Katharsis annotation). This saves extra round trips between a client and a server, under an assumption that most clients will want to know the details of the artifacts owned by a hero. A hero also has a reference toward the matching game. Finally, the available field is a marker whether the hero is controlled by a player or is free.

The Bean validation constraints are checked by Morphia each time a resource is saved into the database. The MongoManagedImpl class's constructor activates this feature by executing the following line of code:

```java
new ValidationExtension(morphia);
```

In the case of a constraint violation, the system throws the ConstraintViolationException exception. All exceptions are caught by the Katharsis exception handler, and are passed to the matching exception mapper (in this case the ConstraintViolationExceptionMapper class). This mapper produces the JSON API error response, as defined in the JSON API specification.

Specifying Resource and Relationship Repositories

Every resource and each of its relationships with other resources must be implemented by the matching resource and relationship repository class, respectively. For example, the previously mentioned Hero resource would require three classes: one resource repository class, and two relationship repository classes (one is for the Hero->Game relation, and the other one for the Hero->Artifact relation). The resource repositories are extended from the BaseResourceRepository abstract class, and the relationship repositories from the BaseRelationshipRepository abstract class. Both of these are so-called annotated repositories. Here is the abridged listing of the former.

```
public abstract class BaseResourceRepository<Resource extends NamedEntity> {
    private static final Logger log = Logger.getLogger(BaseResourceRepository.class);

    private final Datastore datastore;
    private final Class<Resource> targetClass;

    public BaseResourceRepository(MongoManaged mongoManaged, Class<Resource> targetClass) {
        datastore = mongoManaged.getDatastore();
        this.targetClass = targetClass;
    }

    @JsonApiSave
    public Resource save(Resource entity) {
        Key<Resource> saveKey = datastore.save(entity);
        log.debug("Resource is successfully saved: " + entity);
        return datastore.getByKey(targetClass, saveKey);
    }

    @JsonApiFindOne
    public Resource findOne(ObjectId id, QueryParams requestParams) {
        Resource namedEntity = datastore.get(targetClass, id);
        if (namedEntity == null) {
            throw new ResourceNotFoundException("Cannot find a resource with id: " + id);
        }
        return namedEntity;
    }

    @JsonApiFindAll
    public Iterable<Resource> findAll(QueryParams requestParams) {
        return datastore.find(targetClass);
    }

    @JsonApiFindAllWithIds
    public Iterable<Resource> findAll(Iterable<ObjectId> ids, QueryParams requestParams) {
        return datastore.get(targetClass, ids);
    }

    @JsonApiDelete
    public void delete(ObjectId id) {
        datastore.delete(targetClass, id);
        log.debug("Resource with id=" + id + " is successfully deleted.");
    }
```

```
@JsonApiMeta
public MetaInformation getMetaInformation(Iterable<Resource> resources) {
    final List<Resource> resourceList = Lists.newArrayList(resources);

    if (resourceList.size() == 1) {
        final Resource primaryResource = resourceList.get(0);
        return new MetaInformation() {
            @SuppressWarnings("unused")
            public final Date createdAt = primaryResource.getCreatedAt();
            @SuppressWarnings("unused")
            public final Date updatedAt = primaryResource.getUpdatedAt();
        };
    } else {
        return new MetaInformation() {
            @SuppressWarnings("unused")
            public final int count = resourceList.size();
        };
    }
}
}
```

The HeroRepository is a just a small type wrapper around the BaseResourceRepository class:

```
@JsonApiResourceRepository(Hero.class)
public final class HeroRepository extends BaseResourceRepository<Hero> {
    @Inject
    public HeroRepository(MongoManaged mongoManaged) {
        super(mongoManaged, Hero.class);
    }
}
```

An interesting detail in the implementation of the BaseResourceRepository class is the getMetaInformation method. This will attach inside a top-level meta section the date and time when the primary resource is created and last updated, or it will embed the total number of resources (see the count field) encompassed by the request (in the case of a collection of resources).

The BaseRelationshipRepository class is a bit more complex, and has more template (Java generics) parameters. However, it is also wrapped by concrete relationship classes. All type wrappers (as evident from the HeroRepository class) contain an additional annotation @Inject. This is used by the Guice framework, and dependency injection is set up inside the DropwizardService entry class.

The save method is annotated with @SuppressWarnings("unchecked"). Often this should be a warning sign, but it is okay to apply it here. First, this method is part of an abstract class, so all accesses are done from the child classes, which definitely need to provide an extra protection. Second, none of these methods are called directly by client programmers. They are all invoked by the framework itself. At any rate, if it is safe to ignore a particular warning, then it should be silenced.

ANNOTATIONS VS. INTERFACES

Annotations are usually better when it comes to generating code based on their presence, or using reflection to work with them. Generating code requires annotation processors. Reflection is (initially) slow. Besides using annotations, it is also possible to define resource and relationship repositories with interfaces (examine the `ResourceRepository` and the `RelationshipRepository` interfaces, respectively). If you don't want to write an annotation processor, and need (startup) speed, then it is better to use an interface. However, a method signature declared inside an interface is rigid. It cannot accept additional parameters (e.g., JAX-RS might deliver extra parameters, like an instance of `ContainerRequestContext`, an instance of `SecurityContext`, a cookie, or an HTTP header), unless you apply the Request/Response pattern (see `http://wiki.apidesign.org/wiki/RequestResponse`). Likewise, methods listed inside an interface have to be implemented. If a class doesn't need them all, then one option is to "implement" them by dummy methods, or another possibility is to throw the `UnsupportedOperationException` exception. You don't have these limitations with annotations.

You can easily combine annotations, as we have just seen. This is very cumbersome to achieve with interfaces. This becomes obvious when you take a look at those Java marker interfaces (they don't enclose any method signature). An interface has to denote a viable abstraction in the system. If an interface is used to modify the behavior of the class (e.g., the `Cloneable` interface with the broken `clone` method), then it is a clear *code smell*.

Annotations can be applied at different granularities (class, method, or field). This is not possible with interfaces. The JUnit framework switched to annotations (`@Test`) because of TestNg. The idea is to entitle test methods with annotations instead of forcing you to extend the `TestCase` class. Therefore, annotations might even help you to overcome the limitations of the programming language (e.g., single inheritance in Java).

Finally, it is straightforward to implement new annotations, and you could even use them to autogenerate source code.

A Sample Session with the Community Game Service

This section presents a short session with the Community Game service (assuming it is already started up as described earlier). The session includes the following tasks.

1. Create a new game.

2. Try to create another game using the wrong data.

3. Increase the maximum number of players for the previously created game.

4. Delete the game.

The content of the data file `game-1.json` (situated inside the `src/test/resources` folder) for Step 1 is given here.

```json
{
  "data": {
    "type": "games",
    "attributes": {
      "name": "Sample Community Game 1",
      "description": "This is the first game for testing purposes.",
      "minPlayers": 2,
      "maxPlayers": 4
    }
  }
}
```

The matching HTTP request is as follows (some extra newline characters are inserted here to make the formatting nicer, but they should not appear on the command line).

```
curl -v -X POST
-H "Content-Type: application/vnd.api+json"
-H "Accept: application/vnd.api+json"
--data "@src/test/resources/game-1.json" localhost:8080/community-game/games
```

We should get the next response from the server with the status code of 201 Created (only the JSON API document is presented here in a pretty printed form).

```
{
  "data": {
    "type":"games",
    "id":"577057ea5cdc7d272403e199",
    "attributes":{
      "maxPlayers":4,
      "minPlayers":2,
      "name":"Sample Community Game 1",
      "description":"This is the first game for testing purposes."
    },
    "relationships": {
      "artifacts":{
        "links":{
          "self": "http://localhost:8080/community-game/
                   games/577057ea5cdc7d272403e199/relationships/artifacts",
          "related": "http://localhost:8080/community-game/
                      games/577057ea5cdc7d272403e199/artifacts"
        },
        "data":[]
      },
      "heroes": {
        "links": {
          "self": "http://localhost:8080/community-game/
                   games/577057ea5cdc7d272403e199/relationships/heroes",
          "related": "http://localhost:8080/community-game/
                      games/577057ea5cdc7d272403e199/heroes"
        },
        "data":[]
      },
      "players": {
        "links": {
          "self": "http://localhost:8080/community-game/
                   games/577057ea5cdc7d272403e199/relationships/players",
          "related": "http://localhost:8080/community-game/
                      games/577057ea5cdc7d272403e199/players"
        }
      }
    },
    "links": {
      "self":"http://localhost:8080/community-game/games/577057ea5cdc7d272403e199"
    }
```

```
    },
    "included":[],
    "meta": { "createdAt":1466980330160, "updatedAt":1466980330182 }
}
```

The top-level self link points to this game instance (note that in your session the generated id value will be different, and you will need to remember this). The relationship links provide information to a client about what the other associated resources are. This is the HATEOAS in action. Of course, at this point they would return an empty set, but they are clearly symbolized. The artifacts and heroes relationships do have an associated data section because these relationships are not lazy (unlike the players relationship). Issue the next command (again, change the identifier 577057ea5cdc7d272403e199 to the value appropriate for your session):

```
curl -v http://localhost:8080/community-game/games/577057ea5cdc7d272403e199
```

You should receive the same JSON API document with the HTTP status code of 200 OK. Let's now try to create another game with the following wrong data (see the file game-wrong.json).

```
{
  "data": {
    "type": "games",
    "attributes": {
      "name": "Sample Community Game - Wrong",
      "description": "This is the game for testing constraint violation.",
      "minPlayers": 1,
      "maxPlayers": 4
    }
  }
}
```

Because our service is handling community games, it is meaningless to allow single-player games. After executing:

```
curl -v -X POST
-H "Content-Type: application/vnd.api+json"
-H "Accept: application/vnd.api+json"
--data "@src/test/resources/game-wrong.json" localhost:8080/community-game/games
```

the service will respond with the HTTP status code of 409 Conflict, and pass back the following error report:

```
{
  "errors": [
    {
      "status":"409",
      "title":"Min. number of players cannot be lower than 2.",
      "source": {
        "pointer":"/data/attributes/minPlayers"
      }
    }
  ]
}
```

If you look into the @Min constraint, as defined in the Game resource class, you will notice there the exact same message as inside the title field. Moreover, the source field contains the JSON pointer to the culprit. If you want to make a partial change to a resource, then you should issue an HTTP PATCH request. Here is the command:

```
curl -v -X PATCH
-H "Content-Type: application/vnd.api+json"
-H "Accept: application/vnd.api+json"
--data '{"data": {"type": "games","attributes": {"maxPlayers": 20}}}'
localhost:8080/community-game/games/577057ea5cdc7d272403e199
```

The server will respond with the updated game representation and the HTTP status code of 200 OK. To verify that the update was really successful you can issue the following command[11] (it just retrieves the maxPlayers field):

```
curl -v --globoff
http://localhost:8080/community-game/games/577057ea5cdc7d272403e199?fields[games]=maxPlayers
```

The server will respond with the following document.

```
{
  "data": {
    "type":"games",
    "id":"577057ea5cdc7d272403e199",
    "attributes": { "maxPlayers":20 },
    "relationships":{},
    "links":{ "self":http://localhost:8080/community-game/games/577057ea5cdc7d272403e199 }
  },
  "included":[],
  "meta": { "createdAt":1466980330160,"updatedAt":1466982657174 }
}
```

The prior request was an example of a sparse fieldsets usage. It is handled automatically for you by the Katharsis framework. Other features, like sorting, grouping, and paging, need to be implemented in the code. However, even in this case, you will get all input data (parsed from the URL) inside an instance of the QueryParams class.

Finally, to delete our game you should issue the following command.

```
curl -v -X DELETE http://localhost:8080/community-game/games/577057ea5cdc7d272403e199
```

The server will respond with the HTTP status code of 204 No Content. If you now try to read back this resource, then the service will respond with the HTTP status code of 404 Not Found, and pass back the following error report.

```
{"code":404,"message":"HTTP 404 Not Found"}
```

---

[11]Notice the --globoff option in the curl command.

285

Summary

The biggest part in our job of implementing the Community Game service revolved around the Java packages containing model resources and repositories. The rest was all handled by the underlying frameworks, like Katharsis, Dropwizard, and Morphia. This is the main goal that we aim to achieve by using frameworks. We strive to reuse as much infrastructure code as possible, and just add our domain-specific logic on top. In our case, Katharsis handles all the thorny aspects of the JSON API specification, and leaves to us only the details that are application specific. Just imagine how much time we would need to implement the Community Game service from scratch.

This chapter's text with the Community Game service source code doesn't cover everything related to the Katharsis framework. The investigation of the following features is left as an additional exercise:

- The @JsonApiLookupIncludeAutomatically annotation on relationship fields.

- Provisioning of links information in resource repositories (see the @JsonApiLinks annotation).

- Filtering, grouping, sorting, and pagination through the usage of the QueryParams object.

EXTENDING THE TEST COVERAGE

Unit and Integration Testing of Our Service

The Community Game service is shipped with some unit and integration tests implemented with the JUnit framework (visit the src/tests folder). The pom.xml file already contains the required dependencies for this exercise. All tests based on the JUnit framework should run fast in a fully isolated manner (this is especially true for short unit tests). For this reason, the Community Game service uses *Fongo*, which is a faked-out in-memory MongoDB in Java (see https://github.com/fakemongo/fongo). You can see examples of its usage inside the service's code base. Your task here is to extend the number of unit and integration tests to cover most of the code base.

The hardest part of writing integration tests revolves around controlling the database. You cannot just demand to have a test database running somewhere ahead of executing the tests. All tests must be run by the build tool without any user intervention. Moreover, the tests should be performant, so hitting a remote database is out of the question.

Another issue regarding database access is the ordering of tests. Your tests should be independent of each other. It is very bad practice to execute tests in some predefined order. Therefore, before running each test the preconditions related to data inside a database must be satisfied (irrespective of what tests were run before the current one). Again, this is very hard to achieve having a real database running in the background (let alone to think about using the production database, and messing it up).

You might want to boost the build job with a test coverage reporting tool (e.g., Cobertura is very nice and available at cobertura.sourceforge.net). Tracking test coverage is very important to pinpoint weakly tested areas of the code base. As a quality assurance metric it shouldn't be taken out of context; that is, you might end up with 100% coverage, while still having bad tests. The goal is not to chase percentage per se, but to boost your understanding about how well the system is covered with tests. Totally untested parts of your program probably hide bugs, so by increasing the code coverage with tests you're actually lowering the risk of a production failure (risk mitigation technique in action).

AUTOGENERATE TYPE WRAPPERS

There are lots of manually written resource and relationship repository type wrappers in the code base. There is a better way to implement them. Write a build plug-in (or an executable command-line program) to automatically generate these wrappers. One approach is to use a separate input `wrappers.yml` file. This file could have the following structure:

```
resource:
  - Player
  - Game
  - Artifact
  - Hero
relationship:
  Player: [Game, Hero]
  Game: [Player, Artifact, Hero]
  Artifact: [Game]
  Hero: [Game, Artifact]
```

The tool would first create all the specified resource repositories, and afterward the resource relationship repositories. The generated code should look the same as the handcrafted one. Don't forget to add an option for a user to specify the target package or folder for the generated code.

Another approach is to use annotations. In this case, a resource class or a relationship field marked with `@GenerateRepository` would trigger the proper autogeneration process. Annotation processors give you the element structure for free, which is usually enough. Embedded DSL (via annotations and their processors) is a very powerful way to go.

Finally, you might even have an option to analyze the Java source code, and recognize resource and relationship definitions. However, this requires some knowledge from the domain of writing compilers, and I don't recommend it here. Of course, you might want to read about lexical and syntax analysis and examine JFlex (`http://jflex.de`) and CUP (`http://www2.cs.tum.edu/projects/cup/index.php`).

ADD LOGIC TO CHECK ARTIFACT AND HERO AVAILABILITY

The current code base only contains a reserved field `available` for artifacts and heroes. However, it is not currently used when artifacts and heroes are picked up (when setting the matching relationship; e.g., `artifacts` for the `Hero`). Implement the necessary logic to consult the `available` field, and return the HTTP status code of `403 Forbidden` if the artifact or hero is occupied.

PERFORM END-TO-END TESTS

The current code base contains some additional test resources, which are not used as part of the "curl" session. Repeating the whole "curl" exercise in an automated integration test might be very valuable for testing the system from end to end. Using the techniques from Chapter, 10 implement such an automated test suite.

Reference

1.   Richardson, Leonard, and Sam Ruby. *RESTful Web Services.* Sebastopol, CA: O'Reilly Media, 2007.

Index

A

AJAX. *See* Asynchronous JavaScript and XML (AJAX)
Amoeba effect, 6
Annotated repositories, 280
Annotations *vs.* Interfaces, 278, 281
Apache Avro properties, 171–172
Apache Felix framework, 40–41
Apache Kafka
    JMS support, 187
    performance, 187
    set up, 188–190
API documentation
    class diagram, 272
    high-level stable conceptual and
        behavioral models, 272
    round-trip engineering, 272
    source code, 272
application/hal+json, 148
application/json, 153
Application programming interfaces (APIs)
    abstraction, 20
    data, 20, 22
    encapsulation, 22
    meta-process, 18
    quality attributes, 135
    TDD. *See* Test-driven development (TDD)
    type coercion module
        abstractions and encapsulation, 26
        coercing arguments, 24–25
        function-composition.rkt, 23–24
        symbolic algebraic manipulation system, 22
        target-level variable, 26
        type-coercion.rkt, 25–26
        type-tagging.rkt, 23
    use case, 19
Artifact and hero availability, 288
Asynchronous JavaScript and XML (AJAX), 135, 137
Atomicity, consistency, isolation, and durability (ACID), 278

Autogenerate type wrappers, 287
Automated integration tests, 203
Automaton-pick feature, 222–223
Avro's DatumWriter, 182

B

Bean validation API, 277
Behavior-driven development (BDD), 81–87
Billboard URL, 162
Black holes, 173
Broken windows theory, 5
Bulk extension, 258

C

Client-controlled asynchrony, 135, 137
Client/server model, 187
ClientServerTest class, 185
ClientServerTest Test Case, 204, 206
closeClient methods, 184
collectionReference, 167
Comma-separated values (CSV), 171, 216
Common information model (CIM), 232
Community Game service
    aim, 270
    architecture, 273–275
    artifacts and heroes relationships, 284
    command, 285
    conceptual model, 270–271
    configuration, 275–277
    configurations, 271
    CRUD operations, 270
    error report, 284
    execution, 284
    game-wrong.json, 284
    HTTP request, 283
    microservices architectural style, 272
    @Min constraint, 285
    multiple artifacts and heroes, 271
    parameters, 271

E. Varga, *Creating Maintainable APIs*, DOI 10.1007/978-1-4842-2196-9

■ S

Get the eBook for only $4.99!

Why limit yourself?

Now you can take the weightless companion with you wherever you go and access your content on your PC, phone, tablet, or reader.

Since you've purchased this print book, we are happy to offer you the eBook for just $4.99.

Convenient and fully searchable, the PDF version enables you to easily find and copy code—or perform examples by quickly toggling between instructions and applications.

To learn more, go to http://www.apress.com/us/shop/companion or contact support@apress.com.

Printed in the United States
By Bookmasters